The Power of Reason: 1988

Sponsors

Renée Beard
American Friends in the Philippines
Shirley Biddison
Elliot Boyce
Helen Altgelt Boyce
Canadian Patriots for LaRouche
Flora Carmine
L. I. Chapman
Roland Dickman
L. Farley
Des Moine Field
James Gaines
Creda Glenn
Kevin Gribbroek
Dr. Herbert Griffith
Hubert H. Hutchinson
Doris Kimbrough
Terry Klingel
C. E. Leisey
John Perricone
Sigmund Pfeiffer
Elizabeth Roark
John K. Shrader
Clarence Smith
Ray B. Younkins
Walter Worth

The Power of Reason: 1988
An Autobiography

by Lyndon H. LaRouche, Jr.

Executive Intelligence Review
1987

copyright © 1987 by
Executive Intelligence Review

Designed by: World Composition Services, Inc.
Cover design: Virginia Baier

Cover photographs (clockwise from upper left): Lyndon LaRouche during
a 1982 visit to the Escorts Tractor Plant, Faridabad, Haryana, India
(NSIPS/Uwe Parpart); Lyndon LaRouche, spring 1986 (NSIPS/Philip
S. Ulanowsky); Lyndon and Helga LaRouche visit the Seabrook, New
Hampshire nuclear power plant, autumn 1979 (NSIPS/Virginia Baier);
Lyndon LaRouche, spring 1986 (NSIPS/Philip S. Ulanowsky).

FIRST EDITION
2nd Printing
Printed in the U.S.A.

For more information contact the publisher:
Executive Intelligence Review
P.O. Box 17390
Washington, D.C. 20041-0390

Library of Congress Cataloging-in-Publication Data

LaRouche, Lyndon H.
  The power of reason, 1988.

  Rev. ed. of: The power of reason.
  Bibliography: p.
    1. LaRouche, Lyndon H. 2. Democratic Party 3. Politicians—
  United States—Biography. I. LaRouche, Lyndon H. Power of
  reason. II. Title.
    E840.8.L33A36   1987   324.2′092′4   [B]   87-7894
    ISBN: 0-943235-00-6

Contents

Author's Foreword

During the course of the past nearly twenty years, I have become perhaps the most controversial among the influential international figures of this decade.

Unlike all of the other leading candidates for the U.S. presidency since 1945, I am an influential original thinker. This is not to suggest that such prospective candidates as Vice President George Bush and Senator Robert Dole are lacking in intelligence or executive abilities. For the past forty years, the successful candidates for the presidency have been persons who, in the customary manner of speaking, advanced their political career up to that point, by doing "the right thing at the right time," saying and doing nothing which will make enemies among important factions of the "establishment." Bush and Dole, for example, have adapted to those rules for success under ordinary conditions.

However, this is a crisis; in such crises, what is customarily successful becomes a failure. Our nation has once again entered into a time when only the unusual succeeds, and the usual fails. We have entered into a period of crisis, in which only original thinkers are qualified to lead.

On paper, our nation is a constitutional democratic republic. In reality, it has not been such a republic for approximately one hundred years, certainly not since the sweeping changes in our form of government introduced during the presidency of Theodore Roosevelt. Most of the time, the policies of government, the selection of most leading candidates for federal office, and the majority of popular opinion, have been regulated by behind-the-scenes committees representing what is called "the establishment."

Under this arrangement, candidates for leading office present themselves, like job applicants for corporate executive appointments, to this "establishment." The "establishment" either gives such candidates permission to campaign, or "not at this time." If given such permission, the candidate so "authorized" seeks backing for his or her election by the "establishment," by proving to the "establishment" that he or she can "sell" the policy which the establishment has decided to push at that time.

For myself, I began to understand this in 1947. At that time, I wished General Dwight Eisenhower to campaign for the 1948 Democratic nomination. The general replied to me, stating agreement with my policy arguments in support of his candidacy, but informing me his candidacy was not appropriate at that time. There is no doubt that Eisenhower could have won the 1948 nomination and election by a landslide, had the "establishment" permitted him to campaign.

During the 1970s and 1980s, I came into the position of influence in which I was consulted by "establishments" on such matters as the suitability of prospective candidates for high office. Those discussions took the form of, "What should our policies be, and what possible candidate do we see who might be a suitable figure for selling that policy to the electorate?" Naturally, I had no vote in such matters among "establishment" ranks, but my opinion was increasingly among those surveyed by members of the "establishment," as a view to be taken into account in their making their own decisions in such matters.

Although I am not a member of "establishment" councils myself, I have become an insider of the policy-shaping processes, and therefore situated to observe the way things are done.

So situated, I have been told, as other prospective candidates have been told, "We do not think your candidacy is appropriate at this time. It would be wise of you to stay in the background for the coming period." Often, there have been warnings of the very unpleasant things which some sections of the establishment might do to me if I refused this advice not to run. I was permitted to run, in 1980, with the advice that I would not come within reach of the nomination. I was forbidden to run in 1984, and one can see today the pattern of attempted Justice Department and federal court frame-ups against me and my friends which have resulted from my refusing to obey that order from the "establishment."

Do not delude yourself. The Justice Department and the federal courts are the principal arms of the liberal wing of the establishment. The control is exerted through the channels of a collection of major law firms, which are agents for the power of cartels of both U.S. and foreign major financial interests. Since Theodore Roosevelt and Woodrow Wilson's presidencies, the Justice Department and federal bench have been under increasing control of this portion of the establishment. Establishment decisions determine who is prosecuted, and what evidence will be considered or ignored in deciding who is or is not the winner in politically sensitive legal proceedings. Recently, through "ABSCAM" and kindred operations, the U.S. Congress has been terrified, by and large, into submission to the political pressures from the FBI and related functions within the Department of Justice. Congress and the presidency have the legal power to break this control, but so far they have not shown the collective courage to do so.

During the 1970s and 1980s, "former" leftists of the 1960s and 1970s, such as the Justice Department's Stephen Trott and William Weld, have risen to key positions within government. This is part of an international pattern, in Western Europe and North America, called in Western Europe the 1960s leftists' "march through the institutions." Leftists whose efforts were funded by McGeorge Bundy's Ford Foundation and the Institute for Policy Studies back during the 1960s and 1970s, have been introduced to lower-ranking positions in state and federal offices, and have been promoted, step-by-step, to key positions in high office.

So, Trott, now engaged in efforts to destroy the research capabilities of major U.S. defense contractors, rose from the ranks of the Communist-linked "Highwaymen" folk-song group, through channels linked to Soviet agent Armand Hammer in California, to head a powerful special committee within the Department of Justice. Boston leftist William Weld, was placed in government under the sponsorship of Elliot Richardson, and steered by Harvard Law School crony-circles into the position of Boston U.S. Attorney, and into a high position, under Trott, in Ed Meese's Department of Justice. These two cases are notable, but not exceptional.

Usually, these days, the popular vote may decide the final margin by which a candidate for leading office is elected or not. It is the "establishment" which decides which candidate will be permitted to come in reach of being elected.

There are no democratic governments in any part of the world today, at least not "democratic government" as popular opinion defines it. Nations are ruled by a combination of contending and also overlapping "councils" of competing factions of behind-the-scenes power, councils which function somewhat like a board of directors of a corporation, a board of directors which selects approved candidates for high offices, and which decides which assortment of contending policies will be tolerated or not. Presidents are like the corporate presidents appointed by a board of directors. The board may allow the voting stockholders to choose among a short list of approved candidates and policies, but that is the limit of power of the electorate.

Throughout known history, governments have always been organized in this way. Elites continue in power over many generations, and these elites determine what forms of government, what leading candidates, and what assortments of policies will exist in the short term. Mankind has yet to reach the level of popular education, at which ordinary citizens assume the responsibilities and competencies of formulating the compositions and policies of governments. At the most, popular opinion is able to exert a limited degree of veto-power over the decisions made among the ranks of those ruling combinations which are the nation's elites.

Over the centuries, since the reforms which Solon introduced to ancient Athens in 599 B.C., there have been many influential persons and groupings which have sought to change this state of affairs. The American Revolution is one of the outstanding examples of such efforts. One of the most notable efforts is that of Germany's Wilhelm von Humboldt, who proposed a system of universal education intended to transform the entire adult population into a qualified elite. Humboldt's reforms were excellent for that purpose, and are a model of what U.S. public education should be transformed to become today. His educational system worked, but his kind of classical and scientific education was never permitted to reach more than an elite minority of Germany's youth. Mankind will not enter the long-awaited Age of Reason, in which true democratic republics exist, until the overwhelming majority of the adult population is educated and motivated to constitute the national elite.

I am a democratic republican. Yet, I know that such

a happy state of affairs cannot be simply wished into being. It must be built up, through educational reforms and other measures, and this must be done by dedicated leaders who mobilize the population to demand such reforms in education and popular opinion. First, we must reestablish the best qualities of that electorate which brought our independent nation and federal republic into being: fiercely independent farmers, entrepreneurs and working people, each of whom enjoys that degree of economic independence indispensable to speaking one's own opinion publicly without fear of reprisals. As President George Washington and others insisted during that past time, we must have a system of education which qualifies our citizenry in knowledge of statecraft, as well as the principles of scientific and technological progress. We must have a people which is truly free, and sufficiently educated and well-informed to be capable of making those kinds of decisions now made by relatively tiny elites.

I am such a free citizen. I came from out of nowhere, so to speak, from an obscure background, and became influential through my acquired capacities as an original thinker, through producing and working for ideas which have become increasingly influential. Although I am consulted, increasingly, by portions of the world's elites, I did not come up through establishment channels. I came into a position of increasing international influence from the proverbial "outside." It is the way in which I have become influential which makes me essentially different from any ordinary sort of leading candidate for the presidency.

Even those among elites who admire at least some of my accomplishments, view me as an "outsider," as someone not to be trusted, because he is outside their control and resistant to such control. I have been invited to join the establishment, provided I would accept the kind of control to which it was demanded that I submit. I rejected those terms, and was thus viewed as an incorrigible outsider. On this premise, even portions of the elite who admire aspects of my policies and work, join with their factional adversaries within the establishment as a whole, in agreeing that I must not come into a powerful elected position.

The result has been an establishment decision to portray me as a mysterious sort of outsider. Taking into account all of the wild lies circulated against me in the major news media and other gossip channels, the common theme underlying all of these libels, is the message: "Beware, he is an outsider, with suspiciously mysterious connections."

I am not one bit as mysterious as some contemporary coverage would seek to imply. If one looks back to the leading figures of the eighteenth and early nineteenth centuries, and imagines that those figures were living today, or I living then, there should be no great difficulty in recognizing rather quickly exactly who and what I am. As an economist and statesman, I belong to the tradition of the nineteenth-century American Whigs; I represent the tradition of such as John Quincy Adams, Henry Clay, Henry C. Carey, and Abraham Lincoln. The chief difficulty is, that I do not seem to fit into the mold of our twentieth-century politicians.

As I have already indicated here, the controversy surrounding me has two overlapping causes. By the standards of the twentieth century, I am an "anti-establishment" figure, which is not pleasing to our establishment. Most of the controversy attached to me by the major news media and liberal factions of our two major parties is simply a desire to destroy anyone who is viewed as a serious potential threat to the current policies and interests of the establishment. In addition to being "anti-establishment," I am also a significant original thinker of our time, and thus an irritant to those, especially among economists, whose pet theories I tend to upset.

Most of what is alleged concerning me in the establishment's news media, is to be written off as simply the sort of malicious lying the establishment invariably directs against any person it views as a potential threat to its interests. Apart from such outright lies, the most important misrepresentations of me take the form of the establishment's desire to leave unmentioned the issues which motivate its hatred of me. For both reasons, most citizens can discover almost nothing about me from either the principal news media or the stream of insider gossip wholesaled among the institutions of government and diplomatic channels.

Fortunately, for those who care to know, there have existed two biographies which include those kinds of principal facts which a citizen would wish to know respecting a presidential candidate. The first is a book-length autobiographical essay, *The Power of Reason,* written in the autumn of 1978. The second is a book published by the editors of the international newsweekly, *Executive Intelligence Review (EIR), LaRouche: Will This Man Become President?* during the 1984 Democratic campaign. In addition, I have published more books and articles than any twentieth-century candidate for the presidency. Although the content of none of these writings has been reported in the establishment news media, those who take the time and effort to know where I have stood over the recent decades could discover and verify that for themselves.

Although the two extant biographies of me are factually accurate, I find neither adequate for the present circumstances. On two counts, these biographies are an inadequate presentation of the total picture of what is relevant to the readers at the present time.

First, since the beginning of the 1984 presidential campaign, I have been at the center of some among the leading crisis-developments affecting current history, including the Soviet and liberal establishment efforts to destroy the U.S. Strategic Defense Initiative. In particular, since early 1984, there has been massive interest in the subject of my rumored behind-the-scenes influence on the shaping of our nation's policies, and also my associations with governments and other influential forces abroad. The truth about this aspect of my life must be given much greater emphasis than I could have foreseen in 1978, or the editors of *EIR* in 1984.

Second, neither biography satisfies fully the standard I now consider essential. It is not sufficient to answer the obvious questions of "What?" "Who?" "When?" and "Where?" What ought to concern the voter is the way in which the candidate thinks, how the candidate is likely to respond to challenges of the years immediately ahead. What must be emphasized are those aspects of the candidate's past which have made him what he is today.

What I am likely to do as President is presented in the current book, *Program for America*. The continuity of my past and present policies is shown clearly enough there. A biography must begin with what that book leaves out: the inner development of the man which leads me to such policies. The earlier autobiographical essay identifies this connection, but, in my opinion, does not develop the connection adequately.

For me, "current events" do not exist. Only the present connection between past and future history exists; this might be restated, "only present history, rather than 'current events,' exists." What biography ought to do, is to bring into the foreground those aspects of a person's past which bear directly on his or her development as a figure affecting the processes of present history. Only biography written in this way, uncluttered by the pornography of distracting, gossipy details, enables the reader to trace a process of development in public figures.

I give one illustration of what I mean, the case of that wicked stage-biography of the composer Wolfgang Amadeus Mozart, *Amadeus*. This drama's portrayal of Mozart's personality was a deliberate fraud, from beginning to end.

Mozart's life was dominated by three political developments, none of which was acknowledged in *Amadeus*. The first was his father's commending Mozart to associate himself with Benjamin Franklin in Paris. The second was the rise and defeat of the sweeping reforms of Austria's Joseph II. The third was Mozart's attachment to the faction of Johann Sebastian Bach, and the revolution this caused in Mozart's method of composition from 1783 onward. Mozart, like Beethoven, and also the circles of Friedrich Schiller, was a member of a political faction in Europe which tied itself to the cause of the American Revolution, a faction which hated the French Jacobins, and rightly viewed Napoleon Bonaparte as an enemy of those principles which the American Revolution symbolized. The musical tradition of Bach, was the instrument used by those great classical musicians who were members of this political faction.

Also, Mozart, like Beethoven, was deeply religious. Their masses were not adaptations of music to religious occasions; they were religious in and of themselves. The treatment of the Credo in Mozart and Beethoven's masses, especially the treatment of the *Filioque,* makes this clear to anyone familiar with the rudiments of classical musical composition.

These political and musical issues were the dominant feature of the lives of both Mozart and Beethoven, in such a way that all aspects of this are expressed in their musical work. Thus, the character of neither can be brought to the surface without identifying what is creative in musical composition, as distinct from acceptable schoolbook composition, and the fight of each to introduce specific creative principles of composition.

The life of each, Mozart and Beethoven, is potentially the subject of a great classical drama in the mode of Aeschylus or Schiller. Such a drama would be truthful only if it accomplished two things. First, it must identify dramatically the raging fight for and against classical well-tempered polyphony in Europe, from the time of Leonardo da Vinci through the eighteenth-century campaign of the House of Hanover to stamp out the very existence of Bach's music. Second, the drama must show the connection of this life-and-death struggle within music to the brutal struggle for and against the influence of the American Revolution, struggles centered in political factions of which both Mozart and Beethoven were a part. The difficulty is, that the composing of such a drama would require an author familiar with the musical principles involved, as well as the more explicitly political issues.

The result would be magnificently entertaining drama. Although Mozart was murdered by the apothecary's trick of subclinical doses of mercury, which was standard political practice during the eighteenth century, and although the impairment of Beethoven's hearing was probably the result of similar poisoning, neither of them is a tragic figure in Hollywood's sense. Both were magnificently successful in accomplishing what they set out to accomplish. Yet, the circumstances under which an almost starving Mozart died, persecuted by the enemies of Joseph II, is itself a tragedy in the Aeschylan or Schiller's sense.

Any other approach to a biographical treatment of Mozart is a fraud, whether intentionally so, or merely out of the author's inability to grasp the subject matter.

The author and producers of *Amadeus* commit a deliberately libelous hoax, by misrepresenting bits of gossip, each taken out of context, and by representing the musical genius of Mozart as a forerunner of the irrationalist romanticism of a Richard Wagner. (In fact, every Mozart composition is thoroughly worked-out, and rigorously so, by principles of composition as rigorous as those of mathematical physics. There is no wild inspiration involved, but rather an aesthetical power analogous to the works of scientific genius.) *Amadeus* is bad, fraudulent television soap-opera.

Most modern biography written is shaped by misconceptions and bunglings similar to those of *Amadeus*. There is no competence shown respecting the process of development which governs the way the subject's opinions and commitments are shaped at various points in his or her life. The result is disgusting gossip, tuned to the degraded tastes of Harvard faculty cocktail parties.

My purpose is to present my development as I would recommend a biography of Mozart be written, or the biography of any other notable historical figure. My purpose is to show the mainspring of my behavior, to present what might otherwise be regarded as my innermost secret.

The Making of an Economist

1

I make no great claim when I insist that I am the leading economist in the world today. "In the world of the blind, the one-eyed man is king."

Although there are thousands who bear the title of "economist," what is taught as "economics" in our universities, and practiced by most among so-called economists, has no resemblance to political-economy as that subject was understood by U.S. Treasury Secretary Alexander Hamilton, the two Careys, Henry Clay, Friedrich List, or Abraham Lincoln, for example.

Economic science was founded by Gottfried Leibniz during the period 1672–1716. Leibniz designed the principles of what was later called the "industrial revolution," known then as the principles of heat-powered machinery, and known more broadly as the "physical economy" curriculum which Leibniz introduced to the branch of university instruction in statecraft known as cameralism. In this connection, Leibniz discovered the conception of "technology," and was the first to supply a rigorous mathematical-physics definition for technology.

Leibniz's economic science was adopted by the founders of the United States, and incorporated in what Alexander Hamilton was first to name "the American System of political-economy." This economic science was adopted in explicit opposition to the doctrine of the British East India Company's Adam Smith, and was the economic policy on which our constitutional republic was founded. Following the War of 1812, the contributions of German economists, and French economists Chaptal, Ferrier, and Dupin were incorporated into the American System. So, by the 1830s, all economic science was known worldwide by the name "American System of political-economy."

Beginning in the 1870s, with the passage of the treasonous U.S. Specie Resumption Act, the control of U.S. debt and currency was taken over by foreign bankers centered in London and Switzerland. These bankers viewed the American System as a threat to their power over the government of the United States. These wealthy interests used their control over leading universities to eradicate the teaching of economic science from both the university curriculum and the economic profession. During the period of Theodore Roosevelt's presidency, the suppression of teaching and practice of economic science was almost complete. Economic practice was limited to management principles for agriculture and industrial firms, and the war-planning functions of our military. With the rise of influence of institutions such as Harvard Business School and the Wharton Institute, competent management economics was driven out of even our industrial firms. Robert S. McNamara drove economics competence out of the Defense Department, with his dogmas of "systems analysis."

During the postwar period, U.S. national income accounting was reorganized under the so-called Gross National Product system. This system, which is intrinsically incompetent as a way of measuring economic performance, took over the economic reporting functions of government, and shaped the practice of the economics profession. During the 1940s and 1950s, an absurd doctrine concocted by John von Neumann, "linear systems analysis," became the basis for what was known generally as "econometrics." This concoction then became the basis for most applications of accounting and economics practice to computer systems.

One of the results of the incompetence so introduced in place of economic science, is the situation of the recent years, during which the U.S. economy has been consistently sliding deeper in a new depression, a situation which the Reagan administration has insisted is an "economic upsurge." Although the President's own utterances on this subject are chiefly wishful thinking, reports of U.S. GNP appear to support the President's arguments, at least superficially. The reason that GNP shows economic growth, when the economy is sliding into a new depression at an accelerating rate, is that GNP is a totally incompetent yardstick for measuring economic performance. However, since economists base their economic theories upon this GNP doctrine, they have assured the President that the economy has been growing, when it has been collapsing in fact.

I am the only public figure in North America or Europe who teaches the American System of political-economy today. If that were my only accomplishment, I would be, automatically, one of the world's leading economists. "In the land of the blind, the one-eyed man is king."

I have the good fortune to have made two discoveries which are, combined, a major contribution to economic science.

Since Leibniz, we have known the general nature of the cause-effect relationship between the introduction of an advancement in technology and a resulting increase in the productive power of labor. Improvements in technology enable us to reduce the amount of labor consumed in producing a good. It was not known, until my work of the early 1950s, how to show that this cause-effect relationship itself could be measured.

Once I had discovered how this cause-effect connection could be measured, I was faced with the difficulty of finding a mathematics suited for such work. The kind of mathematical function my discovery required, is of a class which mathematicians term "nonlinear." The conventional mathematics taught in universities today, is intrinsically incapable of solving such functions directly. This was a contributing factor in John von Neumann's adopting the absurd dogma, that all important functions of economic analysis could be accomplished in terms of "linear mathematics": what are called solutions to systems of linear inequalities.

The second part of my original discovery in economic science, was to recognize that if the mathematical physics of Bernhard Riemann is understood as Riemann understood it, Riemannian physics provided the mathematical method for measuring the cause-effect connection between quantified amounts of new technologies, and proper measurement of increases of the productivity of labor. Hence, because of the order in which the two parts of this discovery were made, it is known today as "the LaRouche-Riemann method."

Thus, I am the world's leading economist, first because I am among the very few economists who have mastered the American System of political-economy, and also because I have contributed the only valid discovery in economics during the past hundred years.

For a New World Economic Order

Although I am fascinated by every class of problem in applied economics, my life's work has been concentrated on effecting sweeping reforms in monetary institutions and economic policies. All among my other work in public life, has been centered in these proposed economic reforms.

The center of my proposed reforms, has been the establishment of the kind of international gold-reserve monetary order needed to promote high rates of growth of productivity in what are called today "developing nations." The flow of exports into developing nations, so fostered, will promote high rates of growth in advanced industries among the "industrialized nations." Thus, these reforms provide for a worldwide economic prosperity, centered upon a massive and growing flow of capital-goods exports from industrialized into developing nations.

Up to that point, my proposed reforms are nothing but a modern application of the American System of political-economy to international economic relations, as well as to the domestic economic, credit, currency, and taxation policies of the United States itself.

My original discoveries in economics enable us to measure the rates of growth resulting from various mixtures of technological priorities. The ability to make these predictions is extremely important. Development involves capital investments in agriculture, industrial capacity, and economic infrastructure. Each such investment has an economic half-life of from about seven to twenty-odd years; mistakes in investment policies cannot be corrected easily in the short term. Governments and private investors must reach a consensus on which sorts of long-term investments are most desirable; to make such choices, they must be able to precalculate the results of various choices over periods of seven to twenty years. My original discoveries in economics make possible reasonably accurate predictions of this sort.

The most important feature of my past life is that combination of personal experiences which has led me to such discoveries and such commitments. To make this connection clear, my biography must deemphasize those experiences which have little relevance to this point. The names of persons I knew, when, where, and how, have no relevance except as that experience bears upon shaping the development of my intellectual capacities and the inclinations leading into my principal past and present commitments. I am also persuaded to adopt this selective approach, because I abhor public figures' passing judgment in any way on persons who are not able to respond with the resources available only to public figures, unless that be a person who is cited as an authority in circulating a false report of my past actions and associations. If private persons do not bear in some essential way on my development and commitments, and if I suspect they might resent this book's intrusion upon their privacy, I choose not to abuse my advantage as a public figure, and to leave them in peace.

During the first forty years of my life, everything that has been of importance bearing upon my outlook, commitments, and activities during the past twenty-five years, can be efficiently listed under five categorical headings. First, that I was born a member of the Society of Friends (Quakers), and the issues of my break with that creed. Second, my 1948–1952 determination to refute the morally unwholesome "information theory" dogma of Professor Norbert Wiener, the undertaking which led directly into my original discoveries in economics. Third, my association with a management consulting career during about twenty of the twenty-five years beginning 1947. Fourth, my experience in India, during the concluding portion of my military service abroad. Finally, my reaction to a 1949–1954 association with a tiny Trotskyist group, the Socialist Workers' Party.

During the past twenty-five years of my life, the most decisive features of my development and commitments are found under three categories. First, my mid-1960s commitment to combat a "New Left" philosophy which I saw as the greatest evil of our time, and the international association which grew up around those who joined me in this commitment. Second, my launching of an increasingly influential international campaign for comprehensive monetary and economic reforms. Third, my collaboration with my wife, Helga Zepp-LaRouche.

For the present and future, all that is important falls under a single category, my elaboration of what conventional usages term a "grand strategy" for the United States, both to check the Soviet attempts to establish a world-empire, and to accomplish the founding of a permanent colony on Mars by approximately the year 2025 A.D. Everything of importance recently added to my development and commitments falls under this single heading.

These nine categories constitute the topics of this autobiographical report.

In the remainder of this chapter, I shall cover as much of those nine categories as fall within the first twenty-five years of my life. This includes my Quaker background and the developments leading into my break with Quaker theology, as well as the impact of my experiences in India. In the second chapter, I shall take up the period 1947–1957, including my entry into management consulting, the process of reaching my discoveries in economic science, and my encounter with Marx and the Socialist Workers' Party. In the third chapter, I shall cover my political and counterintelligence activities of the period 1957–1971. In the fourth and fifth, the principal developments from 1971 through 1979. The sixth chapter is an intermezzo, providing the reader the key to some of the stranger things which happened to me and my friends up through 1974, and some stranger things which occurred later, up to the present time. In the seventh my development of the U.S. Strategic Defense Initiative and the worldwide ramifications of that development. In the seventh chapter, I resume the narrative, up into the beginning of 1981. In the eighth chapter, the key features of my collaboration with my wife, and her emergence as a key international figure in her own right. In the final chapter, I shall present my programmatic view of the future of the United States in a changed world.

I now begin the narrative.

I was born into the evangelical faction of the Religious Society of Friends, in Rochester, New Hampshire, on September 8, 1922. From my earliest recollections, my parents' household was steeped in five generations of family traditions.

My father, Lyndon Hermyle LaRouche, Sr., deceased in 1983, was the native-born son of a Joseph LaRouche, who had immigrated to the United States, by way of Paris, France, from a remote region in Quebec. Joe LaRouche, a vigorous bantam of a man, was the son of a violin-maker. He had held careers as a pharmacist and international representative for the United Shoe Machinery Corporation, and had accumulated enough to be among the well-to-do. My father's mother, Ella, was of mixed French and Irish descent. During my childhood, my father was employed by the Haverhill office of United Shoe, servicing shoe manufacturing firms in a territory centered around Rochester.

My mother, Jessie Weir LaRouche, was of mixed English and Scottish ancestry.

The English side of the family, the Woods, were Quakers who had settled in Pennsylvania during the 1670s. My great-great-grandfather, the Reverend Daniel Wood, was of the same generation as President Abraham Lincoln, and like Lincoln, attached to Henry Clay and the American Whigs. Daniel Wood, a Quaker abolitionist, had moved from the Carolinas to north of Columbus, Ohio, to become the local squire of a community named Woodbury, in Delaware County. He had run the "underground railroad" station for escaping black slaves in that vicinity.

My mother's father, the Reverend George Weir, had come into the United States at the age of two. His father, a professional Scottish dragoon with traditional affiliations to the Greys, had left Scotland to volunteer in the First Rhode Island Cavalry, and to become a familiar of relevant drinking places in Fall River, Massachusetts, after the war. His saber was legendary in Fall River at the time, until my great-grandmother prevailed upon his brother, Cunard Captain William Weir, to remove the saber so terrifying to the drinking circles my great-grandfather habituated.

Young George Weir had been caught by an evangelical revival passing through the vicinity, had taken up the ministry, and moved to Columbus, Ohio, to run a mission in the skid-row district there. He had married Martha Wood, the granddaughter of the Reverend Daniel Wood, and had spent most of a long adult life, until 1940, traveling from one assigned Ohio parish to another, as a minister in the United Brethren Church.

For reasons which I understand only partly, I acquired more of my character from a blending of my two grandfathers than from either of my parents. In part, both grandfathers were very strong personalities, far more so than either parent. Although my father had a strong sense of humor by spurts (my mother did not), for a hearty sense of humor, few I ever knew could rival the two grandfathers'.

I recall some instances of Joe LaRouche's humor very vividly today, although he died in 1931. Two cases are sufficient. The first was the instance of the afternoon hunt for Snooky's missing tail.

Snooky's very existence was already a sample of my grandfather's sense of humor. Snooky was a large, not really domesticated bobcat, who would permit only my grandfather to touch him with impunity. Snooky spend most of his hours under the iron stove in the kitchen at President Street in Lynn, Massachusetts. One discovered his presence under the stove by moving into the vicinity; a very impressive, menacing growl boomed out from under the stove.

My grandmother could feed Snooky, but not touch, and she could command him in certain ways.

During the 1920s, it was commonplace for hoboes to go from door to door in a neighborhood, soliciting a meal, a contribution, or making an offer to work off the value of food or other contributions to their well-being. My grandmother would turn from such a caller, calling "Here, Snooky," in her girlish soprano. Snooky would emerge from under the stove, and make a fair imitation of a tiger's lunge at the unwanted caller. On two occasions, I saw a hobo scuttling down the street in terror, with both Snooky and my grandmother each registering their own variety of self-satisfaction at the sight.

At the age of seven, I was bemused by the fact that Snooky did not have the tail which I thought all cats should have. I took this up with my grandfather. After a bit of exchange, back and forth, he ventured: "Maybe Snooky's tail is down at the dump. We should go and find it and give it back to Snooky." So, that summer's day in 1929, off we hied, I in the sidecar of my grandfather's motorcyle, visiting several junkyards in succession. Failing to find Snooky's tail, my grandfather suggested that perhaps if we fed Snooky enough fishheads, Snooky would be able to grow back his tail. Off our motorcyle moved, to Fisherman's Beach in adjoining Swampscott, where I was entrusted with the relevant bag-full of fishheads which Snooky dragged under the stove to devour, snarling with delight.

My grandfather retired early, because of the onset of cancer. He decided he would do something he had not done in his life so far. He took a trip to Brazil, up the Amazon, and did a bit of hunting. Among the trophies with which he returned were a pair of alligator skins. How, I inquired, had he managed to get his bullets through that armoring hide? He gave an elaborate tale of inducing the alligator to open his mouth.

That day in 1931, I knew my grandfather was dying, the day my father put me in the Ford beside him, and we drove from Rochester down to Lynn. My grandfather wished to see me once more before he died. The priest had been there when I was admitted to the upstairs bedroom. He seemed so pathetically weakened. His voice was weak, too. He took my hand in his and blessed me in his way.

So, we said goodbye. We drove back to Rochester. My mother had a meal waiting for us. She put grapefruit halves on the kitchen table there at 3 Coxeter Square. The telephone rang. My grandfather was dead. My father tried to eat the grapefruit. He took one spoonful, and then set his spoon down. He cried, "Jessie, I can't eat; all I can taste is my father's body." I hugged him, trying to console him, and as I did so, I wept silently, uncontrollably.

This incident was to play a decisive part in the shaping of an important aspect of my personal character. After my grandfather had died, beginning the day of his funeral, there was a squabble over the division of his estate. I was stunned by this. My father's words of pain over the grapefruit haunted me, the taste of his father's body. The squabble struck me as like an act of cannibalism. I immediately hated the zeal for acquiring wealth, and struggles for position. It is a habit which has remained with me all of my life. I have adhered to that habit, because I know I am both happier and a better person because of it.

George Weir's Christianity appealed to me much more than my parents' variety of evangelical Quakerism. He took responsibility for the condition of mankind, and was legendary in his time for such things as intervening to prevent bloodshed in a strike in his parish, an intervention for which his own life was threatened as an unwanted meddler. Maybe there was a bit of the Scottish dragoon in his courage, but it was also his view of Christian duty. It is no childish delight in grandparents which prompts me to report, quite objectively, that George Weir was a thoroughly loving and lovable man, with a hearty, rolling sense of humor I shall never forget.

Even before school age, I was drawn more into the adult world than that of peers of my age. The center of our household's life was "church work," a disposition my mother had acquired as a minister's daughter, and in which my father supported her to the point, in 1978, she collapsed in the illness leading to her death some weeks later. I never

liked being classed as "my mother's little man"; I was
persuaded even then, that I was an independent personality
with a destiny of my own. However, I accepted and adapted
to the activities into which I was plunged several nights a
week and nearly all day Sundays.

Those who know what Protestant "church politics"
used to be, will recognize more readily what impinged
upon my life during my childhood and adolescence. My
mother and father were among the Protestant establishment of 1920s Rochester. Religious figures who wished to
have Rochester included on their itineraries were advised
to touch base with my parents, and were usually dinner
guests at 3 Coxeter Square during their visits to the community. Those conversations accelerated my interest in
adult reading fare, so that I was more well-read than most
adult members of society by the time I entered adolescence.

In those days, in the process of courtship leading toward probable marriage, there was a condition only less
definite than an announced engagement, which was described as an "understanding." Later, among the pupils at
Lynn, Massachusetts' English High School, a similar state
of affairs was called "going steady," a term which acquired
more suggestive overtones during the course of World War
II—at least, that is my recollection of such a shift in con-
notations. In a similar way, during my childhood and adolescence, it was "understood" that I was destined to become
either a minister, or, permissibly, a scientist. Adult readings
bearing upon such destinies were permitted to me as early
as childhood. These topical areas were those in which it
was approved that I ask questions and enter, albeit modestly, into discussion.

In this course of developments, I entered first grade
at Rochester's School Street elementary school. The day
began with a solemn family ritual.

My mother led me into the small dining room where
my father was eating his breakfast. My mother watched,
as if she might be preparing a report on the proceedings

for some mysterious agency, while my father performed the ceremony. I recall only snatches of the actual words my father spoke, but enough to report confidently the gist of the matter. I can recall the effect most vividly, if not the exact words. The word for my experience that moment is "awesome."

What he said was, more or less exactly: "You are a Friend. At school, boys are going to fight with one another. You will not get into any fights, even if someone hits you."

I was stunned. I took in the implications of the words.

A few years later, I heard a story about the way a goat happened to appear one morning in the bell tower of the elementary school which my great-grandfather Wood administered in Woodbury. My great-grandfather had retained a new teacher for the school year. On the first day of school, the new teacher had laid down the rules to the student body. According to the account of the affair I received some forty-odd years after the fact, the list of "do's" and "don'ts" were mostly "don'ts." For some reason which no one could explain afterward, one of the teacher's "don'ts" was a prohibition against putting any of the goats of my great-grandfather's farm into the school's belfry. Inevitably, a goat went into the belfry one night.

Until that moment in the dining room, I had no mental image of fighting at school. It was somewhat like being instructed not to put a goat in the school's belfry. However, I was able to construct a mental image of what "fighting at school" might signify. I grasped much more clearly the solemnity of the instruction I had just received. I pledged to be a good Friend. My parents looked at one another, silently. My father said goodbye, with a final admonition to "be a good boy." My mother took me off to school.

All of these circumstances of birth and early life had a distinctive sort of combined effect. I was by no means what was sometimes popularly described in my childhood and youth as a "regular guy." Having to receive blows, without returning them, and being obliged to endure even extreme provocations, were an important part of the molding of my experience, but only a secondary part.

Although my family was relatively well-off during the 1920s, and scrimped through the 1930s Depression years without the devastating crises many other households endured, the intellectual standpoint of my family was "genteel poverty." It was as much a family tradition as anything else. My mother had been raised in a minister's household, and Joe LaRouche, although well-to-do, believed in a Canadian-French variety of miserliness. Joe LaRouche was generous, whenever his sense of obligation or an amiable impulse prompted this, but he had a strong belief in "keeping down expenses." My father, who lacked his father's unquenchable self-confidence, was, I think quite naturally, stingier than my grandfather.

There were two other important features to this policy of "genteel poverty." On both sides, my family was "American squirearchy." The Woods of Woodbury were definitely Quaker squires. That was the general level of Joe LaRouche's standing in the community. He was a man whose achievements, status as a landlord, international travels, independence, and carefully stored accumulation of wealth, made him a man whose opinion was to be reckoned with both among his French-speaking cronies and the other circles in which he moved. Joe LaRouche was a man who did things, such as constructing one of the first radio receivers existing in Lynn, Massachusetts, or scandalizing the family with his taking up wild riding on a motorcycle at the beginning of his sixties (the adding of the sidecar was a concession to family pressures).

The same tradition of "American squirearchy" enveloped me, when we moved from Rochester, to Lynn, in 1932. One of George Weir's sisters, Jennie, had married a wealthy shoe-box manufacturer in Swampscott, Massachusetts, which is why my mother happened to know of the Hollywood actor Walter Brennan as an older classmate from Swampscott High School, during her stay with her aunt there. (Walter Brennan movies ranked somewhat higher in the social scale with my family, because Brennan had attended Swampscott High School during a time that high school was considered very respectable.) Typical of the American squirearchy from those generations! The particular importance of the shoe-box fortune was that it was part of the chief trust fund on which the Lynn Society of Friends depended, a fund which had vanished, in part to the nominal advantage of the liberal American Friends Service Committee, during the course of the early 1930s. Thus, as a surviving representative of her uncle's family, my mother was part of the Lynn Friends' squirearchy, and, supported by my father, a nemesis of the American Friends Service Committee.

I was given to understand, throughout childhood and later, that I was part of such a squirearchy, encumbered with the moral and other responsibilities implicit in that status.

Of relatively greater weight was the fact that my sense of social identity, from childhood, was partly adult, and of course, also that of a child and youth. I was much better read than any I knew years beyond my age, and by adolescence, better read than most adults. All of these circumstances combined to make me extremely resistant to the popular American ideology described by David Riesman as "other-directedness." The fact that an opinion was putatively a popular one, was more likely to prompt me to view it with suspicion, than to adopt it. I was definitely not what Lynn school days identified as a "regular guy."

Here one sees quickly, an essential difference in personality between me and President Ronald Reagan. However much the two of us might tend to agree on many issues, especially those of traditional American family values, he is essentially a populist. This shows most clearly in his efforts to explain his "economic agenda." His tendency to argue that economic policy is as simple on principle as managing a family's household budget, does not really signify that he lacks intelligence, but rather that he is ideologically a populist. Nearly all ideologically consistent populists will tend either to exude hostility, or drift to sleep, if confronted with an argument whose exposition requires more than two or three short paragraphs of exposition in, mostly, short declarative sentences. Any conception which demands more than an appeal to popular common sense, causes a consistent populist to view the proponent as "one of them," an outsider whose motives are subjects of dark suspicions. My inclinations are directly the opposite, and have been since early during childhood: Anything too simply explained, by an appeal to popular common sense, I suspect to be some sort of a swindle—and, usually, my instinct in this matter has proven sound.

My father was predominantly a populist in this sense, and my mother inclined to that, too, whereas both grandfathers were not. The endemic conflict between my father and me, was his hostility to what he called "theory," with a strong note of derision in his using the term. He was by no means "anti-intellectual" in other respects. He was a strong Anglophile in literary, musical, and plastic-arts tastes, as were most who acquired their education and general prejudices in the Greater Boston area. He was simply anti-Socratic in the strictest sense of the term. He was a man for established tastes, established values, and of ideas readily conveyed by appeal to popular common sense. Whenever he suspected my intellectual purposes were veering into Socratic directions, he would find ways to interrupt that activity, preferably by assigning some chores to take me away from such mischief. He would have found President Reagan's style more agreeable than he found my own; he admired Nixon on precisely those grounds.

The development of my Socratic method

From earliest relevant sorts of memories, dating from approximately the period immediately before and after my entry into the first grade at School Street, my attitude toward ideas was one fairly described as "Socratic." The source of this method of mine was originally theology. Even a relatively simple theology examines particular beliefs as flowing from underlying assumptions. Western Christian theology has always been Socratic (Platonic), or, since the thirteenth century, Aristotelean, or a combination of both. For whatever reason, my inclination was toward the Socratic, from a very early age.

In the simplest approximation, the Socratic method for exploring the validity, or error of ideas, involves two successive steps. On the first level, we must answer two questions. Is the proposition represented by that idea consistent with the set of assumptions used? If the proposition is consistent with the assumptions, is it also consistent with the facts? If we find the proposition consistent with both the assumptions and the facts, we cannot prove the proposition to be in error unless we can show that one or more of the assumptions used is false.

This was the general form of my attitude toward ideas from about the level of the first and second grade at School Street. At first, this took more the form of a way of reacting to ideas than a definite method. By early adolescence, a definite such method was developed. This emerged clearly beginning my twelfth year.

I had begun poking into the writings of philosophers. After a few readings, I decided to begin all over again, this time reading a selected list of philosophers in chronological order. I began with selections published in the Harvard Classics, a set given to me by grandmother Ella LaRouche that year, and supplemented that with other texts. The list ran, Francis Bacon, Thomas Hobbes, René Descartes, John Locke, Gottfried Leibniz, David Hume, Berkley, Jean-Jacques Rousseau, and Immanuel Kant.

Bacon, Hobbes, Locke, Hume, Berkley, ahd Rousseau I hated. Leibniz moved me with a sense like that of coming home after a long homesickness. I read the *Monadology, Theodicy,* and the Clarke-Leibniz correspondence again and again, going on to writers later in my series, and back to Leibniz again. By fourteen, I was an avowed student of Leibniz. After my evangelical Christian upbringing, this encounter with Leibniz was the most important intellectual experience of my childhood and youth. The two encounters have been the most defining experiences of my development.

About the same time, I encountered the issue of the American Friends Service Committee (AFSC). By my twelfth year, my parents and their friend, Dr. Leroy Austin, were involved in a raging fight with the AFSC. The Austins had been friends of my parents. It had been Dr. Austin's father and my mother's uncle, who had established the Austin-Crosman trust fund, the fund which had vanished. My parents and the Austins wished that the AFSC would act to restore the fund, so that this sum might be used to meet some urgent requirements of the consolidated Friends meeting in that city, the Silsbee Street Meeting House. The AFSC's vindictiveness against my parents and me over this issue reaches down to the present day, in such forms as Judge Lawrence E. Wood's vicious action against Lewis du Pont Smith.

Judge Wood is a descendant of ancestors we share in common, and, in addition to being allied to the AFSC faction among Friends, is part of a faction of the Wood family from which my ancestors broke long ago. Any honest judge would have recused himself from the Smith case, given such and other prejudicial features of his own personal connections. I find his actions typical of the AFSC faction of the Friends, as I have known them over more than fifty years.

The issue of the Austin-Crosman trust fund inevitably overlapped two distinct but interrelated quarrels between my family and the AFSC. The first was political. The AFSC had attempted to recruit my father and other young Friends to support Soviet communism shortly after the October 1917 Revolution. My father and others knew "where the monkey slept" around AFSC headquarters, a character which the AFSC continues to the present day. The second was theological. The AFSC was not a part of the Society of Friends, although it was headed by individuals who were members. Within the Society, the AFSC represent a faction of gnostic "liberal theology" whose doctrine was essentially consistent with William James' *Varieties of Religious Experience*. The issue of the Austin-Crosman trust fund brought these political and theological issues quickly into the foreground.

The issue between the Christian and liberal factions within the Friends national organization, the so-called Five Years Meeting, was focused upon the fundamental difference between the religious "conscientious objection" to military service, of the evangelical Friends, and the pacifism of the AFSC and the liberals. The pacifist view was not only akin to Bertrand Russell's, but the liberal Friends had been directly associated with Russell from early during the present century. The liberals were committed to a global political order of pacifism, and the AFSC functioned as a part of the Soviet "Trust" networks, allied with Theodore Roosevelt's faction in the U.S. intelligence services built up around the Russell Sage Foundation and the World War I-period National Civic Federation. In contrast, the religious Friends' doctrine of "conscientious objection" was one closely linked to a Calvinist notion of God's Will. My parents and other religious Friends saw the pro-Soviet leanings of the AFSC and the liberals' pacifist political dogma as essentially inseparable; essentially, my father was correct in this estimation.

This quarrel within the Friends played a large contributing part, but only a contributing part, to my own process of breaking with the theology of the religious Friends. The factional affray, into which I was drawn as a principal even during my early adolescence, forced me to think through the theological issues. Through this process,

I came to reject the Friends' view, that God is accountable for human history. I came to the view that God holds man accountable for human history, and that each of us, to the limit of our talents, is personally accountable to God for what we do and fail to do respecting the human condition. Although I did not adopt Catholic doctrine on this point in its entirety, my views were consistent with what I came, much, much later, to recognize as the Augustinian standpoint, as argued by the great sixteenth-century canon of the papacy, Cardinal Nicholas of Cusa. It is our calling to participate in the work of the Living God, in the labor of continuing Creation.

The great problem for me, during the late 1930s, was the conflict between my own then-developing theological views and a deep loyalty to my parents. The two most gripping memories in my relationship to my parents, are, first, my father's tears on learning of the death of his father, and the long and tearful hours among the three of us, as I sought their blessing for my desire to renounce "conscientious objection" to military service. I bent temporarily to their will, especially out of love for my father. I could not stomach it for long after that, and betrayed my father—in his eyes—by asking Selective Service to reclassify me for immediate induction into military service.

That was one of the two most important, and profound decisions I have made in my lifetime. The second was my decision to undertake a refutation of Norbert Wiener's "information theory" dogma. Those two decisions are the crucial turning-points in my life, decisions which, more than anything else, determine what I am today. The importance lies not only in the fact of those decisions, as such, but in the effect of the process by which I worked through those decisions.

Among the important decisions we make in our lifetimes, there are two classes. The first, relatively less profound, are those important decisions we make because of what we are. The second, more profound, are those processes of decision-making which make us what we are. The two decisions I have just cited are of this latter class.

I do not wish to, and must not oversimplify these matters. I have presented my break with Quaker theology in its essentials. It is necessary that I do so, in order that the reader may identify the most essential feature of the decision. I must stress, that the full effect of this decision did not appear all at once. The same is true of my decision to devote myself to refuting Wiener's "information theory." By sticking to those decisions, especially through personal crises which put the continuation of those decisions into jeopardy, and the fact that those decisions prevailed in each such crises, I hewed myself as a blacksmith hews hot metal. Over years, various nooks and crannies of my personality were brought into coherence with the implications of those decisions. Indeed, the process continues through the present day. Over the years I became more and more what those two decisions caused me to become.

As a result of my increasing tendency toward a Socratic method, I was a brilliant but poor student in public school and university. This was evident rather clearly by the third grade at School Street. I was a good, conforming student in the first and second grades, but a poor student in the third and fourth. I became a much more brilliant, and much poorer student by the eighth grade, at Eastern Junior High School, in Lynn, Massachusetts. The reason for this paradoxical pattern became clear to me at Lynn English High School. I first understood the cause for the paradox in Plane Geometry I, in a class taught by a fellow Friend and longstanding personal friend of my mother's, Louise Richardson.

The significance of Louise Richardson was that she was a thoroughly sympathetic personality, whom I did not wish to embarrass in any degree. Yet, I could not accept plane geometry as it was taught; I could not accept the axioms and postulates. They were not self-evident to me;

therefore, I refused to believe a theorem deductively premised upon such axioms and postulates. My wrestling with Leibniz helped me to understand the significance of this.

I shall step outside 1937 for a moment, and lean on what I learned of this problem much later in life. It is indispensable that a clear understanding of this issue of method be introduced here, to expose the essential connection between my reaction to deductive method, in high school, and my attack on "information theory" later.

Cusa: founder of modern science

In his 1440 *De Docta Ignorantia* ("Of Learned Ignorance"), Nicholas of Cusa introduced a discovery on which all fundamental progress in physical science since depends. In the simplest of the features of this particular discovery, Cusa presented for the first time what has been known since the eighteenth century as the isoperimetric theorem of topology. The immediately most relevant features of that discovery are as follows.

Cusa, working over a problem considered in various aspects by Parmenides, Plato, and Archimedes, showed that the only geometrical form self-evidently existing in visible space is circular action. Circular action is simply the minimal amount of perimetric action required to generate the relatively largest area. This and other discoveries in the method of physical science contributed by Cusa, formed the starting-point for a remarkable collaboration at Milan, Italy, between Luca Pacioli and Leonardo da Vinci. The combined work of Cusa, and the Pacioli-Leonardo collaboration, was the basis for the contributions to mathematical physics by Kepler and Desargues, and in turn provided the basis for the crucial discoveries of Leibniz, the Bernouillis, Euler, and Gaspard Monge.

On this combined basis, under the sponsorship of the two Humboldt brothers, Wilhelm and Alexander, Gauss and others created a new mathematical physics. The central feature of the mathematical side of Gaussian physics is a discipline known by the names of either "synthetic geometry," or simply "constructive geometry." In such a geometry, no axioms or postulates of the Euclidean type are permitted, and the use of logical deduction is not allowed. One must start with nothing but the isoperimetric principle, and derive the entirety of mathematics from that starting-point, by constructions, with no external assumptions ever introduced.

What is permitted, is the assumption that circular action can be acted upon continuously by circular action. This is called "multiply-connected" circular action. In this case, doubly-connected circular action. We can also assume triply-connected circular action. Such multiply-connected circular action creates straight lines and points. Starting from this, every form which could be constructed in Euclidean plane and solid geometry can be constructed, without axioms, postulates, or methods of logical deduction.

Gauss introduces a higher form of circular action, expanding (or contracting) circular action. The result is the special form of circular action which can be drawn as a self-similar spiral on the outer surface of a cone. Gaussian physics is based on multiply-connected self-similar-spiral action, the Gaussian form of what are called elliptic functions, the Gaussian mathematics of what is called the complex domain.

Therefore, "ideal," "infinitesimal" points do not exist. The existence of "ideal" points is not self-evident. Neither is it self-evident that a straight line is the shortest distance between two points. The methods of Euclidean geometry, and also the methods of axiomatic algebra and arithmetic, are simply wrong.

The way in which I became a poor student, is rather easily explained. Most of the education to which I was exposed, demanded that I assume that certain things were true, and that I accept as also true whatever might be logically deduced from such assumptions. I reacted to this in two general ways. First, as a child and adolescent I was already sufficiently well-read on an adult level, to know that certain among the things I was asked to accept as true assumptions, were simply not true. I dug in my heels at the point I was confronted with such assumptions, and was bored by every effort to derive anything from such assumptions in a deductive way. In mathematics, this resistance developed somewhat later than it appeared in other topics of education. The issue within mathematics became clearly defined only by my encounter with high school geometry.

This was closely related to my resistance to the idea of a "big bang" sort of Creation. I could not believe that God created a variety of things out of nothing all at one stroke. I demanded that there be some principle, by means of which a continuing process of creation unfolded. This view emerged in a clearer form of expression in connection with my attacks on Wiener's "information theory"; it was the drift of my thinking already during the 1930s.

During that period, I located the formal representation of this objection to a "big bang" notion in my wrestling efforts to find a common basis for treating both Descartes and Leibniz. Descartes assumes that Creation is a "big bang." He assumes that the rubble generated by that "big bang" is dumped into empty space and empty time. He assumes that the movement of the particles is initially supplied by the dumping of the "big bang's" rubble into this empty container. He assumes that changes in motion are caused by the action of one piece of material upon another. This makes no sense; so, Descartes adds something else to the picture. He assumes a force acting upon the material universe from outside that universe, a *deus ex machina*. In Leibniz, no such difficulty exists. My concern was to discover how to represent the *deus ex machina* in the terms of Leibniz's *Monadology*.

For me, points and lines could not simply exist. They could only exist if they were brought into being in some definite, lawful way. Nor, could I accept the notion that the so-called "natural numbers" existed in a self-evident way. For related reasons, I refused to accept logical deduction as proof of anything real. Thus, I loved mathematics and physics, but could not tolerate the form in which either were taught.

I would not suggest that my instructors at Northeastern University, in Boston, lacked competence, but they lacked the competence to teach me on conditions I was willing to tolerate. During high school days, I had assumed that those features of the instruction I rejected there, were to some degree or other the result of high school's efforts to give students a smattering of knowledge, by descriptive methods, and that in university I would be exposed to the "real stuff." What enraged me in my encounter with Northeastern was that it was the same stuff I had hoped to put behind me, leaving high school, all over again. Thus, Northeastern incurred my resentment, perhaps not so much for what it did, as pent-up resentment, accumulated over years, which I unleashed upon them.

My mother's heart was set implicitly upon my becoming a minister. My father supported her nominally in this, but his real desire was that I learn the "shoe business," in preparation for going into his consulting business with him. Since his father had apprenticed him to a shoe factory, where he had become a foreman at sixteen, during 1938 he decided to apprentice me to working my way up from the bottom, during summer vacations. I took out the working papers the law required for a minor, and found myself in the lowest rank of production, "hand-dinking" insole-fillers at Benny Shapiro's Peabody factory, the New England Slipper Company. I never had reason to regret this experience, or knowing Benny Shapiro.

It was my first real exposure to a view of the world from a standpoint other than the Anglo-Saxon squirearchy outlook of my family household. Benny was a Polish-Jewish immigrant, who had once earned a living as a professional boxer, and who peopled his employment-roster with relatives and others from first- or second-generation Polish extraction. You may assume, that during the three summers I worked there, I picked up a large dose of Yiddish slang and culture, and felt the impact throughout the shop on the day that Hitler invaded Poland.

Benny was the first to educate my father and me on the subject of Nazism. Benny felt the Jewish question very strongly, of course, but he emphasized to my father that the Nazis were a threat "not just to my sister, but yours, too." Benny could be rough, brutally so, but I recognized that there was a certain philosophy behind this, rather than the sadism some might take it to mean. Benny thought the world was a jungle, and that those who were not constantly alert and tough would not survive. If he acted to toughen you up, he sincerely thought he had the right to do so, and that he was doing you a favor by teaching you to be tough. He took pride in believing that he might be helping you to succeed, by making you a bit tougher. Being tough was a very practical matter for Benny. It was not just a matter of the perils of being part of a Jewish minority; he lived one step from economic death at the hands of the usurers most of the time.

About 1940, my father's relationship to me became strained. My school record was a disappointment to him. This angered him, not only because he thought he had made a psychological investment in the "chip off the old block," but because he was a fearful person generally. He could be courageous, stubbornly so, but he was a brooding man, who would pace the house, talking with my mother for hours, late in the evening, talking through his fears and his tentative plans for coping with what he feared. He was not physically fearful, but psychologically fearful. This weakness of his went with his belief in the "Invisible Hand," not only in economic matters, but in life generally. He was not convinced he could control his fate to any significant degree from such quarters, and tended to substitute propitiatory sorts of rituals for real action in matters he associated with these irrational sorts of psychological fears. It was a quality of fearfulness he acquired from his mother, not his father.

He took my poor school performance as a "bad omen." He was less concerned with the reality of the matter, than the vague fears engendered by his suspicion that this was a bad omen. It grew nasty. I flew down to New York City for the day, to scout the area for a possible sudden change of residence, and took the train back to Boston that same night. I needed to get away from my parents and Northeastern for a while. The way to do it, was to leave a note to my parents and go. On the train back to Boston, I had not yet made a final decision on this action, but the option was more clearly defined in my mind.

I waited until the proverbial "last minute." I was working at Benny Shapiro's during that school vacation period, an employment which Benny and I had preagreed would end at the time I was due to return to Northeastern. Weeks later, on Sunday, December 7, 1941, I entered the lobby of a hotel, intending to meet some acquaintances with whom I had business. Just a few moments earlier, the news of the attack on Pearl Harbor had come over the radio. I stood there, amid the stunned occupants of that lobby area, more fascinated by the way in which I watched those people change almost in that moment, than by the dreadful news itself. Naturally, my first two thoughts were of Benny Shapiro and of the ongoing break with Quaker theology going on within me.

During the weeks immediately preceding, I had resolved tentatively to take an assignment constructing a military base in Africa. That was the business which had brought me to the hotel lobby that fateful Sunday morning. I was not yet prepared, psychologically, to undertake military service proper; so, I thought of taking up civilian duties of a sort which would not represent a total break with my parents on this point. That fateful Sunday, I decided that seeking the construction job in Africa would be an evasion of the question of military service, which I must

remain to face directly. Shortly after that, I saw my acquaintances off to their construction assignment. A few
days after that, I encountered my father in New York City.

We talked as we had not talked together before. My
father summed up his views on personal relations in family,
among friends, and in business affairs, by sundry applications of the formulation "to do right by." He wished "to
do right by" me. On my side, independence taken had
served to put my parents in perspective in my mind. I saw
them as much weaker than I was in every respect, and that
it were my duty to help them. Instead of being smothered
by their efforts to dominate the details of my mental life,
I felt the chains of obligation to their needs. I capitulated
on the perspective of returning to Northeastern, and capitulated to "conscientious objector" status during that
hours-long, tearful session back at the family residence, 23
Pleasant View Avenue, in East Lynn.

It was not entirely a capitulation. Emotionally, I had
been a "conscientious objector" since that morning in the
dining room at 3 Coxeter Square, the day I entered the
first grade at School Street. The numerous beatings taken,
without blow returned, over the intervening years, had
reenforced that initial conviction and pledge. Intellectually,
I had broken with Quaker theology; emotionally, I had
not. The idea of killing another human being was an abomination; emotionally, I was prepared to be killed rather than
save my life at the risk of killing another. The intellectual
decision would win out, but it would take time for that
decision to seep into the relevant emotional nooks and
crannies of my personality. This was not a matter of a
decision to do one thing or the other; it was a matter of
choosing a different identity than I had adopted during
childhood into adolescence. I had made the choice, but I
had to grow into it.

My early management consulting career

I entered a Quaker conscientious objectors' camp in West
Campton, New Hampshire a few days before Christmas,

1942. During the months preceding that, two things occurred which strongly affected my later life. Much of the year was spent assisting my father in his consulting practice. Second, whereas I hated and resisted the way in which differential calculus was taught, I prospered brilliantly in the first course in integral calculus. The first gave me the most essential qualifications for entering a consulting career after the war. The second gave me a deeper insight into my quarrel with axiomatic-deductive methods, and thus contributed in a most important degree to my successful attack on Wiener's "information theory" dogma later.

Among the most important of the classes of assumptions upon which our judgments are based, is the psychological standpoint from which we view a problem. The most important aspects of one's psychological standpoint are two. The first is one's philosophical world-outlook, one's method of thinking, including the yardsticks used to judge which is an acceptable or unacceptable performance. The second, is the way in which one locates one's personal social identity in respect to the area in which the problem lies. If one has adopted the proper form of these two classes of assumptions, one is probably qualified for a career in either management consulting or some analogous occupation. I gained the proper sort of second type of assumption through my 1942 experience with my father.

In first approximation, consulting work prompts one to view problems from the standpoint of management. More important, it prompts one to rise psychologically to a higher vantage-point than corporate management. The response of the management to the problem, is the subject on which the consultant's attention is focused.

This standpoint was most consistent with my Socratic world view. Given the technological and other facts of the situation, most management problems occur not because of the management's lack of technical expertise, but because of mistaken assumptions underlying management's policies of response to technical and other problems. The most important function of the consultant, is to discover the assumptions underlying the policies under review, and to discover which among those assumptions are misleading managements in their policy-responses.

The technical side of consulting is indispensable, of course. Without technical competence, the consultant could not define the problems, or the optional technical solutions to those problems. The consultant must have such technical competencies, but such competencies do not yet qualify him as a consultant. He must also have a Socratic disposition for examining underlying assumptions of management, and approach these matters with the right sort of habituated psychological standpoint.

During the late 1930s, what was called the "penny loafer" became a popular style in footwear. The distinctive feature was the moccasinlike vamp (forepart) of the upper part of the shoe. The machine conventionally used to sew this moccasin vamp was the United Shoe Machinery Corporation's (USMC's) ORL, a machine designed to sew the sole of a Goodyear-welt shoe to the strip of welting attached to the upper part. The USMC had devised an attachment, to adapt this machine to the sewing of the moccasin vamp. The disadvantages involved in the use of the USMC machine were cost per thousand stiches sewn, and a lack of flexibility in the stitching which was a source of great frustration to designers. My father devised an attachment, used on a much cheaper machine than the ORL, which not only reduced the cost greatly, but permitted designs not possible using the USMC's device.

Adapting my father's device to the new range of production problems caused by the greater flexibility in designs, was the problem which kept my father long hours in the factories of his clients. Causing a linen thread to form a neat lockstitch, especially during turning of the work in the process of sewing, is not quite the simple problem it might appear to be. The tension exerted upon the threads must be proper at each point in the operation. It is done simply in lockstitching by hand, as in the case of hand-sewn moccasins; causing a machine to replicate the hand-sewer's manual adjustments of the tensions, was not so simple. A master at handling the adjustments of the machine can solve this readily enough; the problem is to ensure that the ordinary machine operator will succeed as well.

The added problem was that these machines were introduced from the beginning to ongoing production of scheduled lots. All the problems encountered had to be solved in ongoing production, without incurring spoilage or delays. The underlying cause of the problem was the USMC's virtual monopoly.

The basic design of shoe manufacturing machinery was completed at the beginning of the twentieth century. The only major improvements in those designs had been accomplished by Tom Plant, an inventive shoe manufacturer operating in the vicinity of Boston. The USMC had taken over Tom Plant's inventions, and so shoe machinery in the 1940s was essentially what it had been about World War I. The USMC had used its virtual monopoly over all areas but those dominated by Singer, to hold back technological progress in the industry, and to reap much higher profits by so doing. Thus, the machinery with which my father worked was very crude, relatively speaking, and required correspondingly greater technical resourcefulness by technicians and machine operators.

The problem confronted by my father and his clients, was forcing crude machinery to do its job despite its crudeness.

My father was an expert in the methods of various modes of construction of footwear, and under his direction, I mastered this knowledge rapidly. I also learned to enter a factory whose production was in disarray, whose machinery was in deplorable condition, and to whip that sort of mess into working order, if I had to spend the entire weekend rebuilding the plant with a few hands to assist me. A good consultant's delight is doing what appears impossible, and having the business working, to everyone's astonishment, the following Monday morning. Most people do not recognize what the possible is, until they have worked through such undertakings. The only branch of industry in which I have seen such habits commonly practiced, is among the independent farmers the U.S. Department of Agriculture is now working to make extinct.

The technical chores on the factory floor were complemented by late evening sessions with management. So, I learned the rudiments of the point of view of management, and gained some familiarity with the problems of policy assumptions, largely through my oversight of the combined efforts of my father and his clients to outwit a USMC which was treating my father's invasion of a lucrative area of its business as an affair of corporate honor.

The problem with the calculus is the prevailing obsession to prove, that Newton, rather than Leibniz, discovered the calculus. Knowing this, and what this involves, accounts for the reasons I assimilated the integral calculus so easily after rejecting the axiomatic assumptions of taught differential calculus.

The specifications for a differential calculus were developed by Johannes Kepler. Kepler saw this need from two interrelated standpoints. Primarily, he developed these specifications as a byproduct of his founding of astrophysics. To assist him in his calculations, Kepler devised the first calculating machine. Kepler's machine was destroyed during the course of the 1618–1648 Thirty Years War, but Kepler's design was reproduced by Blaise Pascal, and Pascal's machine was the starting-point for Leibniz's design of the modern mechanical calculating machine, and of the principles of a differential analyzer.

The task of developing a differential calculus according to Kepler's specifications was undertaken by Pascal, who worked through principles of ordering of number-interval-series from the standpoint of what we recognize today as elementary differential geometry. Leibniz had undertaken some preliminary investigations in the same direction prior to 1672, and had also composed his first paper on economics, "Society & Economy." His serious work on the calculus began in 1672, in collaboration with Christiaan Huygens, in Paris, under the patronage of France's Jean-Baptiste Colbert. Leibniz gained access to the unpublished papers of Pascal, and completed the specifications for a differential calculus in a paper delivered to a Paris publisher in 1676. Investigation of the unpublished papers in the Hanover Leibniz archive, shows that Leibniz's development of the calculus, during the 1673–1676 interval in Paris, was far more advanced than anything known in the public domain until about the period of the Carnot-Monge Ecolé Polytechnique of 1784–1814.

What Newton published, approximately a dozen years after Leibniz's 1676 paper, was not a differential calculus. No one would have thought to argue that it was, unless Leibniz had been considered for the post of Prime Minister of England. The Marlborough faction in England, the opponents of Queen Anne and Leibniz, sought to discredit Leibniz's scientific accomplishments as a way of blocking Leibniz's appointment as Prime Minister. Queen Anne insisted that the scurrilous gossip against Leibniz stop, and ordered Leibniz's critics to conduct a public debate with Leibniz over the matter of their allegations against his work. So, the Marlborough faction invented the myth of Newton's original discovery of a differential calculus. The result was the Clarke-Leibniz correspondence, and a paper by Leibniz on "The History and Origins of the Calculus."

If one proceeds from the standpoint of a constructive geometry, and treads the path of Kepler, Pascal, and Leibniz, there is nothing axiomatically deductive about a true differential calculus. If one attempts to define such a calculus in terms of infinite series and the standpoint of axiomatic algebra, a large number of nonsense-assumptions must be introduced to make such a concoction appear to work in the manner a calculus requires.

By the beginning of the nineteenth century, Newton was discredited among scientists on the continent of Europe, virtually a laughing stock. This changed, beginning 1815, as a result of political decisions made at the 1815 Congress of Vienna. Lazare Carnot was exiled from France. Monge was thrown out of the Ecolé Polytechnique he had created and led, and Monge's curriculum, which had made France the world's leader in science, was ripped out of the institution. LaPlace and his protégé, Augustin Cauchy, took over. In parallel to this, during the 1820s and 1830s, a movement, including Charles Babbage, emerged in England, warning that science was virtually dead in Britain, and demanding that Britain learn science from the continent of Europe. This faction pronounced Newton's so-called calculus an absurdity, and demanded the adoption of Leibniz's differential calculus, instead. What appeared, both in Britain and France, was a parody of Leibniz's calculus, based on the neo-Cartesian nonsense which Cauchy introduced to be perpetuated to credulous students of calculus textbooks today.

The operations of an integral calculus are immediately referenced to conceptions taken from constructive geometry, and can be mastered readily, conceptually, without reference to the standpoint of what is called the axiomatic-deductive reductionism of Cauchy's method. Hence, I was fascinated by, and happy with my initial exposure to the integral calculus, where I had been plunged into a funk by the differential.

This experience turned my attention back to my readings in Leibniz in a fresh way. Something was percolating, which would come to the surface only after the war.

I enter the Army

With few exceptions, the conscientious objectors I met were a bad sort of the worst hypocrites I would have cared to meet. One exception was F. Porter Sargent, a man whose parentally shaped philosophical outlook was in every respect directly opposite to my own, but who was nonetheless a person of the noblest qualities of personal morality in dealings with other human beings. Porter was a dear friend, and remained so until my deep shock at his death in 1975. With a few other exceptions, the conscientious objectors I knew were personally immoral, in contrast to Porter, for example, and represented varieties of philosophical outlook which I abhorred. Worst of all were the camp administrators, officials of the American Friends Service Committee. The AFSC used the fact, that I was in their administrative custody, to attempt to set up vengeance against my parents. I discovered documentary proof of their nasty little operation, and gained transfer to a government camp. This was worse, because the unit was smaller, throwing me into closer association with more of the AFSC types.

There was a fellow from Queens College, who had transferred to the government camp with me from West Campton, Quentin Stodola. I talked with him, playing out my inner beliefs with him as an aid in formulating my decision. His philosophical standpoint was not my own, but we decided jointly to take up military service. I acted first, sending a telegram to Selective Service in Washington, and was promptly inducted at Fort Bliss.

I later turned down two offers for Officer Candidates' School, reflecting my habituated abhorrence of seeking wealth or position. In the course of events, I was sent to Indiantown Gap, for assignment in Europe, and then shipped to the Pacific Coast, for a voyage on the Admiral Benson to Bombay. From Bombay, we were shipped by train to a camp outside Calcutta, waving en route to Mahatma Gandhi, and admiring the glow above the steelworks at a nighttime Jamshedpur. By rail and portage, I made my way to Ledo in Assam, and bummed a ride on a quartermaster truck, down the Ledo Road to the ruins left in the wake of the last battle at Mitkynia in northern Burma.

I saw death often in the emergency ward of the 18th General Hospital, but received one battle star having experienced no risk but one hazardous encounter with a stray hand grenade. I missed one amoebic dysentery epidemic which hit the ranks of the hospital's staff and patients, picked up a minor tropical infestation, and one illness caused as much by exhaustion as the probably inherited vascular problem brought to the surface under these conditions. So, the end of the war came. I was flown by DC-3 to Ledo, and soon after, given custody of a stock of 10-in-1 rations for a group of GIs hitchhiking our way by train back to Calcutta.

I recall only two experiences during my service in the CBI theater which are noteworthy today. The first was brief, a mere incident, but with lasting impact. The second, more extended, was my experience in Calcutta during the early months of 1946.

The incident occurred at the replacement depot outside Calcutta, prior to my trip to Burma. The news had come that President Roosevelt had died. It was evening. I was called over to a group of about two dozen GIs, and asked to express my views on what the death of the President would mean for the immediate future. The mood of the occasion was a wake. Our wartime President had died, and we wished to react to this fact in some appropriate, personal way. I expressed the view that Vice President Truman was a much smaller man than the deceased President, and that I was worried about the future on this account. There was general assent to that view.

I was surprised by the fact that I was selected to provide political leadership of that sort. I was surprised by my response, too. I had not recalled thinking out anything of this sort; it simply came out of me in response to the request. The idea occurred to me then, that there might be something within me which impelled me in the direction of playing some sort of role of political leadership in the future. I thought about this occasionally during the months which followed, always referencing the image of that impromptu wake. I liked the idea of being useful in that way, but I objected to the idea of pursuing personal political position. This idea rattled about within me, with no particular consequence until I returned to the vicinity of Calcutta at the end of the war.

It was this experience, in Calcutta, in 1946, which defined my principal lifelong political commitment, that the United States should take postwar world leadership in establishing a world order dedicated to promoting the economic development of what we call today "developing nations."

The combination of rail travel and portages, from Ledo in Assam, to Calcutta, brought me, filled with a 10-in-1 rations' turkey dinner, to the Kanchrapara replacement depot outside Calcutta. Passes to Calcutta were available. I made a list of political organizations in Calcutta which I wished to visit, to learn as much as possible of the situation in India. These explorations were informative, but the important contacts developed after my transfer from the camp, to an ordnance unit in Calcutta.

One day, I was approached by a delegation of GIs. I had been selected to represent the camp at a GI rally. I had had no prior contact with the group which nominated me, although I suspected which of my acquaintances might have had a voice in the nomination. The next day, I was informed that I was being transferred to a unit in Calcutta, thus eliminating my role as a representative to the conference to which I had been nominated. Later, a friend of mine in the MPs told me I had been placed under watch by military intelligence, on recommendation of British intelligence. I suspected that my transfer to the ordnance unit had had that sort of inspiration.

The simmering fear among the GIs in postwar India, was that we were being held there for possible support to British forces in case of hostilities involving Indian independence forces. That, at least, was the barracks latrine rumor, and it made a lot of sense to most of us at the time. The prospect of such an assignment was revolting to most of us. This was an added reason for desiring that we be pulled back home as quickly as possible. My known pro-Indian views had certainly been a consideration in nominating me to represent the camp at the GI conference.

The ordnance unit was bedded in what had been a girls' school, a short walk from the southern extremity of Calcutta's central park, the Maidan. Off duty, in the evening, I made my way to Chowringhee, the fashionable street running beside the Maidan, to observe and to pick up conversation with those among the Bengalis curiously probing GIs for their views on India's prospects for independence. At the same time, I developed a circle of fellow GIs, also sympathetic to India's cause, who tended to follow my lead in these matters.

By day, I was assigned to a warehouse, staffed by two Indian babus of the Brahmin caste. My duty was to assist in consolidating the movement of stores, in connection with preparations for U.S. forces' withdrawal. I had at my disposal a tractor, a flatbed trailer, and about two dozen Indian coolies. I had excellent collaboration with the two babus, and excellent labor relations with the section of coolies assigned to me, until a sergeant with a racist streak spoiled it all. It was an unpleasant incident, but it turned out to be the proverbial "ill wind."

This sergeant took it upon himself to bypass channels, and pick a quarrel with one of the two babus. It went beyond ordinary abuse, into some vilely racialist invective. I ordered the sergeant out. He studied my mood, and obeyed. He ran whining to the first lieutenant in charge, and an impromptu hearing on the incident was convened. The sergeant screamed for my hide, but he didn't have a chance against the corroborating witnesses obviously available. I was simply relieved of my assignment, and given no other. Thus, my freedom to explore Calcutta was greatly enhanced.

The Bengali as I knew him, was characterized by exemplary devotion to curiosity. The sight of my uniform was sufficient to prompt the beginning of an acquaintanceship two or three times within the distance of walking a single block. My willingness to enter into discussion resulted in my gaining access to anything I might have desired to know respecting the finest details of the circumstances and tempo of developments then building up. The Anglo-Indians, persons of partial or total European ancestry, were more Bengali than many among them would have wished to profess. I soon became involved in both Indian and Anglo-Indian political circles simultaneously.

A fellow GI, Gene Schramm, and I were riding a tram to attend a function at the Red Cross center. The tram had few passengers at the moment. One of them was an Anglo-Indian, a struggling writer named Ken Stuart. Ken approached us and struck up a conversation, which led to invitation to Gene and I to share a whisky and soda at his club. Ken and his friends at the club introduced us to the inner circles of Anglo-Indian politics in Calcutta. They were pleasant people, but, generally not disposed to integrate within an independent India. Some thought of obtaining the Andaman islands as an Anglo-Indian particularity. Others simply planned to emigrate to England. It was a shame, I thought; they could have adapted to a useful role in an independent India.

There has been a certain sadness in most of my meetings with Indians during recent years. In 1946, the Congress Party represented a vitality of optimism which has been chiefly lost over the intervening years. In 1946, those were exciting people.

One of the most memorable illustrations of my point, is an encounter I had with a group of coolies on the Maidan, a few weeks prior to the outbreak of what was called the "Calcutta riots." I was chatting with two of my acquaintances, as we were approached by this group of coolies. The spokesman for the group asked if his group might ask "the American sahib" a question. Would the United States export textile machinery to India once India had its independence? One has to have a sense of Calcutta as I knew it then, to grasp the powerful impact of this question upon me.

The plight of Bengal's coolies was among the questions I had explored with the assistance of friends. The poor fellows, illiterates, had an income of a few annas a day, a wage set by the British prior to the savage inflation of the immediately preceding years. I had priced the buying power of this income, and found that it could not purchase decent nutrition for even a single person in the available markets. Many supplemented this wretched income by begging, and slept where they could. For them, being employed in a textile factory symbolized escape from their general condition. Most U.S. yuppies today lack the quality of patriotism and good sense these poor coolies expressed by their question to me.

I replied that I was only an unimportant soldier, who could not decide such things, but that I believed that my country should help an independent India secure machinery for its development. My questioners seemed pleased with that response.

Calcutta: a lesson in politics

If I needed to grow up politically, the Calcutta riots left me no choice but to do so. Coincidentally, I was involved at the beginning, and at the end. I learned a lesson in real politics, which seems to frighten some among my vocal Soviet and other enemies and critics to the present day.

The sequence of events began on the Maidan, near the place where the local trolleys ended one leg of a journey, before undertaking the return trip. I met two young Indians I knew. They pointed to the several score of Indians gathering near them. The two students were leading a routine demonstration for India's independence in front of the governor-general's palace. We would, hopefully, meet later to talk about some matters of mutual interest. Some of those demonstrators never returned.

Such demonstrations were routine, noisy in a Bengali way, but essentially peaceful political protests. This time, the guards mounted a lathi attack on the small group of demonstrators. A lathi is a piece of metal on a long, flexible pole. Swung by an expert, it is a most lethal weapon. The attack was an obvious provocation, ordered by someone as an intentional provocation.

The result was essentially predictable. A large demonstration was assembled to protest this brutality. Along Dharmatala, some blocks from the governor-general's palace, the protestors were met by machine-gun fire. There was a restive calm in Calcutta immediately following. Then Bengal exploded. The roofs and sides of the trains coming into Calcutta were heaped with incoming demonstrators. For days and nights several million Bengalis marched in solid queues stretching from one side of the street to another. The British forces left the city. Only the U.S. military remained. The persistent cries of "Jai Hind!," from hundreds of thousands, sometimes millions of throats, filled the city. Had anyone cared to take that step, an independent government of India could have been established in Calcutta then and there, and the bloody communal outbreaks of the next year averted.

Except for the incidents more or less unavoidable in such a circumstance, nothing happened. The exhausted demonstrators dispersed. The nationalists had the situation in their hands, and did nothing. Why? I was perplexed by this. I asked everywhere I might find an explanation. I received my explanation from P.C. Joshi's Communist Party headquarters. Stalin and Churchill had agreed on India's independence in 1947. I really saw into the Communist mentality in that moment; in later years, I have had abundant demonstration that my judgment of the Communist mind, formulated then in 1946, was an entirely accurate one. The Communist mind conjures up the mental image of a poisonous snake; never be fooled by the smile, they will betray without notice.

What most of the world desires and needs, is a world order based on those same principles which we avowed in our 1776 Declaration of Independence, a world economic order consistent with that American System of political-economy which George Washington's administration formulated in U.S. Treasury Secretary Alexander Hamilton's reports on Congress on the subjects of public credit, a national bank, and manufactures. With the power our republic represents, we are untrue to our heritage as a nation, unless we adopt it as our principal national purpose, to bring such a world order into being, and to defend such an order against all who would seek to destroy it.

Talk of our national interest, our national security, in any terms you choose. Our essential national interest is to be, and to perfect ourselves as the quality of nation our founders sought to establish with our federal constitutional republic. If we are not that, we become nothing morally, and shall probably become nothing physically, sooner or later. Our republic was established by an international conspiracy allied with Benjamin Franklin. It was established by those international forces to bring forth on this planet a new kind of constitutional republic, to be a temple of liberty, and a beacon of hope for all mankind. To defend the perpetuation of those principles, we must spread them among nations, and establish them as the dominant form of relations among states on this planet. Our security in the world at large, and our vital domestic interests depend upon this. Any contrary conception of our national interest is a delusion, and the pathway to a national tragedy.

That, and much more, I learned by the time I boarded

the troop ship from Calcutta, for the journey through the Suez Canal and back home. Since then, that has been my consistent and principal political commitment for our nation. It will always be so.

The Case of
Norbert Wiener

2

In the spring of 1947, Pacific Mills was exploring its marketing to medium-sized shoe manufacturers. Trade sources suggested to them, that my father was the best person to advise them on supplying technical services to New England firms. My father, in turn, suggested that I was most suited to conduct the particular sort of survey they requested. I severed my unhappy relationship with Northeastern, and took the assignment. For about twenty of the following twenty-five years, management consulting was my sole source of income.

In 1949, I went in a somewhat different direction, taking employment in the jet-engine production division at the Lynn General Electric plant. I had joined a tiny group of acquaintances constituting the local branch of the also tiny Socialist Workers' Party, who strongly encouraged their associates to take employment as a means of access to trade-union activity. During the first three years of my 1949–1954 association with that political group, I took several forms of employment outside management consulting.

In 1952 I was struck with a very serious case of infectious hepatitis. It was suggested, during my convalescence, that I help my friend Porter Sargent cope with a troublesome investment he had made.

This was suggested to me by a mutual friend, Porter's cousin. Porter had taken over his deceased father's Boston-based publishing venture. One of the firm's vendors, the Coleman bindery, had gone into bankruptcy. Since the firm represented some handcraft skills on whose preservation Porter placed a high moral value, he had bought the firm out of bankruptcy at an excessive price. The cousin asked if I would be willing to step in and help put the bindery on a breakeven basis. Through this mediation, I assumed the job, and managed to reach the assigned objective by early 1954.

Once I had completed that assignment, I was asked to help pull a New York machinery firm out of its financial mess. The client was an amiable fellow, who was willing to change almost anything but those habits which were digging him deeper into the hole. The relationship ended one day in early 1955. The client countermanded my instructions, and substituted a cheaper tailgate-lift truck for a winch–truck: the tailgate collapsed, with $7,000 of broken machinery on the New York street. As I received the telephoned message from the driver, telling me what had just occurred, I decided that my further efforts to aid my penny-wise, super-salesman client would be futile.

In the meantime, I had moved to New York City in October 1954, where I remained, but for one brief period, until 1982.

From the point of my assistance to Porter, I remained in consulting until developments of 1972. Shortly after my stints of 1947, I had undertaken a venture which made consulting the most agreeable basis for ordering my personal life.

I had struck up an acquaintance with Louis B. Mulvey at Northeastern shortly before leaving the place in 1947. By early 1948, Lou had moved on, too. Boston University had established what it called a communications curriculum, and Lou had joined that. The significance of these facts, is that at Boston U., Lou had struck up an acquaintance with the daughter of MIT Professor Norbert Wiener. For that reason, one particular meeting with Lou had enormous significance for my life thereafter.

Lou had been a specialist in radar in his wartime military service, a profession to which he had returned at the time. Years later, I lost track of him. Professor Wiener's daughter had become aware of this aspect of Lou's background, and had loaned Lou a copy of the paperbound, Paris edition of her father's *Cybernetics*. Lou was absorbed by the book. He reported this development to me, and suggested that I skim through the book then and there. To a large degree, I shared Lou's fascination with the book, except for one feature which infuriated me, Wiener's evil "information theory" dogma.

I became absorbed with this issue. It was not until I read a later book of Wiener's, his *Human Use of Human Beings: Cybernetics and Society* that I suspected an evil streak in Wiener himself. I merely assumed that Wiener had gone wrong on this one issue of "information theory," and that he was otherwise an amiable and brilliant fellow. Years later, I learned that Wiener had been thrown out of a seminar at Göttingen University by the great Hilbert, and that for a specific piece of stubbornly repeated incompetence bearing directly on the method he employed for his "information theory" dogma. I had a growing sense of the importance of destroying this dogma. Over the months, into the autumn of that year, a plan of attack began to form in my mind.

My plan of attack was influenced strongly by an issue which had absorbed my attention during late 1946 and early 1947, the doctrine of biological negentropy of Lecomte du

Nouy. It had been a leading topic in an Anglican-sponsored discussion group in which I had participated during that period. The book of du Nouy's is of no importance in itself; the issue which that book merely restates, in its own fashion, is of crucial importance.

Since classical Greece, the principle defining beauty of form has been those harmonic divisions of the circle which correspond to the harmonics of living processes, the harmonic proportions of the human form most emphatically. In other words, beauty is life, and death is ugliness. In Plato's lifetime, an acquaintance of his, working at the Cyrenaic temple of Amon, had proven that only five regular solids can be constructed in what we call "Euclidean space." The construction of these so-called "Platonic solids" depends upon the construction of the circle's Golden Section. For reasons I shall come to in due course, harmonic orderings congruent with the Golden Section are the underlying characteristic of beauty of form in classical art: painting, sculpture and architecture, poetry, and music. The harmonic orderings associated with sequences of the five Platonic solids, are a special aspect of this.

In Milan, Italy, in the last decades of the fifteenth century, Luca Pacioli reconstructed a proof that only the five Platonic solids are constructable regular solids in Euclidean space. The work by Pacioli played a central role in the collaboration between him and Leonardo da Vinci. It was central to Leonardo's work in every branch of physics and art from that Milan period onward. Among the discoveries developed by Pacioli, Leonardo, and their collaborators, was the observation that all living processes' morphology of growth is harmonically ordered in a manner consistent with the Golden Section, and that of all nonliving processes not.

Today, we must qualify this. If we exclude the two extreme cases, astrophysics and microphysics, then we can state, that if a process is harmonically congruent with the Golden Section, then that process is either a living organism or is a special kind of work done by a living organism. However, what are ostensibly inorganic processes, at the extremes of measurement, astrophysics and atomic and nuclear physics, are governed by the same harmonic orderings characteristic of living processes on the ordinary scale of measurements. Otherwise, if a process does not have such characteristics, it is not a living process.

This discovery, by Pacioli and Leonardo, combined with the work of Nicholas of Cusa on a solar hypothesis, was the starting point for Kepler's development of mathematical physics. Since God is a living being, His work must be harmonically congruent with the Golden Section. The entirety of Kepler's mathematical physics is based upon this. The illustrative points are, at a bare minimum of explanation, as follows. Kepler placed the planetary orbits at intervals defined in terms of a series of Platonic solids. Discovering that the orbits were elliptical, rather than circular, he stipulated that the ratio of perihelial and aphelial angular velocities of the planets must be in harmonically ordered series consistent with a musical scale defined by the Platonic solids.

Admittedly, over the centuries since, superstitious fellows who do not understand the principles of physics involved, have attempted to give a magical interpretation to both the Golden Section and the harmonic ordering of the planetary orbits. There is nothing magical or simply arbitrary or accidental involved. All of the efforts to show something magical or accidental in these orbital values are simply the result of using the wrong physics. If one assumes that Newtonian physics is competent, which it is not, then these orbital values are very, very mysterious. From the standpoint of the physics of Leibniz, Gauss, and so forth, these orbital values are simply pathways of what physicists know as Leibnizian Least Action in Riemannian physical space-time.

The relevant observation on Kepler's physics immediately to be added, is that Kepler's mathematical physics is accurate to its degree of development, whereas the contrary, Newtonian approach, leads only to absurdity in astrophysics. This was proven conclusively by Karl Gauss, whose treatment of elliptic functions from the standpoint of self-similar-spiral action, enables us to show why the astronomical orbits must be determined approximately to the values determined by Kepler's three laws.

From the standpoint of Gaussian physics, Keplerian harmonic orderings of both living processes and at the extremes of physical scales of measurement, are the characteristic of those kinds of processes which modern statistical thermodynamics calls "negentropic." Wiener was correct, up to a point, in seeing intelligent behavior as "negentropic" in the sense that statistical thermodynamics defines "negentropy." The trouble is, that the way statistical thermodynamics explains "negentropy" is absurd. Although Wiener's argument was based directly on the false arguments and assumptions of a late nineteenth-century mathematician, Vienna's Ludwig Boltzmann, the issue has been one of the central conflicts within science since Descartes, and was the central feature of the Clarke-Leibniz correspondence, the source from which I first came to understand the issue during my adolescence.

My understanding of this error of Wiener's, is the key to my original discoveries in economic science, and is therefore the key to everything which has made me an influential international figure today. I have learned more and more of this over the past thirty-five years, and am still learning new things almost weekly, through my role in promoting certain important research programs in physical science. In 1948 I knew the rudiments of the issue, and my view of the error of Wiener's work was already a sound one, then.

Although Wiener's error originates with Descartes, the problem was put into focus first by Newton. Newton warned his readers that a central feature of his own mathematical physics was absurd. He warned, that if his choice of mathematics were used, the result must be a physics picture of the universe which was, he stressed, an absurd one. The use of his mathematics leads to the false assumption, he warned, that the universe is winding-down in the sense of the winding-down of a mechanical timepiece, such as a spring-powered clock. This is what modern writers mean when they use the term "entropy." Physicists and others who are ignorant of the problems inherent in an axiomatic-deductive form of mathematics, insist that our universe began with a "big bang," and that the universe as a whole has been winding down ever since. They argue that the age of the universe can be measured, thermodynamically, in terms of an increase of the statistically measured entropy of the universe as a whole. So, some popularizers speak of entropy as "time's arrow" in physics.

These true believers in "universal entropy" are embarrassed by the fact, that, within the universe as a whole, there exist processes, such as living processes, which violate the doctrine of "universal entropy." The behavior of these processes, they call "negative entropy," or, for convenience, "negentropy." Boltzmann's chief work was the effort to explain how "local negentropy" might arise in a process defined by "universal entropy," using statistical gas theory as the point of reference for his argument. Wiener's "information theory" is based on Boltzmann's argument, as are the dogmas of "dissipative systems" of the contemporary Ilya Prigogine.

So, within the confines of taught modern statistical thermodynamics, the issue takes the following form. Using the wrong definition of the problem, the statistical definition, they insist that the argument is whether the universe as a whole is governed by "statistical entropy" or "statistical negentropy." In science, if you ask the wrong question, you end up with the wrong answer, no matter what answer you develop. The issue of entropy versus negentropy is not a question of statistics.

As I have already reported here, all processes which

are characteristically "negentropic," statistically, are actually processes defined by a progressive harmonic ordering congruent with the Golden Section. It was shown, as early as Kepler's discoveries, that the laws of astrophysics are determined by such an harmonic ordering. This tends to prove that the laws of the universe are of a form which statistical thermodynamics calls "negentropy," not "entropy." As Philo Judaeus of Alexandria was the first to attack Aristotle's "big bang" dogma on this point, a "big bang" form of Creation could not have occurred. Rather, the laws of the universe, including Creation itself, are based on an underlying, creative principle, with the implications of "negentropy."

Gauss enabled us to correct Kepler's hypothesis, without throwing out the most essential feature of Kepler's physics, and to prove the corrected view conclusively. Today, a proper study of those phenomena associated with special relativity (as distinct from the errors in Einstein's understanding of Riemann on this point), including quantum phenomena, is conclusive empirical proof that our universe as a whole is a negentropic one.

Newton was correct in identifying the source of the problem as a defective mathematics. If we use an axiomatic-deductive method, such as that of Descartes, to attempt to describe physical phenomena, the picture of the universe presented in that way will always suggest "universal entropy." If we use a different choice of mathematics, derived from constructive geometry, the physical phenomena prove that the universe is governed by a law of "universal negentropy." Also, the attempt to represent axiomatic-deductive mathematics as a universal language for physics, leads us to generate an array of absurdities within physics, insoluble paradoxes such as those at the center of James Maxwell's defective view of electrodynamics. From the standpoint of the physics of Gauss, Riemann, et al., we are able to prove empirically that the insoluble paradoxes of an axiomatic-deductive mathematics vanish if we examine the same physical phenomena from the vantage-point of a mathematics based upon constructive geometry.

The information will cause a deep emotional crisis among some readers. Graduates of modern education are so much conditioned to interpret physical phenomena in terms of a deductive sort of algebra and arithmetic, that they are unable to separate their knowledge of physical phenomena from their habituated algebraic way of describing the phenomena. It is almost impossible for them to separate their knowledge of experimental physics from the mathematics they have customarily used to describe those experimental results. To view the same experimental results from the standpoint of a different choice of mathematics, constructive geometry, implies going back to about the seventh grade in public school, and learning mathematics all over again in a new way. Their emotional attachment to those years of public school and university education, and to the professional or kindred status they have gained by using a defective sort of mathematics, drives them into a rage whenever their personal investment in axiomatic deductive thinking is put into doubt.

From my experience, only a minority of brilliant mavericks among scientists has shown the intellectual and emotional strength to accept the physical evidence which places axiomatic-deductive method itself in doubt. Perhaps a new generation of scientists, educated in Gaussian constructive methods from the ground up, is needed before scientists generally will be able to understand the physics of Gauss and his collaborators.

The entirety of the mathematical physics of the complex domain of physical space-time can be constructed using nothing but methods of constructive geometry, prohibiting the use of axiomatic-deductive methods at any step. This requires a foundation in elementary synthetic geometry beginning no later than the secondary-school level. With that foundation, the student must move on to the Gaussian domain, defined in terms of multiply-connected, self-similar-spiral action, rather than a simple circular action. From that standpoint, we have an entirely different view of the meaning of the phenomena associated with negentropy or entropy.

On the frontiers of science today, we are exploring new classes of physical phenomena. These include, most prominently, thermonuclear fusion, coherent pulses of electromagnetic radiation, and the phenomena of optical biophysics. Some limited accomplishments can be obtained using so-called conventional methods, but however useful are some among these results, the useful application of an axiomatic-deductive method is a limited one. We shall not master these domains in a comprehensive way, until we have shifted our choice of mathematics back to the Gauss-Riemann tradition.

Creativity and scientific progress

The foregoing background briefing presents the problem from a standpoint more advanced than my knowledge in 1948, but my knowledge then was in the same direction, and consistent with what I have described the issues to be thus far. That same qualification applies to the following, added background briefing.

My tentative hypothesis, during 1946–1949, was that those functions of the human brain which account for creative mental activity, must be based upon the same mechanisms responsible for development of the fertilized egg into a human individual. The best way in which to test this hypothesis, was to pose the question, whether the form of development of economies caused by technological progress, had the "negentropic," harmonic characteristics of healthy living processes. Since scientific and subsumed technological discoveries are the paradigm of creative mental activity, if the effects of such mental activity are negentropic in form, then creative thinking is characteristically negentropic. A rigorous demonstration required that it also be shown, that such forms of economic growth occur only as the result of technological progress.

This drew me to an extended study of the mathematical biophysics of Nicholas Rashevsky. Rashevsky's work was defective, for reason of its adaptation to axiomatic-deductive methods. Nonetheless, it was most useful. By studying Rashevsky's work, and cross-gridding this with other relevant sources, I sought to develop a comprehensive mental image of biological processes which would have something better than what Wiener describes as "heuristic" relevance for studies of the cause-effect connections between technological progress and economic growth. My tactic was to follow Rashevsky through every step of his argument, aided by cross-referencing to his cited and other sources, to drive his conception up to the point that his arguments collapsed into paradoxes. This is my habituated application of Socratic method to the thorough analysis of any subject matter.

This approach to Rashevsky's work forced me to develop a sense of what mathematics terms "discontinuities." By "discontinuities," I mean the case in which a well-defined mathematical function generates a case in which ordinary sorts of mathematical analysis breaks down. In mathematics, the model of discontinuity presented by Karl Weierstrass, illustrates the point most simply. The paradoxes in Rashevsky's "modelings" of living processes all centered around this problem of discontinuities. The living process continues to function beyond the point at which ordinary mathematical analysis can follow this development. So, I reasoned, there must be a higher sort of function, which includes ordinary sorts of mathematical functions as special cases.

It was clear that my hypothesis, concerning the negentropic form of healthy economic growth, was the right one. It was also clear that only technological progress generated such patterns of growth. It was also clear enough, that all fundamental scientific discoveries involve discontinuities of the type I associated with the paradoxical features of Rashevsky's modelings.

In the course of scientific work, it is more frequently the case, that existing theories are discredited by showing that, either the conclusions are not fully consistent with the assumptions used, or that the facts are in some degree not consistent with the conclusions reached. This is the everyday, but more superficial side of scientific work; it occurs only as an incidental, if often indispensable feature of fundamental scientific work. Truly fundamental scientific discoveries involve overthrowing a generally accepted, axiomatic sort of assumption. Such modifications of assumptions, are discontinuities in the strictest sense of the term.

Although much of technological progress occurs as a result of mental activity on the level of day-to-day scientific work, in the broader sweep of technological progress, this is not the case. Each particular technological innovation belongs to a family of such innovations, which altogether represent the unfolding of what we often describe as a scientific revolution. It is these "scientific revolutions" which are the underlying driver of technological progress, such that all advances in human productivity are, in the last analysis, an unfolding of the internal process of generating scientific revolutions.

We distinguish, today, between those advances in technology which represent the introduction of a "new scientific principle," and those which are merely a more advanced expression of a scientific principle already well established. It is the introduction of a new scientific principle which represents, at once, both a discontinuity in scientific thinking, and which generates a generalized discontinuity in the course of technological-economic growth.

In this way, I formulated the first part of my two-step discovery in economic science. On the one side, the characteristic features of creative mental activity are negentropic and therefore implicitly so measurable. Advances in technology, as mental conceptions, could be measured implicitly in this way. The introduction of these advances in mental conceptions, to production, causes economic growth, the which is also negentropic in form, and measurable. So, measurable negentropy in the first instance, causes measurable negentropy in the second instance. By reducing this causal connection to a single functional expression, the causal relationship between technological progress and economic growth is measurable, and this in a way which admits of predicting the benefits of adopting a specific form of technological progress.

This was the first part of my discovery.

The problem posed by the discovery, was the question: where to find the mathematics appropriate to such a function?

At first glance, I recognized that Georg Cantor's notion of transfinite orderings touched directly upon the kind of mathematics needed. I spent the greater part of every available moment, over approximately a year, fighting my way through Cantor's work. I had stabbed at Riemann's work years earlier, by way of Eisenhart's text. Working through Cantor, I saw Riemann in the right way for the first time. I read Riemann's famous 1854-published inaugural dissertation, "On The Hypotheses Which Underlie Geometry," with what can be described only as an empyreal quality of excitement. From that moment, everything I had sought began to fall into place.

Thus, during the period of my prolonged convalescence from hepatitis, in 1952, was born what is known today as "the LaRouche-Riemann method" in economic analysis.

During the same period, 1948–1952, I was exploring the same topic along a parallel track. This touched significantly on my personal friendship with Porter Sargent. Our principal common interest was music, paralleling my friendship with one of a pair of friends, Felice and Edmond Manna. The exciting part of these friendships, with the

Mannas and Porter, was the sharing of some of the latest discoveries by any of us among compositions and performing artists. If I dug out any such "find," I had an immediate, compelling impulse to share this with those friends. I delighted in the finds they presented. This activity overlapped a provocative observation I made during that period, that after a few hours saturating myself with a working-through of a Beethoven composition, most emphatically, or fighting through my critical thoughts on the competence of one or another performer's treatment of such compositions, my own mental productivity was considerably enhanced.

This prompted me to seek out a parallel between artistic and scientific creativity. I chose the intersection of music, classical poetry, and classical drama, as the target-area on which to focus attention. Two aspects of artistic composition stood out, beautiful form and the creative element within the elaboration of that form. I adopted the thesis of Shelley's "In Defence of Poetry" as a point of reference.

I reduced music, poetry, and drama, to three distinct philosophical types: the "Dionysian," typified by Nietzsche and his ilk, the "Apollonian" submissive type, and the "Promethean." The terms I chose reflected the fact, that I undertook this as an attack on Nietzsche's doctrine. These are the same three "types" which Dante Alighieri assigns to the respective "Inferno," "Purgatory," and "Paradise," of his *Commedia*. These are the three types identified by St. Augustine. They are the three types, respectively, of "bronze," "silver," and "golden" souls in the Socrates homily appearing in Plato's *Republic*. Bach, Mozart, and Beethoven, typify the "Prometheans" in music.

I focused, naturally, on the questions of form and creative features of "Promethean" art-types. From this standpoint, I attempted to reconstruct, in my own terms of reference, the "transfinite" progression from "Inferno" into the concluding, empyreal canto of Dante's *Commedia*.

Creative classical composition is based upon two seemingly irreconcilable principles. As in constructive geometry, the composer must introduce no element which is arbitrary. Yet, he must supersede the forms flowing simply from the established rules by a creative innovation analogous in nature to a creative scientific discovery. For example, as Friedrich Schiller explains this for the case of dramatic composition, the entirety of a great classical tragedy begins from the author's discovery of a central feature of the entire work, which Schiller references as the *punctum saliens*. In the language of biology, the *punctum saliens* is the central moment of the process of mitosis. The entire existence of the cell, is a process leading into mitosis, and the daughter cells flow from the mitosis. The author, or classical composer, begins with a *punctum saliens*, the creative discovery, and then elaborates the composition in such a way as to build toward this event, and to append its consequences.

In bad art, the absent creative mental activity is replaced by the purely arbitrary intellectual or sensual effect, as in the romantic method of Richard Wagner. It is pure fraud, to accept the classification of any part of Beethoven's compositions, or of Schubert, or Chopin, or Schumann, as "romantic." Such characterizations were applied to these musicians after their time, as musical criticism became corrupted by the wide influence of the "historical" school of Karl Marx's law professor, Friedrich Karl Savigny. They are falsely labeled "romantics" because the "historical school" wished to argue, in a Hegelian or Marxist way, that there are no rational principles in aesthetics, but only a mysterious evolution in popular opinions and tastes. Mozart, Beethoven, and so forth were "Bachian" composers, who based themselves on the strict limitations of Bach's well-tempered polyphony, and on the principles of form adopted from classical poetry, classical strophic forms of Italian and classical German poetry most emphatically. The innovative features of their compositions can be shown, by methods of analysis associated with classical Bachian polyphony, to be rigorously defined scientific discoveries, rather than anything arbitrarily produced for either intellectual or sensual special effects.

For example, a mode appears in the "Lachrymosa" of a particular Mozart Mass, which is parodied by the romantic Hector Berlioz in his virtually Wagnerian travesty of the singing of the Mass. To the musician, Mozart's Lachrymosa is rare beauty, and Berlioz's parody painfully ugly. Berlioz parodied Mozart to produce a special sensual effect; what he parodied had none of this.

As I have already indicated earlier here, it happens that the notion of beauty in art in western civilization, has been premised since classical Greece, on harmonic orderings consistent with the Golden Section. This includes the forms of poetry, the harmonic proportions of a great classical tragedy, and is the basis for both the well-tempered scale and for the rules of classical polyphony as well as the scale itself. This same principle, governing beauty of form, is the underlying principle of creative mental activity, too.

A briefing of the reader on this subject, is in order at this point.

A negentropic process is one characterized by an increasing richness of singularities. To measure the increase or decrease of the density of singularities per chosen interval of action, is one valid way of measuring the relative negentropy or entropy of a process. This is reflected in the fact that statistical measurements of negentropy or entropy are possible, a possibility which is understood rightly if we underscore the geometrical basis for Gaussian probability distributions, rather than the more popular ones derived from LaPlace. There is only one way, in mathematics, in which functions of this sort can be constructed. They occur in the complex domain constructed by Gaussian, multiply-connected, self-similar-spiral action.

Here lies the key to the significance of the Golden Section. If you construct a self-similar spiral, on a cone constructed of transparent material, and stand that cone on a sheet of white paper, a very simple, but crucial point is demonstrable. The shadow of that spiral, appearing on the paper, is also a spiral. The projected spiral, on the paper, has harmonic ordering consistent with the Golden Section. Golden Section harmonics in visible space, are characteristic features of reflections of conic self-similar-spiral action, occurring in the real physical space-time of the complex domain, upon the shadow-world of the world as we imagine ourselves to see it.

The only mathematical function which describes what has been occurring within the U.S. physical economy during the recent eight years, is the function known as the LaRouche-Riemann method. Every other published forecast analysis, by either the government or private agencies, has been proven repeatedly absurd by the collapse of manufacturing, agriculture, basic economic infrastructure, and actual physical content of average market-baskets—at a rate of less than 5 percent per year over the 1983–1985 period, and by more than 15 percent during 1986.

The overall, accelerating downslide in the U.S. physical economy (as opposed to an almost meaningless GNP) takes the form of an alternating series of ups and downs, looking very much like the ups and downs in the downhill run of a roller-coaster ride. Each of the turning-points, up and down, over this period, is associated with the dropping-out of significant elements of our nation's physical economy. Each of these turning-points is a mathematical discontinuity in the function used to measure the economy's simple rates of growth and contraction. In structure, the U.S. physical economy is becoming less dense in singularities; in other words, our physical economy is collapsing, entropically, into a more primitive physical state.

On the way up, in a genuine period of physical growth, the reverse sort of process occurs. The economy becomes more complex structurally, and these structural changes are associated with ups and downs like those of a roller-coaster ride downhill, but in reverse. Take a motion picture of a roller coaster's downhill ride. Play that film in reverse; that is a fair description of what economic growth looks like.

The generation and elaboration of new scientific principles, the mental source of the technology causing economic growth, reflects the same sort of increasing density of singularities. This is the characteristic geometry of all creative mental activity, whether in the physical sciences, or in classical forms of art.

My association with the SWP

In the midst of this scientific activity, I became associated with a group of about two dozen persons in Lynn, Massachusetts, the Lynn branch of the tiny Socialist Workers' Party. I was brought into contact with this group by an acquaintance I had known for more than thirty days on a troop ship returning to the United States from Calcutta. The track leading into the renewing of this contact started at Northeastern in 1946, but I paid little attention to occasional contact with this handful of Trotskyists until October 1948. It is of some practical importance to show the association as it developed and proceeded, rather than the absurd interpretation I have read in some published locations.

In 1946, I was recruited to join in founding the Northeastern chapter of Cord Meyer, Jr.'s American Veterans' Committee (AVC). Some months later, a group of my friends, members of Hashomer Hatzair, approached me, explained that they were emigrating to Israel, and asked me to take over the leadership of a Students for Democratic Action chapter on the campus. I replied, that I thought the American Veterans' Committee duties were as much extracurricular responsibility as I could competently fulfill, especially since I was commuting to campus from Lynn daily; but, I offered an occasional helping hand, if it were needed. The Communists were the major factional issue inside AVC at the time, but the Trotskyists had also sought to gain an influential foothold. The Lynn branch of the SWP, predominantly Jewish, was then actively involved in pro-Israeli circles. So, these Trotskyists took notice of me, and discovering that I had a former acquaintance among them, encouraged him to develop a contact with me. Nothing more came of it until October 1948.

The blame, if any, for my becoming associated with the SWP later, falls upon Dwight D. Eisenhower's failure to seek the 1948 Democratic nomination. Had he done so, I am certain that my future would have been steered accordingly. Experience had not lessened my early 1945 doubts about President Truman's administration in the least. His administration had done a great deal to demoralize the postwar population, and his foreign policy, as well as his domestic, was a horrible failure on balance. Wallace had looked interesting briefly, for saying some things that others seemed unwilling to mention, but that favorable impression did not last for long, especially as he became more deeply involved with the Communists. Dewey presented himself in his campaign as an unmitigated disaster. I felt very sad for the United States, and saw little likelihood that matters would improve for some time to come.

I dropped any interest in what some might call "mainstream politics." In my view, things would tend to become worse in that area, and there was no point in my wasting my time attempting to influence matters there as a tiny voice from within. When I was invited to attend an election-campaign meeting for the Socialist Workers' Party vice presidential candidate, Grace Carlson, my interest in maverick politics led me to attend. Her assurance to me, that the SWP was a movement open to exploring new ideas of the type I identified, changed my earlier inclination to keep away from the SWP.

She later dropped out of the SWP herself, in 1952, to return to the Catholic Church, but just before she did, she contributed one thing of rather lasting impact upon me. I happened to be in Minneapolis, on business, during the period preceding my bout with hepatitis. I saw her occasionally during my stay there, at the time she was considering, secretly, leaving the SWP. For some reason, she chose to confide in me, not the fact that she was leaving, but the inner state of mind which prompted her to do so. She spoke of the "little priest" she met occasionally, and in that context of reference, quoted from Isaiah: "If the trumpet shall sound an uncertain note, who, then, shall heed the call to battle." Only conceptions which are deserving of expression with great pungency and force, and which are uttered and acted upon accordingly, are worth the giving of a life's service.

The Lynn SWP was more of a social club, which met in an office on Central Square once a week, than the popular image of a Trotskyist organization. I joined it in 1949, not by intention, but because I saw no reason not to when the offer was presented. There were differences in philosophical outlook, but no visible differences of any more importance than I was accustomed to in most day-to-day associations with friends and others, earlier or then.

The stock-in-trade of shared beliefs, was that Stalin had established a brutal dictatorship in the Soviet Union, that Trotsky had been the leading opponent of Stalinism, and that conditions in the U.S.A. were becoming rotten, and would probably remain so for some time yet to come. The rule was, "dont't become excited about anything, poke about doing some modestly useful project after another, make friendly contacts among working folk, and run an occasional 'educational' political campaign." They regarded liberals as hypocrites. They radiated the policy: "Those of us who see things this way ought to stick together." The meetings were weekly and brief, usually. The rest, most of the time, involved private readings of the history of the Trotskyist faction, and a reading through of the writings of Marx and Trotsky. Otherwise, I was a member of the club, and found the rules of the club generally agreeable or scarcely a burden.

This changed when Senator Joseph McCarthy's traveling roadshow reached Boston. This motivated me to serious action. More by default than anything else, I became the active tactician in our brawl with McCarthy.

I developed a different view of the SWP when I moved to New York City to take up my consulting assignment there. I saw in the SWP leadership a collection of hard-nosed, bigoted, petty bureaucrats, resembling the worst sort of trade-union bureaucrat. They pretended to have command of some precious stock of ideas. The ideas proved, on closer examination, to be a populist's sort of gossip about this or that book, and a fanaticism which was actually nothing but Riesman's "other-directedness" run to extremes. Few of them actually thought, except as tactical issues of factional maneuvering provoked them to do so. Since McCarthy had been ruined, and since the new projects resolved upon disgusted me, there was no reason I should remain.

It was not a formal break. I have rarely made a show about breaking from any business or other association. Such shows are a waste of energy. If I find something to be a mistake, I learn my lesson quietly, and simply walk away. Why pour new efforts into what has proven a bad investment of one's energies? I busied myself in consulting work, and used as much spare time as I could muster to follow up on my discoveries.

My issues with Marx and Engels are much more important than my differences with the 1949–1954 SWP, and much more relevant to my development over the years. Since I had already completed the initial form of major discoveries in economic science, I thought it useful to attack Marx's economics in a thorough way, in the same spirit I had worked through Rashevsky, for example. Since I was a Socratic dialectician, and since Marx asserted that he based himself on a dialectical method, I thought it useful to work through that aspect of Marx, too.

I never encountered a member of the SWP who understood anything of Marx's economics or method. An SWP class in economics was a person reading from a few pages of one of Marx's pamphlets, or a passage of *Capital,* and commenting, in the manner populists do, on the appreciation to be placed on each paragraph recited: "What Marx is trying to explain here, is . . ." In method, there were academics such as George Novack, putatively the oracles on such topics. It reminded me of those Appalachian elementary schools called "blab schools," from which students emerged with borrowed opinions, and no experience in actually reading a page. Poor George was a student of John Dewey, who simply imposed the commonplaces of American pragmatism on textual references, to much the same effect SWP "economics teachers" conducted their "blab school" classes.

It could hardly be said that I disagreed with the SWP's economics or method. There was nothing of that sort worth disagreeing with; most members were simply not interested in such matters, beyond picking up and regurgitating a few catch-phrases. Their ideology was essentially a radical variety of the populism which has strongly influenced the changes in U.S. popular culture over the past hundred years. They constituted a club of persons, without any original ideas, who wished the club to become respectable and influential among chosen sets of peers, and who thought that by adhering to the memory of a few putatively successful radical figures of the past, some of the magic of the past might sooner or later rub off on the club.

The fraud of Marx's economics

Marx's economics, itself, is nothing more than a variety of the political-economy of the British East India Company's Haileybury College. British political-economy, as associated with Adam Smith, Jeremy Bentham, Thomas Malthus, and David Ricardo, was imported to Britain from

French-speaking Switzerland. Smith was picked up by the Second Earl of Shelburne in 1763, and assigned to work on Shelburne's project for destroying the economies of the English colonies in North America. In training for this project, Smith was sent to study under David Hume's cronies in France and Swiss banking circles, and thus learned the Physiocratic doctrine of Dr. Quesnay, and produced a book, *Wealth of Nations,* which is essentially no more than a plagiarism of the *Reflections* of the physiocratic writer A.M. Turgot. This became the doctrine taught at Haileybury, constituting what Marx presented as the "only scientific political-economy" before his own work.

Marx was recruited to British political-economy by an agent for British intelligence, Friedrich Engels. Engels was the son of a textile manufacturer whose income was based on the system of slavery in the cotton-producing states of America, and was politically affiliated with the Cambridge circles identified with the Apostles. This circle was part of Charles Babbage's backing in the fight against the excesses of Malthusianism which erupted in Britain during the 1820s. So, Engels was a follower of the Haileybury school, but took special exception to the work of one leading economist of that school, Malthus. Engels broke Marx to his will in this matter, by inducing Marx to undertake a vile libel against the leading German economist, Friedrich List. Marx, recruited to Guiseppe Mazzini's Young Europe conspiracy at Berlin, remained an asset of Mazzini's until the point Mazzini dumped him about 1869. In London, Marx came under the control of the section of British intelligence which coordinated its actions with Mazzini's operations, specifically Palmerston's agent Urquhart, operating out of the British Museum. Urquhart was Marx's controller during Marx's work in the British Museum, and guided Marx's work in economics and other subjects.

Marx's economics differs from that of Ricardo et al. only on several secondary points. First, Marx draws out the implications of Haileybury political-economy to its limits, in his linear mathematical model of "extended reproduction." Second, Marx's *Capital* is pervaded by the influence of what is commonly described as Marx's "historical materialism." Third, Marx attempts to portray himself as an original thinker in economics, by plagiarizing, although badly, certain notions from the work of Friedrich List and Henry C. Carey. Marx was a scholar; he was often a vicious liar on scholarly matters, but a scholar beyond doubt. He had some potential for originality, but his reputation for originality, apart from a scissors and paste sort, is highly exaggerated by both his admirers and those who denounce him most strongly.

Marx's notion of "extended reproduction," on which his theory of the business cycle depends, is a clever hoax. As Marx himself emphasizes repeatedly, his model of investment leaves out of consideration technological progress in the succession of these investments. On this basis, he pretends to show, that as the capital-intensity of production increases, the net effect is an inflation of costs, which lowers profit rates, and thus causes a self-feeding contraction of investment and employment levels in production. This sort of development does appear in economies which inhibit technological progress, but it is not a natural tendency within modern agro-industrial economies. Naturally, because of my own discoveries in economic science during that period, it is this centrally thematic feature of Marx's *Capital* which I recognized most immediately as a fundamental error.

Essentially, Marx's so-called historical materialism is nothing but a parody of the irrationalist dogma of "historicity" which was the central doctrine of Marx's Berlin law professor, F.K. Savigny.

Savigny was the closest collaborator of Metternich's spy at the University of Berlin, Prussian State Philosopher G.W.F. Hegel. He was a leading among those followers of the notorious Madame de Stäel, who introduced the form of irrationalist dogma called Romanticism into nineteenth-century Germany. Savigny was also a fanatical anti-Augustinian, who devoted his career to reviving Roman imperial law's tradition as a replacement for Augustinian natural law. His particular notability was his largely successful influence in Germany, and more widely, in insisting that in art, law, and politics, there existed no rational principle analogous to law in the physical sciences. On this premise he proposed to eliminate constitutional law of the sort adopted by the United States, and insisted that the law must be based, instead, on changing tastes in popular opinion. This irrationalist doctrine of popular opinion, called his *Volksgeist* dogma, was later the basis for Nazi law.

Savigny's *Volksgeist* dogma is also known as the dogma of "historicity." Marx restated this in terms of that doctrine of class struggle which had been introduced by certain German Jesuit circles during that period. Marx developed a theory, that social classes each underwent an irrationally evolving series of changes in popular opinion, and of evolution of subordination and resistance to the currents of opinion associated with temporarily dominant classes. He elaborated his economics to conform to that view.

The principal term he plagiarized from List and Carey was the notion of "labor-power." The plagiarized term originated with Gottfried Leibniz's founding of economics, in which the relationship among technology, heat-power supplied to machinery, and the productive powers of labor, is at the center. This notion of determination of the productive powers of labor was formally adopted by the administration of President George Washington, as the central feature of U.S. economic policy, in Treasury Secretary Hamilton's December 1791 "Report to the Congress on the Subject of Manufactures." The conception is central to the writings of all leading American System economists, including Mathew and Henry Carey and Friedrich List.

Since Marx excludes technology from an integral role in the process of extended reproduction, it was inevitable that his use of the term "labor-power" would be an empty parody of Leibniz's conception. This fallacy is made clear at the outset of the first volume of *Capital,* where Marx purports to define the "cell form" of economic value.

Marx's "dialectical method" is a chimera.

The notion of a "dialectical method" originates with the Ionian and Athenian Greeks. It appears in a rigorous form in the dialogues of Plato, in which Plato causes his Socrates to speak of "my dialectical method." The term signifies nothing other than "the method of these dialogues." After Plato's death, the sophist Aristotle developed a different sort of dialectical method, especially for the purpose of his commentaries upon Plato's dialogues. Where Plato's dialectical method is based, as he insists, on the methods of a constructive geometry, Aristotle's is based on the reductionist method of the axiomatic-deductive method.

The Platonic dialectic was the preferred method of Western European Christianity until the Aristotelian dialectic was introduced, by way of Venice, during the thirteenth century. A strict Platonic dialectical method was employed by the leading thinkers of the Golden Renaissance, such as Cusa, Pacioli, and Leonardo. Leibniz was an exponent of this method. Descartes was an exponent of the Aristotelian dialectic, as were the eighteenth-century opponents of Leibniz, such as Immanuel Kant.

From the standpoint of physics, the most obvious difference between the Socratic and Aristotelian dialectic, is that the former is consistent with the method of constructive geometry, and the latter is strictly an axiomatic-deductive method. The former is the scientific method of Plato, St. Augustine, Nicholas of Cusa, Leonardo da Vinci, Johannes Kepler, Leibniz, Friedrich Schiller, Gaspard Monge, Karl Gauss, and Bernhard Riemann, among others. The Aristotelian method is expressed at its best by the famous work of the "false Euclid," Euclid's *Elements*.

The earliest trace which I know of the roots of the Socratic dialectic, is ancient Vedic solar-astronomical calendars, as the ancient Vedic way of thinking and communicating is defined, approximately the fifth century B.C., by the great Sanskrit philologist Panini. Classical scholars among my associates have afforded me conclusive demonstration, that the classical Greek as typified by Aeschylus and Plato, conforms in essentials to the principles defined by Panini. In other words, that the ancient Greek, like the ancient Hittite, derivatives of the ancient form of the Vedic, carried forward a way of looking at and describing man and nature also transmitted into the Vedic culture of India. During the late 1940s and early 1950s, I had but a bare approximation of my knowledge on this topical area today. However, I understood the bare essentials of the matter quite accurately then, by some significant familiarity with key fragments of written classical Greek thought from the Ionian onwards, and by viewing the content of those fragments from the standpoint of my own work on the same issues of method in a more modern setting.

For purposes of identifying the issues to the modern layman, it is accurate to report that the Socratic method, like Panini's standpoint in philology, places the emphasis upon the verb, whereas the Aristotelian method, like all forms of axiomatic-deductive method, places the emphasis upon the noun. In the Aristotelian method, one points to an object and utters a name assigned to that object. In Socratic method, and its kindred, such as Panini's philology, one points to some action by which a process undergoes a change. This change as such is the subject of thought, and that thought is presented, not as a noun, but as a statement defined in terms of a transitive form of a verb.

In the Socratic method, the essential substance of the universe is defined in terms of an action, as expressed by a statement centered upon the transitive form of a verb. In that sense, "substance" is defined as "change." In that view, the existence of the particular objects to which we assign nouns as names for objects, is viewed as a product of change.

In the axiomatic-deductive, or nominalist method, "substance" is viewed as the quality of existence of objects imagined to have a self-evident existence as "things." In this nominalist method, change is defined as the form of interaction among things.

In physics, for example, the nominalist assumes that matter is composed of assemblies of indestructible, very small particles, such as either atoms, parts of atoms, or the imaginary "quark." The physicist in the tradition of Cusa, Leonardo, Kepler, Leibniz, and Gauss, insists that there are no self-evidently existing elementary particles, but rather that particles are what the mathematics of Gauss, Dirichlet, Weierstrass, and Riemann defines as singularities, particles created out of nothing but continuous change. The significance of Hegel and Marx, on this point, is that they were both quasi-Aristotelian nominalists in method, who attempted to account for Sextus Empiricus's fragments of the pre-Socratic Ionian, Heraclitus, on the subject of change, within the terms of an Aristotelian dialectic.

The root of this pseudo-dialectic in the writings of Hegel and Marx, is the role of the *deus ex machina* in Descartes' dogma. Respecting the physical universe, Descartes is a radical nominalist in the footsteps of Aristotle. Yet, Descartes, like Newton, was shrewd enough to recognize that the nominalist's sort of materialism contained an absurdity. The absurdity of the use of formal axiomatic-deductive logic, in the effort to explain the material universe, is that such a universe must be "winding down" from the beginning. A universe based on principles of "winding down," could not have come into existence in the first place. So, to define a universe which could exist, Descartes had to postulate an efficient agency outside that universe, an agency in no way consistent with the laws of the physical universe, which could magically create the universe and keep it running, a *deus ex machina*.

All modern European varieties of gnosticism and agnosticism, Ludwig Feuerbach and Marx's "materialism," as well as British empiricism and modern positivism included, are elaborated on the basis of this argument by Descartes.

In Plato and Christian theology, man's reason is the potential development of a divine spark of reason, which sets man absolutely above the beasts. By virute of his animal-like existence, man is subject to the baser impulses of the beast, expressed as the irrational, hedonistic impulses for seeking sensual pleasure and avoiding pain. Yet, man is also possessed of a divine spark, in the image of God. By developing this divine spark of reason, and by subordinating his hedonistic impulses to that development of reason, man is able to choose to live in ways which are suitable for a creature in the imitation of Christ. The development of reason enables us to know the Will of God, the *Logos* or "Holy Spirit," if only in an imperfect way. This effort at perfection of knowledge of God's Will, is merely typified by scientific progress. By governing our behavior in a manner consistent with knowledge of the Logos, we govern our actions according to the influence of God's Will, and so participate, to that imperfect degree, by manner and intent, in God's work. Such was the theological standpoint from which I broke with Quaker theology.

Johannes Kepler's founding of modern mathematical physics, is an expression of this point of view in science. We are able to discover, with lessening imperfection, those lawful principles which reflect the way in which God is continuing to create the universe. We are thus able to adduce the lawful form of the act of creation. We can do this only from the standpoint of adopting the action of change itself, rather than particular things, as the essential form of universal substance. This was passed down to modern European civilization chiefly through the *Timaeus* dialogue of Plato, one of the chief references in classical Greek philosophy adopted by Christian theologians, including St. Augustine. The only essential difference between Plato and these Christian theologians, as St. Augustine states this explicitly, is the person of Jesus Christ, as identified by the inclusion of the *Filioque* in the Latin Creed.

The issue is the mechanistic materialism which Descartes introduces. As Philo Judaeus showed, in such a neo-Aristotelian schema, God could not be an efficient existence in the universe once the "big bang" sort of Creation had occurred. God might intervene in some magical way from time to time, but only in violation of the laws of a material universe as defined by Descartes and his followers.

From the adoption of Descartes' argument followed the empiricist immorality of a John Locke, a David Hume, an Adam Smith, and Jeremy Bentham. Marxist materialism is an outgrowth of the same conceit. If God is not efficient within the material universe, then, as material beings we cannot know God's law bearing upon this material universe, and are not responsible for acting in a manner consistent with God's law in these matters. Adam Smith's immoral dogma of economics, a dogma fully supported by Karl Marx, the "Invisible Hand," is directly a product of this materialist line of argument. The atheists' and agnostics' view of a universe without God, is merely a consistent, if radical extension of Descartes' argument.

The most important eighteenth-century codification of this Cartesian dogma within German literature was the work of Immanuel Kant. Kant's original intellectual influence was as a popularizer of the doctrines of David Hume, as part of the eighteenth-century effort to rid Germany of the influence of Leibniz, most immediately. However, Kant believed strongly in a rational form of customary morality. When Hume shifted toward that sort of radical break with the principle of custom typified by Jeremy Bentham later, Kant objected, and began the writing of his *Critiques,* both as an attack on British radical forms of empiricism, and as an exposition of those views on which Kant had based his earlier adherence to Hume's dogmas.

The clearest expression of the earlier Kant in the later

Kant, was underlined in Kant's last *Critique,* his *Critique of Judgment.* In this latter work, Kant featured two wicked arguments, that man could not know the principles governing the discovery of a valid new principle in science, and that matters of beauty in art were merely an arbitrary choice of changing popular tastes. These arguments are central to all of Kant's *Critiques,* but are brought forth with a bold nakedness in the last one. These were the two interrelated issues in my own rejection of Kant's arguments. They were also the arguments attacked thoroughly in Friedrich Schiller's aesthetical letters, the aesthetical letters which, more than any other single source shaped the development of German educational reforms and Germany's nineteenth-century emergence as the world's leader in scientific work. I was not familiar with Schiller's role during the early 1950s, but I had developed the same general thesis in my postwar period attack on Wiener's "information theory" dogma.

Hegel was a consummate fraud. On the basis of knowing the program in historical studies which dominated Jena univeristy during the period Hegel was there, we know that Hegel's account of history and of the history of philosophy, was not simply a mass of ignorant errors, but deliberate fraud. Hegel's influence depended greatly upon the influence of the two objectionable theses of Kant, which I have just identified, as did also the influence of Hegel's accomplice, Savigny. Both Hegel and Savigny worked, with only slightly different emphasis, to elaborate these two arguments of Kant's into a comprehensive system of philosophy. In the effort to establish himself as a major philosopher, Hegel attacked Kant, and announced himself the replacement for Kant.

Hegel ridiculed Kant, by insisting that Kant's system was based on arbitrary adoption of Aristotle's system of categories. This is essentially true. However, on this point, Hegel did the same thing. Otherwise, Hegel's *Weltgeist* was nothing other than Descartes' *deus ex machina,* as Savigny's

Volksgeist was but a more nakedly irrationalist guise for Hegel's *Weltgeist*. The central points of agreement between Hegel and Savigny were two. Both were fanatically anti-Augustinian, adopting Roman imperial law as their ideal. Both were products of and advocates of the same Swiss-centered, Rousseauvian romanticism which they shared in common with Robespierre's Jacobins. Both Hegel and Savigny, especially Savigny, are to be seen as forerunners of Nazism on this account.

Broadly, Hegel's dialectic is a neo-Aristotelian dialectic. The key feature of Hegel's work, is his effort to systematize the Cartesian *deus ex machina*.

Marx's dialectic has certain hereditary connections to Hegel's, but these connections have been greatly over-emphasized by most among the relevant, putative scholars. The principal intellectual influences on Marx at Berlin, were the Savigny from whom Marx derived his "historical materialism," and circles of nominally Protestant and Jewish gnostics associated with the Berlin neo-Hegelians of the early 1840s. Among these gnostics, theologian Ludwig Feuerbach was the most influential, but Strauss very important. To understand the peculiarities of Marx's "dialectic," one must have grasped the essential features of Feuerbach's *The Essence of Christianity*, a work which is the principal influence, together with Max Weber's, on the development of gnosticism among German and some other Protestant churches to the present day. Feuerbach's book is the principal model for the spread of the "feminist" theology among Catholic schismatics of the Americas today. Feuerbach's influence is also relevant to the emergence of the so-called "Christian-Marxist dialogue" movement among the followers of Karl Rahner and others today.

Meet my intellectual ancestors

Although my deeper knowledge of these matters has been built up over the course of decades, what I have described is consistent with the general view of Marxism which I developed in the course of the 1949–1952 period. Since the Trotskyists had almost no knowledge of those aspects of Marx's economics and method which I rejected then, my reactions to Marx had more bearing on certain later activities of mine than upon any feature of week-to-week relations with the SWP during the 1949–1954 interval. The practical effects of my 1949–1954 encounter with Marx and the socialist movement played an important part in later developments in my life. It is for that latter reason, that I have dwelt on these matters as much as I have here.

The question is implied: How much impact did this 1949–1954 association with the SWP have upon my development, during that period itself?

The key to discovering the answer to this or similar sorts of questions, in the life of any person, is to begin with the observation that there are, on the average, three hundred sitxy-five and a quarter days in a year, seven days in a week, and twenty-four hours in a day. We sleep approximately eight hours each day. Other routine functions, such as eating and dressing, occupy about three of the remaining sixteen hours of the day. Ordinarily, about fifty hours or more of the week are associated with employment and traveling to and from work—although my own working week has run to about seventy hours most of the past three decades. What else we do, is sandwiched within the remaining hours.

Once we have situated any particular activity within the limits of such a schedule, we must consider the fact, that not each segment of our waking hours has the same psychological importance as other segments. For some, as for my work in management consulting, and my researches more emphatically, my intellectual life is concentrated in my work. For others, the activities immediately associated with the circle of family and friends are dominant features of intellectual life. For many, entertainments such as spectator sports, or some mix of that and other entertainments, are a central feature of psychological life. Many think they are being "themselves" during those circumstances they "let their hair down." It is necessary to discover how persons see their individual identity as more or less "involved" in various kinds of activities, to estimate with at least fair accuracy the psychological weight of their experience in each among the assorted activities of which the hours of the year are composed.

There is no possible margin to doubt, that the kinds of activities typified by my breaking with Quaker theology and my commitment to refute "information theory," are the activities in which I have located my sense of personal identity since some time during childhood. The identity of "philosopher" was one I began to assume during my twelfth year. My intellectual integrity, as defined by my philosophical development, is the central motivation of my internal life, and my life otherwise is governed by a struggle to bring my practice outside my thoughts into conformity with what I regard as my inner personal integrity. Apart from these two matters, I have never been able to sustain interest in, or much attention to those other matters which seem to preoccupy much of the attention of most people. Most persons in our culture know my kinds of motivations in themselves, but this motivation dominates me much more than all but a very tiny minority of our civilization generally.

Most of the members of the influential elites I have known, "belonging" is the center of their motivations. In many cases, belonging to family, or a certain group of families, dominates the sense of individual identity. Many adopt a substitute for the oligarchical sort of family tie in belonging to an adopted peer-group, or even narrower circle. Many among the elites fuse these two notions of personal identity into one. Various permutations of these and other considerations are commonplace. I don't fit into those categories, nor the kind of "other-directedness" which marked the "regular guy" of my childhood and youth.

I suppose the development of my sense of identity began during childhood. I see a blending of the influence of the image of great-grandparents and great-great-grandparents upon my family's life, and a growing importance of past personalities with whom I became acquainted through my voracious appetite for readings in history, theology, and scientific matters. I transferred early, the sense of personal identification with family ancestors to intellectual ancestors met through such readings. Leibniz, for example, became my "ancestor" in that sense. I could imagine, and often did, standing before an assembly of adopted intellectual ancestors, and being called upon to defend my ideas and actions in their eyes. I came also to imagine, that in future generations, my ideas and actions might be judged by persons of a nature akin to that of adopted intellectual ancestors. My sense of personal identity became what I might imagine those combined intellectual ancestors and future critics might judge the outcome of my life's work to be.

This is no approximation. It is a vivid memory. I have traveled, in this life of mine, much like a living agent entrusted to my present duties by a council of intellectual ancestors long dead. So, is my conscience, and my sense of personal identity molded and defined. I am no slave to the opinion of those intellectual ancestors, but I hold myself accountable to prove to that jury that I am right, whenever I disagree with them.

Over the 1949–1954 interval, my activities with the SWP consumed an average of a few hours, mostly during one day of the week. This includes shorter intervals of weeks, or even somewhat longer with no activity. I never became assimilated into the ranks of those who saw the SWP as representing in some fashion a collective identity, like that of a family, in its own right. For me, it was a collection of personal associations with individuals, most among whom I liked, some deeply. Those personal attachments were my chief ties. I was sometimes a student, much as I was a student in school and university, and never a "follower."

Except for those personal associations, the SWP gave me a tiny, initial access to an aspect of past and present history which had been hitherto unknown to me. The Russian Revolution of 1917 had shaped history profoundly, and the development of the socialist movement up to that time must be seen from that standpoint of reference. Once exposed to this tiny access to that aspect of history, I was fascinated to learn the secrets of socialism and that revolution in every possible detail. A few SWPers, like Vincent "Ray" Dunne, had been located in somewhat key, advantageous positions, and afforded me a more accurate insight into relevant events and personalities they had known first-hand than the plausible, but misleading published myths and legends. This knowledge, although fragmentary and representing only a tiny corner of the whole business, was invaluable to me as I was drawn into counterintelligence work later in life.

While I shall never regret the personal associations I had with the SWPers personally closest to me, and view them with affectionate memory to the present day, my essential judgment on that experience was that without the access it afforded me to understanding certain matters, I could never have come to understand some of the important things I know today, including my strategic insight into the problems posed by the Soviet empire. I have made some important contributions to the formulation of U.S. strategy; ironically, but not accidentally, that 1949–1954 experience with the SWP gave me the first foothold in analysis of the Soviet dictatorship.

Relative to its size, the SWP leadership and general membership was flooded with agents of sundry intelligence organizations, in addition to the FBI's generous representation. This coincided with the special circumstances of the period of McCarthy's sideshow. I began to develop an instinct for counterintelligence, the art of discovering what people are who are not quite what they pretend to be. In this, I was guided by the certainty, that what people really are is the way their minds work. A person can disguise what they appear to believe and what they do; they cannot disguise the way their mind works under intellectual stress. This aspect of the experience, too, contributed the germ of a skill which developed to some importance to our nation during more recent years.

A number of my associates have come from backgrounds representing a kindred experience. The process by which our association was selected, and other associations selected out, defined a kindred sort of capability for strategic analysis and intelligence work. Those among us who had had exposure to the so-called Left, shared a common zeal for discovering "where the monkey sleeps." We received happily any accumulation of evidence proving that, as we had always suspected, many things were not quite the same as they had been represented to be.

For example, the Bolshevik Revolution of 1917 never actually occurred. At least, what did occur had no resemblance to the putatively expert books on the subject, or popular legends. The Bolsheviks inside Russia were one among the various radical organizations, including the Odessa-based Zionist organization, created by, and directed by the czarist secret police, the Okhrana, and backed within the highest levels of the czar's government by officials including the minister of war. From outside Russia, the Russian Revolution was orchestrated by western financial circles centered around Venice's Count Volpi di Misurata, with British and German intelligence drawn in at the highest levels: the British role was relatively the greatest in the February 1917 Revolution, and the German most significant in bringing V.I. Lenin to power. The Communist International was created and run jointly by wealthy western interests, including former President Theodore Roosevelt's apparatus inside the U.S.A. The documentation is massive and conclusive.

Not only is the popular view of communism and of the Bolshevik Revolution a myth false to reality. To understand why certain powerful interests inside the czarist government and the West collaborated to organize and exploit that coup d'état, leads one to "where the monkey sleeps," the great secret of all twentieth-century history to date. I would not have discovered this secret, unless my curiosity had been stirred by certain curious facts in the background of the SWP.

My career in economic forecasting begins

After severing with my New York client, in 1955, I walked into the New York offices of the George S. May Company almost by accident. Within the hour, I was hired. I remained with the consulting firm into 1958, and again briefly after that. During this period, I moved from theory to the first practical applications of my discoveries to economic forecasting.

My career in economic forecasting began in 1955, when I was promoted from the field to become an executive in the New York office. I assembled a mass of standard statistical sources, U.S. government, Federal Reserve System, and key private tabulations. I worked on both the U.S. economy as a whole, and also on designing a much-needed, new sort of management-accounting system for prospective clientele. My general focus was on defining the efficient interdependency between the macrocosm, the economy in the large, and the individual firm, of various types, within that economy.

During the 1952–1954 period, I had done some important preparatory work, a byproduct of my critique of "information theory," on the function of energy in economic growth. That work of the early 1950s was the starting-point for my elaboration of a forecasting "model" started with a critical analysis of the chart of accounts of the national income accounting system. Within a reasonable degree of approximation, it was possible to redefine the national income chart of accounts in a suitable way.

The essential thing to be done, in arranging the statistics, was to make a rigorous distinction between factors of productive costs, and those items of administrative, sales, and services which are essentially "overhead burden" for the economy taken as a whole. In this way, the shifting composition of employment and nominal income flows could be traced in a meaningful way. This gave, if only in useful first approximation, a better way of measuring economic growth than the methods used by leading governmental and private forecasting agencies.

The nature of my executive duties prompted me to direct this work toward two narrow objectives. First, what was the economic function of management consulting services in the economy at large? Second, given the answer to the first question, what were the marketing prospects for management consulting services during the period 1957–1958? Given my answer to the first, my forecast for 1957–1958 was not an optimistic one. My report did not assist in prolonging my employment with the firm.

By the beginning of 1957, it was clear to me that the U.S. economy would slide into a major recession during 1957, presuming that present governmental and Federal Reserve policies were continued. The trends in financing of automotive and correlated categories of consumer durables sales were the warning indicator. The recession would probably be deep and prolonged over several years, assuming major changes in policies did not intervene. By February, statistics showed that such a downturn was already in progress. I so indicated.

The firm had a very strong emphasis on the miraculous powers of salesmanship. Most of the executives, from the owner on down, had come up through the ranks as star salesmen, and shared the view that it was salesmen's skills and dogged determination which carried production through. My report was received among the majority of

relevant company officials as reflecting a "negative attitude," and as contrary to the reports being issued from
authoritative forecasting services. From that point, I was
on the downslide in standing among executives. When I
proposed, later that year, that the time had come to begin
shifting the composition of services offered, to take the
lead in offering electronic data-processing services as an
integral part of the package offered, the management was
listening less and less to any recommendations from me,
although, by that time, the existence of the 1957–1958
recession was generally acknowledged.

I was far more interested in the vindication of my first
attempt at general economic forecasting, than the opinion
expressed by my peers. I started on a more ambitious,
long-range forecast, whose results were to shape my future.

The Long-Range Economic Forecast of 1959–1960

3

By the autumn of 1957, I was certain that the deep recession, then obviously in progress, was a long way from becoming a new economic depression like that of the 1930s. I projected the recession as bottoming out during 1958. I described what I called "the 1957–1958 recession" as "a turning-point in postwar history." The long range which I elaborated, over the course of 1958 and into 1959, was, that the crises leading directly toward a new economic depression would not erupt until the second half of the 1960s. During the second half of the 1960s, the first of a series of monetary crises would occur. From that point on, the international monetary system would stumble through a succession of debilitating crises.

The forecast was premised on two political assumptions. The first political assumption was, that the relevant institutions would continue present trends in monetary policies. The second such assumption was, that the government and banking system's response to a series of monetary crises, would be an increasingly savage austerity, converging upon the methods Hjalmar Schacht had introduced within Weimar and Nazi Germany.

I did not anticipate the way in which the "Kennedy recovery" of the early 1960s would unfold. I expected a more modest growth in productivity rates during the early 1960s. I was not surprised by the Kennedy investment tax-credit program; I had not anticipated the combination of the aerospace program and that tax-credit program. However, the blunders of the Johnson administration compensated for the somewhat unexpected successes of the Kennedy administration.

The British pound's November 1967 devaluation led to a near collapse of the Bretton Woods system, at the beginning of March 1968. Those monetary agreements were destroyed by President Nixon, in a series of decisions beginning August 15, 1971. The direction of Nixon's economic policy was modeled upon the doctrines of Nazi Finance Minister Hjalmar Schacht from the beginning, even prior to the austerity policies of 1971 and 1972. In all the most essential features, the 1958 long-range forecast has been a notable success.

The suggestion, that there might have been a fascist aspect to President Nixon's administration, will be viewed as controversial. There is no exaggeration in the following picture of that matter.

Nixon went through the 1968 election campaign an avowed admirer of Professor Milton Friedman. Friedman's economic dogmas are explicitly fascist, in the sense that Mussolini's Italy and Hitler's 1930s Germany are models of fascist forms of austerity. After the domestic financial crises of late spring and summer 1970, Nixon seemed embarrassed by the name of Milton Friedman, and announced himself a convert to Keynes later that year. Keynes had described his own economic dogmas as fascist, in the first edition of his *General Theory,* published in Berlin in 1936.

Political democracy and Friedman's economic dogmas simply cannot live together for long. Sooner or later, the one must destroy the other. As this conflict, between the choice of political democracy and austerity, reaches a crisis, monetarists such as Schacht or Friedman have insisted that it is political democracy which must be destroyed, to save austerity. So, Hjalmar Schacht traveled to his backers in London and New York, to ask their permission and support for putting Adolf Hitler into power.

Naturally, Milton Friedman is not a doctrinaire Nazi, although Keynes was close to being one during the 1930s; he is a vastly immoral little wretch, and, as I concur with Mrs. Joan Robinson on this point, an amazingly stupid one in economics. Friedman did study, and copy the policies of Nazi minister Hjalmar Schacht, with explicit awareness of what he was copying. On balance, Friedman were better labeled simply a "nasty," than a "Nazi." Fellows like Friedman crawl into bed with fascist regimes, not necessarily because they are fascists, but because their economic policies could not be continued without the help of a handy form of dictatorship. It is in that sense, that all austerity policies such as those of Schacht or Friedman are rightly and usefully labeled "fascist."

President Nixon himself was certainly not a fascist. It had been said of the aging President Hindenberg of Weimar Germany, no fascist himself, "Don't put anything on the desk before him you don't want him to sign." Nixon did have a certain resemblance to President Hindenberg; he seemed to sign almost anything Henry A. Kissinger asked him to. Kissinger was, and is, an out-and-out fascist, in his own written documentation of his philosophy, and in the evidence of his practice; if Kissinger had been a bit older, and had not been of Jewish ancestry, the allies might have hung Kissinger in the course of the postwar Nuremberg trials. Nixon was no fascist; he was, unfortunately, not a very efficient sort of antifascist, particularly where Kissinger was concerned.

The 1958–1959 forecast was based upon two interacting factors, physical economy and monetary processes. Physical economy emphasizes the kinds of employment (and, unemployment) of the labor force, the contents of a standard market-basket requirement for producers' or households' goods, and changes in the physical productivity of labor. For productivity to rise, the average amount of energy consumed must increase, and the capital investment per goods-producing operative employed must also increase. These factors are the real aspect of the economic process.

However, what is bought and sold, and how purchases are consumed, is determined by the way currency, credit, and debt, channel their way through the society.

The physical side of the economy represents real values, whereas money, credit, and debt are merely nominal, or "paper" values. A competent economic forecast is based on knowledge of the interaction between real and nominal values. Since the eighteenth century, the study of the interaction between real and nominal values has been termed "political-economy."

By "economic science," or, for short, "economics," we should understand one another to mean "physical economy" as a branch of the physical sciences. The emphasis is upon physical cause-effect relationships, as if money had never existed. The subordination of physical economy to a particular form of government, anarchy, or some combination of both, is the subject of "political-economy."

For example. An alternate name for "physical economy," is "technology." We can define physical economies in terms of the general level of technology they represent. Two nations may represent the same general level of technology, but their political systems may differ absolutely or merely in degree. Even if the form of government does not change, the policies of government and banking systems may be so much altered, from one period to another, that leading features of the behavior of political-economy during one period differ very much from that of another period of the same nation's history.

Although the physical laws of economy never change, each general level of technology is subject to its own special kind of physical laws. Such special laws do not overturn the general laws of physical economy, but they are special laws in the sense that the characteristics of any general level of technology are functionally different than the characteristics of every other general level. Economies at the same general level of technology, thus have common physical characteristics, even though they may represent different species or varieties of political systems.

Therefore, for such general reasons, we must maintain a rigorous distinction between the real values of physical economy, and the superimposed, merely nominal values of a political-economy. Though many objects which have economic value, also have a price, value does not determine price, and price is not a measure of value. Economic value does have an impact upon prices, and prices have an impact upon the way the physical economy is developed; but the efforts of the Haileybury political-economists, and their follower, Karl Marx, to discover a simply calculable equivalence of value and price, is intrinsically absurd. We must reject the popularized delusion that there is any simple sort of equivalence between price and value, and, instead, concentrate our attention upon what is, usually, the adversary relationship between real and nominal values.

It is a fair estimate, that I expended thousands of hours, over the 1952–1959 period, on composing the 1958 long-range forecast. All of the statistical work was done over the 1955–1958 interval. All of it I performed myself, with aid of a slide rule and long nights using one or another desk calculator borrowed from the outer office for the occasion. It was common for me to remain at the office to somewhere between nine and midnight, when I could concentrate without interruption, and get my best work done. In the field, I would often work through the night during the crucial phase of preparation of a report. The number of those late and weekend hours expended upon my forecast, was thousands of hours in total, a fair-sized chunk of my adult lifetime; yet, compared with the number of persons and computer-hours expended on a short-term, quarterly forecast today, I constructed the long-range forecast with relatively little effort.

The LaRouche-Riemann method

How was I able to develop a long-range forecast so accurate, over "merely" a few thousand man-hours?

More than twenty years later, in December 1978, I proposed and defined the application of my method to computer systems, as a means of producing regular, quarterly forecasts for the U.S. economy. This is what is known today as "the LaRouche-Riemann method" of analytical forecasting. Since the first runs of that quarterly forecast, at the close of 1979, this has been the only reasonably accurate published forecast produced by any public or private agency in the U.S.A. What the computer system does, is, in essentials, nothing but a copy of the mental processes through which the 1958 long-range forecast was constructed.

What was "the mental trick," by means of which I substituted myself for a computer system, so to speak, back in 1958?

I am definitely not a John von Neumann. According to my sources, he was famed already during his early years, for amazing arithmetic calculations. As in every kindred case of which I know, this development of one's brain as a calculating machine, has certain advantages, but is usually also a grave mental defect. His posthumously published Yale lectures, on the subject of the computer and the brain, display the price he paid for his remarkable talent. My brain has never functioned arithmetically; at no time in my life have I shown better than average arithmetic capacities. My mind functions geometrically, as I believe all minds should, under normal conditions and normal development. By conditioning children's minds in such a way as to emphasize a potential for arithmetical thinking, we cause them to lose much of a capacity which is more fundamental, more valuable.

From what I know of the human brain, including study of the way in which the eye maps into the cortex, human memory is not digital, but holographic. I believe that we "store" experience holographically. I believe that we do not recall experience in the way a digital computer searches out a stored datum. I believe that we reconstruct an image of experience holographically. This is what the evidence of optical biophysics suggests; this is what my experience in several successful projects indicates. This is the way in which I put together the interacting images of physical and monetary processes in constructing the 1958 forecast.

What I did, was to construct separate mental "models" of physical and monetary processes. Physicists call this defining a "phase space." Each of these phase-space models, was of the form of cyclical behavior. For physical-economic phase-space, my model was the "roller-coaster" model I described in the preceding chapter. This model was based on what I had learned from Riemann and Cantor. To construct a cyclical phase-space for monetary processes, I treated price of nominal values as a price measured in terms of the physical content of a per capita market basket.

I measured flow of payments in terms of a ratio of the payments on combined nominal capital to nominal capital. Nominal (money-value) capital investment was treated as debt, and debt as such combined with capital investment in this way. Thus, physical output per capita correlated with a price-earnings ratio on account of nominal values, and flows of nominal values, as purchasing power, regulated the flow of investment of labor force and goods in the physical cycle.

So, the result of imposing the monetary cycle on the physical cycle, determined the monetary cycle. Problems of this sort are elementary in seeking solutions to least-action pathway requirements in hydrodynamics.

Constructing the forecast, required two principal sets of assumptions. I assumed an average rate of potential technological progress, roughly that indicated for the 1949–1957 interval. I assumed that the monetary cycle would be consistent with the kinds of decisions which the U.S. government and Federal Reserve had made during the inflationary crisis which erupted during the immediate postwar years, and as typified by the correlation between 1954 tax-code revisions and 1954–1957 Federal Reserve policies. I assumed that all other considerations were essentially reflections of these two sets of assumptions, or were of marginal weight in determining the final result.

On the physical side, there are two key factors of decisive importance. The first is the ratio of number of operatives employed in production of physical goods, to total labor force. The second is the ratio of production of capital goods to total physical output. If one must reduce the number of factors to a bare minimum, the choice of these two provides the smallest relative margin of error caused by simplification. To simplify the analysis of capital intensity, we must select a few categories of investment which are most critical. Among forms of basic economic infrastructure, select general transportation improvements and energy production and distribution. For the rest, concentrate on metals manufacturing, automotive, and machine tool. Such simplifications of the problem do introduce a significant margin of error, but the error is no greater than the margin of error in the available statistics.

This simplified approach to forecasting must be tested. Working out more elaborate calculations for a series of

points in the recent history of the economy, and also working through a few hypothetical cases, seemed to be sufficient testing of my simplified model. The rest was a matter
of concentration.

At a minimum, "concentration" means undistracted
attention to the unfolding of one's thoughts over many
hours. For major work, such as working through that
forecast, it is essential that one's concentration be virtually
uninterrupted over weeks. Except for eating and sleeping,
one must concentrate so intensely on the problem each
day, that one thinks of almost nothing else over the night.
One must fall asleep, exhausted, with the completed work
and unsolved problems of the day's efforts on one's mind,
and resume the work immediately upon awakening. To
do this, one must develop the habit of such extended bursts
of concentration.

The human brain is a very slow-working instrument,
by comparison with the speed of calculations we associate
with modern computer systems, but is a vastly more powerful one. To master a truly important conception, we must
keep the brain highly mobilized, concentrated on that problem, over many weeks. So, a fourteen- to sixteen-hour
day, seven days a week, over several weeks or longer,
sometimes months, is the kind of activity associated with
important discoveries. Such sustained concentration permits one to master in weeks or months, what might otherwise be learned over years, or might not be learned at
all in any different way. What might seem a work of genius,
is really this specific sort of hard work.

I am not "tuned" to working in any other way. I can
deliver good quick decisions, but these decisions are merely
echoes of some earlier, extended working-through of problems of that type. The training and experience of a scientist
or engineer, for example, enables him to make accurate
snap decisions wherever the problem presented is of a type
with which he is familiar. That quality of training and

experience must have occurred prior to the point the immediate decision is made.

   This accounts for the reason I consider becoming President a major personal sacrifice for me. The presidency offers minimal opportunity for extended concentration on specific topics. In the greater degree, the President must make numerous decisions during the course of a day. Unless he is essentially a mere figurehead, in the sense that he depends almost entirely upon the counsel of advisors, he must bring most of his decision-making capacity to the presidency on the first day of his inauguration. He has no opportunity for conducting extended research projects. If I thought another candidate were available, who is qualified to be President under conditions of the crises presently developing, I would seek a position as his or her key advisor, and be much happier personally than as President myself. I have no reluctance to assume responsibility for the consequences of difficult decisions; I should miss greatly the joy of working through major projects over extended periods of virtually uninterrupted concentration. I would seek to become President only if my work in that office were far more important to present and future humanity than the research work I must give up as a condition of occupying that office.

The economic fallacies of the 1950s

My sense that the 1957–1958 recession represented a "turning-point" in postwar history, was the elaboration of a worrying idea already in progress during 1955. Two aspects of my consulting experience had contributed to this worrying thought. The worry was what I viewed as a clinically insane sort of consumer-credit expansion during that period, and the indicative case of a sharp contraction of the metal industry in eastern Pennsylvania.

   As those of approximately my generation will recall,

during the war in Korea, the U.S. government and Federal Reserve copied some of the presumably anti-inflationary, restrictive practices of the World War II period. During 1954, key such restrictions were lifted, and a spiral of credit expansion followed, shaped by the 1954 reforms of the Internal Revenue Code. There was a brief period of relative prosperity, leading into, and causing the severe recession of 1957–1958.

A later study by McGraw-Hill, and parallel studies, showed the error of the first Eisenhower administration's approach to credit expansion. Certainly, Arthur Burns, who exerted a crucial margin of influence over President Eisenhower in matters of economic and monetary policy, must shoulder much of the blame for the result.

The absurd idea behind the 1954–1956 credit expansion, was that by issuing consumer credit, and so increasing consumer purchasing power, an expansion in retail sales of manufactured products, would promote a sustainable recovery. I had seen the folly of this policy first hand, and most clearly, in study of the problems of automobile dealership franchises. What was true of automobile marketing, was also the general case for all categories of consumer durables. During 1956, the point was reached, in an increasing number of cases, that after two years or so of ownership of a new car, the buyer still owed more on the car than the cost of buying a duplicate from a used-car lot.

Under President Reagan, so far, we have carried this same sort of national economic lunacy to new extremes: the seemingly endless piling-on of new layers of public and private debt, as a supplement to earned income, as a means of attempting to maintain the level of purchasing power. This policy has rotted out our economy, to the point that our nation is essentially financially bankrupt. If we thought the financial head cold of 1956–1958 was painful, we have acute pneumonia today.

The proper way to promote economic prosperity, is to channel savings and newly created credit into investments in capital goods, not consumer goods purchases. The trick is to increase employment of operatives in the capital-goods sector, while increasing the level of technology in all branches of production. It is the increased employment in the producers' goods sectors, which does the most to promote increased margins of demand (earned purchasing power) for consumer goods.

This does not prohibit the use of financing of consumer purchases. However, by the time a consumer durable purchased has used up approximately half its useful life, the debt owed on that purchase should have been reduced to zero. In other words, the ratio of the consumer's equity-holdings to consumer debt, must be rising. If the ratio of indebtedness to equity is rising, such that the consumer's average net equity position is substantially less than zero, consumer-credit expansion has become a classical sort of financial "bubble," akin to the famous John Law "bubble" of the eighteenth century, a "chain letter" of refinancing of indebtedness. That has been the state of affairs under Paul Volcker's position as chairman of the Federal Reserve System. In such a case, the point must be reached, at which the economy must either accept a major recession in retail sales, or proceed to national bankruptcy as an alternative.

The McGraw-Hill and other studies published during the course of the 1957–1958 recession, showed a dangerous accumulation of obsolescence in the U.S. stocks of capital goods. Had we not attempted to expand General Motors and Ford's retail sales so rapidly, and had we concentrated on investment tax-credits for capital goods investments, instead, we might have recovered from the 1954 economic decline more slowly than we did, but a steady and accelerating growth would have been the case, and no 1857–1958 recession.

The complex of metals industries centered around Philadelphia, was developed prior to and during the 1776–1783 War of Independence. It had included, during that period, the production of U.S. weapons from the "bog iron" of the New Jersey Pine Barrens. Following the 1812–1815 war with Britain, the Philadelphia area, and West Point Military Academy, had been the technology drivers of U.S. economic growth. The development of industry had followed the geographic lines of the grand, earlier eighteenth-century, strategic design of Hunter, Spotswood, Franklin, and Washington: shifting into Ohio and the development of what was, until recently, the center of our economic power, the midwestern industrial belt. Although the center of gravity of metals production had shifted to the Midwest, the industrial zone around Philadelphia had contributed a vital part during the two world wars of this century. During the mid-1950s, this portion of our nation's potential was being deliberately collapsed.

Admittedly, the region's relevant industries were riddled with obsolescence. Granted, the argument of Washington bureaucrats and the bankers was, that industry must flee with its investment to where prices are cheapest. Cutting off one's legs does reduce the amount of tissue one must feed to maintain, but I never thought that sort of "economy measure" was particularly advantageous.

In physical economy, two factors determine levels reached by economic growth. The first is the number, and percentile of the total labor force employed directly, as operatives, in the production of new physical output. The second, is the average physical productivity of those operatives. The chief determinant of the productivity of operatives, is the level of technology employed. Chopping away a chunk of the nation's productive capacity, can have no effect but to lower the level of the national economy as a whole, and to reduce the average level of productivity of the labor force taken as a whole. To chop away a chunk of a state's, or region's economy, is a blow against the well-being of that part of the nation. Anyone who considers the act of shutting down a section of our economy, for whatever reason, to be sound economic policy, has to be some kind of an idiot.

If a section of our industry is obsolete, obsolescence is overcome in only one way, by investment in technological progress.

It was argued that the section of industry being closed down in eastern Pennsylvania was redundant capacity, as well as technologically backward. Excess capacity may be real, or only apparent. For example, if a portion of the food produced remains unsold in a world in which starvation abounds, some foolish people will pronounce unsold agricultural output as "excess production." The "excess" is only apparent, not real. Or, in other cases, the type of capacity may be truly redundant. For example, at the present rates of family formation and birth rates, the U.S. new-car market has a sales capacity of about 4 million U.S.-made, quality passenger automobiles a year (more if the quality is poorer). Automotive capacity in excess of optimal population requirements, is truly excess. In such cases, rather than eliminating that capacity, it should be converted to technologically advanced production of a sort of product for which there is an unfulfilled need.

What was wanted, in the relevant industries of eastern Pennsylvania, was a reorientation of production, combined with a retooling. This case illustrated a pattern affecting many other localities.

In constructing analytical forecasts, during the 1950s, I correlated the statistical patterns with reference to physical cases, such as the two I have referenced. One hears, from pompously self-styled experts, that one is a specialist in "macro-economics," and another a specialist in "micro-economics." Professor Gorge looks at economies only in the large, and Professor Nibble only in the small. The idea that there is a different theory for the economy of the particular firm, than for the economy as a whole, shows that those who believe such things understand the economy of neither the firm nor the society as a whole. The individual firm must always be studied as an integral feature of the economic process as a whole; if a statistical trend seen in national figures, does not have a concrete expression in someone's back yard, then that statistical analysis is absurd. Good economic analysis obliges the analyst to adopt both points of view, alternately and simultaneously.

The erosion and dropping-out of productive subsectors of the U.S. economy, under conditions of putative economic growth, was a warning sign. If existing policy-making trends of the government and banking system continued, the 1957–1958 recession was going to be the starting point for a long roller-coaster ride, downhill. If any major injection of new technologies occurred, this would tend to produce a genuine economic recovery, of course. Except for rather large doses of such technologically advanced retooling of physical production, the post-1957 U.S. economy was headed into a series of recession cycles, and recurring monetary crises, a ride downhill with no long-term bottoming-out in sight.

Such an economic trend was in sharp conflict with established moral values. By "established moral values," I refer to a combination of traditional family-centered values and emphasis on scientific and technological progress. This is the established set of values of western civilization, and of the United States most emphatically. The U.S. citizen was faced with the prospect of a transition from a policy of more and better, to a policy of less and worse. In that way, the economic trends implied a tendency toward crises in moral and political values, and in institutions.

For that combination of reasons, I adopted the opinion that the 1957–1958 recession was a turning-point in post-war history, a turn away from the incompletely fulfilled objectives of the American heritage, to new, and ugly objectives. My conclusion was, that there was no worthwhile policy, except a policy of recognizing these trends, and finding effective ways to reverse them as soon as possible.

This was my view of current history, from the 1957–1958 period, until the events of 1971. I did not abandon this view after 1971. Rather, the dollar crisis of early March 1968, and the 1971 collapse of the Bretton Woods gold-reserve agreements, while they confirmed the accuracy of my 1958 forecast, had also brought the 1957–1971 period to an end. After the events of 1971, and the Azores monetary conference of 1972, the world was operating under a new monetary order, what is called the "floating exchange-rate system." Not only had the economy been changed—for the worse; politics, too, had been changed.

The postindustrial strategic agenda

My sense that 1957–1958 was such a turning-point, has been shown to be a most accurate estimation. Yet, it poses the question: Was the gradual adoption of a "postindustrial" policy, as adopted by the Johnson administration beginning approximately 1966–1967, a result of economic trends, or was there not a decision to adopt such a radical change for the policy which had defined the American character and heritage since the Massachusetts Bay Colony? Which came first, the economic-trends chicken, or the postindustrial egg?

The Eastern Establishment which has established a virtual dictatorship over our nation's leading policies, is not so stupid as the dismal results of its policies might often suggest to be the case. Often enough, at first, the results of its policies do catch that establishment off guard. However, if the policy responsible for unpleasant results is continued over a period of years, we must assume that the results are either a condition the establishment intends to bring into being, or that the establishment views the painful features a price it is willing to have us pay for the sake of its policies.

London Chatham House, which owned Henry A. Kissinger at that time, assigned Kissinger to its New York branch, the New York Council on Foreign Relations. McGeorge Bundy sponsored Kissinger's appointment. George Franklin has insisted that Kissinger was appointed to work for him. Kissinger was brought, then in a junior capacity, into some of the discussions of a new policy, a new strategic agenda which Bertrand Russell had negotiated with the Soviet dictatorship of N. S. Khrushchev. This was the same new agenda which was being negotiated with Moscow through the channels of the Pugwash Conference, a Pugwash Conference to which Kissinger was later assigned. In view of Kissinger's demonstrated illiteracy, Kissinger's Harvard dissertation, a book written by Gordon Dean, was published in Kissinger's name. This book reflects the changed strategic agenda, under whose influence the "postindustrial society" dogma was developed during the late 1950s.

This "postindustrial" policy was promoted explicitly in a 1960 book by James R. Schlesinger, in Robert M. Hutchins' *Triple Revolution* report, and through sundry other channels. It was adopted by President Johnson, and launched under the mask of the "Great Society." "Postindustrial" policies blossomed while Kissinger was national security advisor, as a complement to Kissinger's introduction of the Pugwash Conference's "arms control" agenda in such forms as SALT I and the 1972 ABM treaty. A "postindustrial" agenda was the principal theme of the Carter-Mondale administration. The long-range objective of Bertrand Russell, certainly since no later than his 1902 tantrum at a dinner meeting of the future London Round Table, was the establishment of a "one-world government." By the end of World War II, Russell announced, in the October 1946 *Bulletin of Atomic Scientists,* that he saw nuclear arsenals as a way of bringing world-government into being, step by step. What Russell proposed, was what some today call a "bi-polar world," or what the Trilateral Commission advocates as a "Global Society" run by "world-class" leaders of no well-defined national loyalties.

In 1955, Khrushchev gave a public signal that his government accepted Russell's proposed strategic agenda. The liberal establishment of Britain, Canada, and the United States adopted Russell's agenda. By the end of 1958, these liberal establishments and Khrushchev agreed upon building up the nuclear missile arsenals of both powers to such levels of assured destructiveness than general war between the superpowers would become unthinkable. The liberal establishment also agreed that the United States would never develop weapons capable of destroying nuclear-missile arsenals, and would not develop its economy to levels at which the western allies would be capable of winning and surviving a war with the Soviet empire.

What was agreed to, was the goal of a condition of general strategic parity between East and West, which meant a gradual take-down of the economic potential of the West. This was a very important factor in the efforts to make "postindustrial society" the adopted policy-goal of governmental policy. Robert S. McNamara, at the Defense Department, contributed a major part to establishing that policy. The London Tavistock Institute's Rapaport Report, demanding a take-down of large chunks of NASA and other U.S. aerospace development, was accepted an implemented by the Johnson administration, which also introduced Malthusian population policies into U.S. foreign policy.

The strategic agenda negotiated between Moscow and the Anglo-American liberal establishments, was not the only factor behind the efforts to shift the United States to a "postindustrial" policy, but it was a very critical factor.

The other major factor, was the spread of the "New Age" dogma which had been associated with such names as Madame Blavatsky, Fyodor Dostoyevsky, Friedrich Nietzsche, Aleister Crowley, Bertrand Russell, H. G. Wells, and Aldous and Julian Huxley. These cultists proposed that during the twentieth century, a "New Age" would be born, in which Satan would conquer Christ. Both Crowley and

Nietzsche called this the "Age of Aquarius." Nietzsche proposed the worship of the satanic figure of Dionysus. Crowley's name for his Satan was "Lucifer."

This "New Age" doctrine had been a leading factor in the shaping of Bolshevik cultural dogmas at the Isle of Capri, under Maxim Gorky. Fascism was another offshoot of the spread of "New Age" cults. The "Weimar counterculture" movements of the 1920s, out of which the Nazi Party was assembled, are typical of this. The center of this "New Age" current inside the United States was rooted in the "psychical research" cults of the nineteenth century, and such center as the New York Museum of Natural History. The radical wing of President Theodore Roosevelt's political movement, himself closely tied to the New York Natural History Museum cult-circles, called itself blatantly a "New Age" movement.

The postwar "New Age" movement inside the United States was prepared during the 1930s, by Aldous Huxley's California connections and by the collaboration between Bertrand Russell and Chicago University's Robert M. Hutchins, beginning the 1938 founding of the Russell-Hutchins "unification of the sciences" project, in which Margaret Mead and her one-time husband Gregory Bateson were leading figures during the postwar period. Around such postwar projects as California-based MK-Ultra, social projects such as the Beatniks, and the launching of the advocacy of sexual freedom and recreational drug-usage through the founding of *Playboy* magazine, the 1963 eruption of the "rock-drug-sex" counterculture was prepared.

The recruitment of youth to violence-prone cults, directed to destroying civilizations such as those of the Greek Ionian city-states, is a tactic as old as the Phrygian cult of Dionysus. The increasing saturation of the New Left with the "rock-drug-sex" counterculture, is readily recognized by classical scholars as a direct copy of the identical features of the ancient cult of Dionysus.

The "postindustrial society" policy has been promoted as an intersection of the "global society" perspective with the growth of the countercultural youth movement. The parallels to the way in which 1920s Weimar Germany was prepared to become Hitler's Germany are amazingly accurate, and ominous.

In economic and related matters of strategic forecasting, we must never lose sight of the distinctions between economy and political-economy. The laws of economic processes are a branch of physical science; but economies exist only as the activity of a society subject to political processes of government. Political-economy is the reciprocal action of the economic upon the political, and vice-versa.

The liberal Eastern Establishment was well aware of the coincidence between economic trends and the "postindustrial" transformation of the economy's structure. It accepted the former, and promoted the latter. Had it not desired the latter, it would not have tolerated the former.

So, I report that the years 1957 and 1971 represent the third period of my life, as the conclusion of World War II separates the second period from the first.

The hoax of "artificial intelligence"

During 1958 and 1959, I returned to the original point of departure for my economic researches, the issue of "information theory."

Over the preceding years, in addition to my attention to what was called "automation," I had studied the efforts to sell the idea that digital computers could be developed to simulate "artificial intelligence." Various theorists, including Wiener and Turing, had helped to build up a credulous audience for such propositions. The influence of John von Neumann must also take much of the blame for this.

The idea of "artificial intelligence" is readily proven to be an absurd one, but sometimes the work of refuting an absurd idea leads to a useful result. The idea occurred to me: Instead of merely refuting the asburd claim of MIT's Professor Marvin Minsky, et al., why not use the disproof of Minsky's claims as a way of defining the outer limits of capabilities of digital computers? The idea of looking at the proposition in this practical way, was prompted by my management consulting view of the emerging role of the computer as a tool of business administration.

The most commonplace problems of mismanagement practices are those which involve excessive faith in the use of financial accounting for shaping the operating and investment policies of firms. The cult of mismanagement taught at such locations as Harvard Business School and by Professor Lawrence Klein's friends at Wharton, is an example of this pathological element carried to the extreme.

Financial accounting must be maintained according to the professional standards of accounting firms, for several reasons not limited to tax accounting. A firm's financial accounting must show the firm to be competitive with that of other firms, for such purposes as securing investments and loans. The fact that the ratios of expenses and costs, as shown by methods of financial accounting, vary significantly from those of comparable firms, is a fact which must be explained. The fact that such accounting measures an accrued financial profit or loss, is of particular importance. Yet, financial accounting can never show a firm how to change its operating policy; failure to recognize this fact leads usually to errors, even sometimes disasters.

This involves the distinction between physical economy and political–economy all over again, this time in the "microcosm" of the particular firm.

A firm incurs costs and expenses. These costs are incurred by activities. Those activities which incur costs and expenses, have some functional role in a chain of cause-and-effect leading, presumably, to income from the activity of selling a completed service or product. The shaping of operating policy must be centered upon analysis of such cause–effect relations among activities.

It is absurd to think, that the price of what is sold "causes" the costs and expenses incurred, or that such costs and expenses "cause" the price at which the product or service is sold. Why should Mr. Smith, of firm A, buy a certain line of supplies from firm B? Mr. Smith, if he is wise, requires a reliable source of continuing supply, and is willing to pay firm B the price which permits firm B to continue in business as a reliable source of supply. If firm B's costs and expenses seem to play a leading role in determining firm B's prices, this does not mean that the costs and expenses "cause" the prices. The price is "caused" by prudent customers' desire to secure that quality of product from a reliable source of supply.

Among managements which are engaged in production of a physical product, there is more or less easy agreement with the point I have just described. The further we are removed from the point of production, to the position of the retailer or the commodity speculator, the more likely we are to encounter the famous myth, that the essence of business is to "buy cheap and sell dear." Unfortunately, over this century to date, especially the recent thirty years, and the past decade or so more emphatically, control of corporate policy has moved further away from the standpoint of the skilled production executive. The impulse of the financial speculator has not only taken over corporate ownership, but has invaded operating management itself in such guises as the "systems analyst" and the Harvard Business School types.

I had taken up a study of what was called "operations research," as a sideline, beginning 1949, with special emphasis on the methods of "activity analysis" developed during the war. It seemed to me, that if I guised my own views on the subject in terms of the conventions of "operations research," that brand-label sensitive clients would be more comfortable about adopting the innovative approaches to management accounting which I saw as much needed. The trouble was, that what passed for "operations research" theory was awful stuff, but advocates of "operations research" had done an effective job of marketing their brand-labels among circuits such as the American Management Association. It was "activity analysis," and if a sound variety of this could be introduced to appropriate sorts of firms, a considerable benefit would result.

The chief source of difficulty in introducing "activity analysis" into management accounting practice, was that it duplicated existing functions of financial and cost accounting. It was therefore an added administrative cost. Rather than having two accounting systems in a firm, why not provide the data required for most of the routine transactions of financial and cost accounting as an automatic byproduct of activity analysis? The prospective early role of computer systems for administrative functions was therefore promising.

Many among what are called "decisions" in business administration are either of the form of calculations, or can be expressed readily in this form. I designed a hypothetical computer system, which could be expanded logically to incorporate every administrative function capable of being stated as a matter of calculation. I reviewed the present and pending state of the art with representatives of computer manufacturers, and adduced the probable trends of development of commercially available systems for the coming ten years. What were the implied limits of the presently human administrative functions which computer systems might assume? That seemed a more useful way of stating the proposition, than simply arguing the abstract notions of "artificial intelligence."

Logically, a computer system controlling relevant parts of production could reproduce itself, even expand itself. It could "clone" itself. Such a computer could be designed; at least, there is no logical reason it could not be. What could it not do? It could not improve itself in any qualitative respect. It could make its clone faster, with improved connectivity, and so forth. It could be trained to program itself for a variety of functions, and accomplish any sort of "learning" defined within such limits. It could do anything which an axiomatic-deductive sort of geometry permits. It could not perform any function which is nonlinear.

This limit could be exceeded, to some degree, by a certain conjecturable species of analog computer. Today, I am pushing as much as I am able, for the development of such types of analog computers, and of digital/analog hybrid computers incorporating such analog functions. Yet, even such conjecturable devices converged upon upper limits of capability.

The general form appropriate for posing those kinds of questions of feasibility, is associated, in axiomatic-deductive logic, with what is termed "the hereditary principle." In any logically consistent such system, the system as a whole is one giant tautology. The system is constructed, by starting with a system of axiomatic assumptions, like the axioms and postulates of school book Euclidean geometry. The role of logical deduction is applied. Every proposition consistent with those axiomatic assumptions is constructed entirely by logical deduction. So, in such a system, there exists no possible proposition which is more than a restatement of the axiomatic assumptions from which the system starts. Anything true of the axiomatic assumptions, is therefore true of the system as a whole.

So, if we know the axiomatic assumptions built into the design of a digital computer, we know that the system can never do anything which the axioms do not permit implicitly.

By applying Cantor's elaboration of the principles of transfinite orderings, the limits of application of any logical system, or even all possible logical systems, are directly discovered.

A different kind of "hereditary principle" exists in constructive geometry. Nothing can be constructed which is not implicit in the definition of the unique principle of multiply-connected action, from which all construction proceeds. However, Gaussian constructive geometry is unique, in the respect that it is the only system which is capable of generating singularities without breaking down. Cantor's elaboration of the principles of transfinite orderings started from the standpoint in Gaussian constructive geometry represented by Riemann's work, and the critique of the limits of Fourier Analysis by Karl Weierstrass. Cantor's work along these lines drops off during the 1880s, but the extension is implicit.

Gauss-Riemann physics depends upon the demonstration, that multiply-connected self-similar-spiral action conforms to a principle of least action in physical space-time. If this is demonstrated to be true, two conclusions follow. First, for every proposition constructable in Gauss-Riemann physics, there exists a corresponding physical reality. Second, for every real cause-effect sequence in the universe, there exists a constructable proposition in Gauss-Riemann physics.

This permits us to say, that every bit of information reflecting an act of communication by, or to human intelligence, is representable in the adequately extended elaboration of a Gauss-Riemann physics. This signifies that the correct analysis of "information" is uniquely of this form. That fact disproves absolutely the dogmas of Norbert Wiener and John von Neumann.

The overlay of this line of inquiry with my work in economic science, has been the central feature of my intellectual life since the end of the 1950s, and is the focus of my activities today.

I challenge the New Left

Amidst these developments, I was induced to reencounter the SWP.

I had turned from making my routine purchases at the lobby newsstand in New York City's Chanin Building,

when I was accosted by an amiable gentleman who identified himself in a hushed voice as Special Agent Coffey of
the FBI. He must speak with me about the SWP, which
had become the major national security concern of his
bureau. Could we step to one side to speak? Being an
amiable fellow myself, I gestured to the opposite side of
the lobby, where the windows of Longchamps' restaurant
overlooked the morning bustle toward the elevator banks.

Would I work for the FBI inside the SWP? Against
old friends and acquaintances, who were essentially as patriotic, in their own way, as the FBI itself? By no means;
leave them in peace to find their own way. Yet, although
I would not volunteer that fact in an off-chance enounter
with the FBI, there were a few around the SWP leadership
who I thought quite capable of doing things behind the
backs of the SWP membership in general. I offered Coffey
a compromise; I would not be an FBI spy, but I would
not condone acts against national security. He could assume
that I would act accordingly. If he had the chance, would
he convey my regards to an old crony, K., working for
the FBI?

My reference to K. was a test. If someone in the SWP
leadership were actually involved in something nasty, I
would wish to know it, for the sake of affectionate memories of past personal associations. If that were the case,
then any intelligence agency would not miss the opportunity to put me in touch with an old crony among its
own people. K. could have communicated the gist of the
matter, as old cronies can. If there were no contact from
K., I might assume that the FBI was up to another sleazy
bit of political harassment.

I was not entirely certain that Coffey was not reflecting
legitimate cause for concern. Why I was not certain, could
be a complicated story, if explained step by step. I shall
sum it up as briefly as possible.

At the close of World War II, a Trotskyist "Fourth
International" was reconstituted, based in Paris, under the

control of a Soviet intelligence operative, one Michel Raptis, a.k.a. "Pablo." Pablo had been a controller of today's Greek Prime Minister, Andreas Papandreou, since the 1930s, and had been among those who met the boat as Trotsky arrived to begin his exile. This same Pablo was, simultaneously, Papandreou's controller during most of the period of the latter's exile in Canada during the Greek junta period, and a key figure in recruiting Europeans to terrorist training in Syria at the point KGB Chief Yuri Andropov launched Soviet narcoterrorist forms of "active measures."

During the 1953–1954 period, Pablo's KGB-style organizational practices and pro-Soviet apologetics had become more than old Trotskyists generally could stomach. During the course of 1953, there was a formal political break by the SWP with the Paris circle of Pablo, one Pierre Frank, and one Ernest Mandel (a.k.a. Ernest Germain, a.k.a. Ernst Mandelbaum). However, a secret liaison had been maintained between Pablo's number-two man, Mandel, and a few figures in the SWP leadership. The liaison, which continued until a formal "reunification" with Mandel during the early 1960s, was maintained through a fellow using the cover-name of "Trent Hutter," operating as a steward for Sabena airlines, affording him the convenience for functioning as a courier between Mandel and SWP leader Joseph Hansen.

Mandel, a strange, unmarried man, who lived with his mother, was a nasty piece of work in his own right. He was operating out of the circles of former Trotskyist Henri Spaak in Belgium, and also out of a Soviet-linked intelligence operation based in West Germany.

If Coffey was alluding to something involving this link to Pablo, Mandel, and Frank, nastily interesting possibilities had to be considered.

There had been a visible change in the orientation of the SWP leadership following the famous Twentieth Soviet Congress address of N.S. Khrushchev. They had begun orienting, simultaneously, to quasi-dissident strata around the Communist Party, and to curious projects in the orbit of the League for Industrial Democracy. This had accelerated at first indications of a Moscow-Beijing rupture. By 1957, this new orientation had taken the form of a policy called "Regroupment." In fact, the SWP leadership was in the process of adapting to the Soviet intelligence services, an adaptation which the SWP membership could not be induced to accept even into the early 1960s.

K. did not attempt to contact me. I took no action, until the SWP approached me, in my capacity as one on its list of prospective "useful fools." At least, I could make a stab at satisfying my curiosity. My household had contact with one SWP leader of that period, the late Murry Weiss. Murry hated my guts, as the saying goes, but maintained occasional contact for other reasons. I observed, relying on the principle I had already adopted, that what a man cannot counterfeit, is the way his mind works under intellectual stress.

I have frequently advised my friends, that should they encounter a strange, furry blob, squatting in a woodland pathway, do not ask what it might be; poke it with a stick, and observe how it reacts. In intelligence work, passive observation is unavoidable, but conclusions based only on such modes of investigation are intrinsically fallible. One must introduce some selected stimulant, of a sort which the critter under investigation is not trained to expect. Provoke the critter's mind into attempting to solve the problem so created for it; discover thus, how the critter's mind works.

Arbitrary choices of such stimulants are not reliable. The creature must recognize the stimulant as a relevant one, of importance to it in its own terms of reference. Introduce something strange to its experience, but posed in terms of reference and in language to which the creature is accustomed. My knowledge of the SWP, and my mastery of a Marxist economics which awed the SWPers, but which they did not understand, equipped me for my inquiry.

The older SWP membership, excepting a handful of leading figures, was involved in nothing which should have interested the FBI. Those who remained, were staying with the club, and paying money and other sorts of dues for proverbial old time's sake. Among a new element, among the youthful recruits, there were some strange types. They weren't there to join the club, but to take it over and use it as a springboard for something different. There was a simmering dissidence among the older hands, suspicion and resentment against the new youth leadership. One set of minds functioned in a predictable way, with which I was familiar from the past. The youth stratum was a different sort of creature, and a nasty variety.

I focused upon this youth ferment. Some of the leading figures in the youth ferment in and outside the SWP were most emphatically worrying. By 1963, I began to understand what this ferment portended. By 1964, after encountering the Ford Foundation–funded *Triple Revolution* report of Robert M. Hutchins' Fund for the Republic, there was no doubt that this youth movement was being steered in a very nasty direction by some very wealthy and influential agencies.

I decided to act. I had no organized backing or like resources, but I decided to act nonetheless. I am certain that this was not what agent Coffey had had in mind, but, it was consistent with what I had told him I would do. In the "New Left" I had found the leading edge of the major new security threat to our society, and I was acting as my conscience guided me to do. Nothing but useful experience and added knowledge came of my part-time meddling until the summer of 1966. It was a handful of persons, mostly graduate students, meeting in a tiny living room on the lower West Side of Manhattan, that started something important, from very, very obscure beginnings.

To operate amid the New Left ferment, I needed a "passport." My 1949–1954 studies of Marx and related sources had qualified me as an expert on the subject of

Marx's economics. By presenting my views as a critical presentation of Marx's work in the field, I had my "passport." I needed a foothold. A sleazy loft on Manhattan's 14th Street, styled as "The Free University," needed a course in "Marxist Economics." My name was suggested. I used a pen name, "Lyn Marcus," I had used while in the SWP. I began teaching a thirteen-week course in April 1966.

That pen name would be of no significance today, unless much of the news media had not copied a bit of nonsense from a drug lobbyist, Dennis King, an asset of the organized-crime-linked Anti-Defamation League (ADL), and linked with the Yippies' *High Times* magazine.

The myth began in August 1968. The Columbia University chapter of the Maoist Progressive Labor Party, of which King was a leading member, featured a violent attack on me in that month's issue of the national organization's magazine. That item is the source of the myth that "Lyn Marcus" is code for "Lenin Marx." (The "Marcus" was, in fact, short for the "Marco" of "Marco Polo," the only nickname I had acquired.) In 1979, King was employed by a convicted embezzler, Ed Kayatt, then editor of a New York weekly throwaway, an operation run by the Roy M. Cohn of McCarthy-Cohn-Schine notoriety. King was directed to author an attack on me, as part of a *New York Times*-centered dirty-tricks campaign against my 1980 Democratic presidential candidacy. King copied the myth about the pen name from the old 1968 issue of *Progressive Labor* magazine. The organized-crime-linked ADL used its money and political influence to plant the nonsense produced by King in leading news media.

The class on 14th Street soon sorted down to a student body composed chiefly of graduate students from New York campuses, Columbia notably represented. In late August, there was a gathering in the tiny living room. The discussion was the theme, "What should we do?" I offered three projects. The first two were proposals for research into the economy of New York City, including a study of the history of current financial titles in New York real estate. That latter I indicated as the quickest way to discover "where the monkey sleeps" in that city. The third, was my view that one had to challenge the New Left intellectually at the point it was recruiting talented people from amid the antiwar ferment in progress.

The course was continued at various locations, including the New School for Social Research, and at various campus locations around New York and Philadelphia, into spring 1973. Out of these classes an international association grew up, with highly decentralized activities by its participants, until strange events erupted around the end of 1973. Until spring 1968, my personal participation in these activities was nominal or in many cases virtually nonexistent. In 1971, the classes were put down in mimeographed form, and later published, with editing, by D. C. Heath.

The organized form of activity grew up by happenstance.

The name, "Labor Committees," for example, first appeared in the autumn of 1967 at Columbia University. My friends at that campus had decided to intervene in the formation of a chapter of the Students for a Democratic Society (SDS) there. By autumn, matters had settled down to a three-way factional division among my friends, a trio around Mark Rudd, and an assortment my friends referred to as "mush-heads." Since the putative "mush-heads" and Rudd's trio were antilabor, my friends adopted the style of "Columbia SDS Labor Committee."

The name, "Labor Committee," began to take on a life of its own through a second happenstance. There was no regional organization of SDS in New York City, so my friends thought it a shrewd tactical move to form such a body. So, in early 1968, the "New York Regional SDS Labor Committee" was formed. Some friends, at Swarthmore, hearing of this, formed a Philadelphia SDS Labor Committee in a similar way.

I was involved in none of these tactical developments.

A few among my friends at Columbia knew that someone was plotting to organize a student strike at that campus. These few of my friends conspired successively to preempt the action. In the weeks that followed, the real power behind our New Left opponents came to the surface, chiefly McGeorge Bundy's Ford Foundation, operating in part through Thurman Arnold's left-wing Institute for Policy Studies, in collusion with the networks of former CIA agent Herbert Marcuse. These were the forces directly behind Mark Rudd, for example.

By June, it became clear to me that what Bundy et al. had produced around Mark Rudd, was a classical fascist social phenomenon, with the crucial characteristics of the left-wing of Mussolini's 1920s fascist movement and the National Bolshevist tendencies represented by Gregor Strasser's Nazi *Jugendbewegung*. By then, we knew that the New Left was in no sense a sociological phenomenon, but an internationally coordinated project, which had been created by intelligence agencies, from the top down, through participation of the League for Industrial Democracy in the United States and the apparatus of the Socialist International. Infused with a packaged rock-drug-sex counter-culture, introduced by organizing agencies, the New Left's kernel was already a full-fledged fascist movement in the making.

I outlined the evidence of this "left-fascist" character at a meeting of our factional forces that month. I stressed that this was not a matter of denouncing Rudd's factional forces with unpleasant words. The issue was a matter of properly diagnosing the character of this phenomenon, a diagnosis essential for forecasting the probable course of next developments around this kind of political stratum then emerging across the nation. My report met much resistance that evening, but it prompted serious study of the German and Italian precedents to which I referred. Although we had already adduced the hand of McGeorge Bundy and others behind the New Left operations, I would date the nascent Labor Committees' entry into the practice of counterintelligence from that June meeting.

The next topic on our discussion-agenda that June, was the probability of a potential race-riot scenario in New York City, with the opening of school in September. Bundy's Ford Foundation was also behind this operation. We resolved to investigate and prepare accordingly.

The tenor of the situation around the so-called Left that September was strongly conditioned by the riotous events which the Yippies organized around the Chicago National Democratic Convention. That event had contributed to infusing the Sorelian mythos of violence among the already fascist-tending currents typified by Columbia's future Weatherman leaders. Our New Left opponents were spoiling for action. They were scheduled for a leading role in attacks on the allegedly "racist, Jewish teachers" in the New York City teachers' strike that fall. A well-prepared political counteraction by about fifty of my friends, deployed to key points throughout the city, ruined the intended role of SDS in the racial conflict. Amusingly, the fact that the New York Regional SDS Labor Committee was leafletting key sites, warning against plans to organize a racial riot, created a situation in which SDS groups who had come to riot were turned away by those with whom they were assigned to coordinate! My friends' citywide exposure of the role of Bundy's Ford Foundation, hampered the Ford Foundation's actions, especially when teachers' union President Al Shanker picked up my friends' exposure of Bundy's role. There were ugly anti-Semitic noises from various groups, including Progressive Labor's Dennis King, but, despite a massive strike-breaking turnout organized by the Communist Party, no one succeeded in getting serious violence under way.

Bundy's hunger for vengeance against me and my friends, has not slackened to the present day. The first known action against my friends by the FBI occurred, in a later-exposed FBI covert action launched in support of Mark Rudd et al.! When Vice President Nelson Rockefeller's investigating commission exposed this FBI operation against us, some years later, I wondered what agent Coffey thought about that.

It was my friends' role in working to defuse a potential racial conflict in New York City, around the 1968 teachers' strike, which made my friends and me the target of controversy we have remained to the present day. It was Rudd's Bundy-funded faction which launched the first violence against us, at Columbia, early the next year. Other organized physical attacks against my friends would follow, inside the United States and abroad. Communist Party goon-squad attacks began in Chicago, in summer 1972, and continued sporadically up to the concerted assault launched during March 1973. During 1972, there was also a goon-attack on associates of mine by the SWP.

The Labor Committees is born

The establishment of the Labor Committees as a national organization occurred during January 1969, at a meeting to discuss this option, held on the University of Pennsylvania campus. It was chiefly a defensive measure. We were justly concerned with the possibility that our loose association might be seen as an opportunity by provocateurs. It was necessary to resolve on broad principles of association, to define what sorts of advocacies were and were not condoned by the association as such. We adopted the descriptive name of "National Caucus of SDS Labor Committees," with the stipulation that we would drop the "SDS" as soon as SDS itself had been essentially dissolved, a development we expected to occur during the first half of 1969.

However, there was no additional attempt to constitute the Labor Committees as an organized body until events of 1971, when a loose organization of journalistic and related functions was established. A formal kind of general organization was established in January 1974, in response to some very remarkable developments around the previous January 1 conference of the association. However, the Labor Committees ceased to function as a formal membership organization by approximately 1978, and became to a loose international philosophical association. Publishing functions were assumed by voluntary bodies distinct from the Labor Committees as such, and political activity was conducted more or less ad hoc through formation of political-action or electoral-support bodies.

To this day, the only definite form of organization associated with the Labor Committees as such, is deliberation of philosophical outlook and strategic perspective. It began through the medium of an educational program, and has persisted as essentially a philosophical association to this time.

Although our ideas had a much broader influence, until the summer of 1971, the total number of persons who might be considered "members" of the National Caucus of Labor Committees did not exceed 120 persons at one time. A rapid growth began during the late spring of 1971. When the monetary crisis of August 15–16 exploded, the recruitment zoomed in response to the perception that my forecast of this breakdown of the Bretton Woods agreements had been uniquely vindicated. The registration for at the last class I gave, at Columbia in 1973, was over 200. By that time, the Labor Committees had become an international philosophical association.

From the outset, this association which later developed into the International Caucus of Labor Committees, resembled more a university than any other sort of organization. There was nothing resembling an "ideology." Reference to my course was the only clear common denominator, but even that course's content was viewed with some qualifying reservations by most. I think most from that period would agree, that the common denominator of the association with me, was my jokes. Those who liked my jokes, tended to collaborate with me. This blows apart most of the conjectures among sundry outsiders, about my personal role in this association, but it is a strictly true report nonetheless.

I was probably an exceptionally effective university lecturer. My advantage in this respect, was that I concentrated upon the false assumptions I knew to be commonplace in the general area I covered, and built my lecture-plan around an ironical treatment of those kinds of assumptions. It was a derivative of the method of the Socratic dialogue. I had learned the method of irony in large degree from my study of classical poetry during the late 1940s and early 1950s. My pedagogical objective was, "Get them to think," by encouraging an impulse to unmask pompous absurdity cloaked in the mask of respected, or merely popular opinion.

Many liked some of that wit, and regarded other instances as perhaps exaggerated. Whatever their quibbles with this or that aspect of my lecture-hall irony, they liked the general idea of such an ironical view of matters. They learned perhaps more than they learned in the usual classroom, and learned the profitable fun of fostering a similar practice for themselves. In that sense, we became an association of people tending to share in common a certain quality of sense of humor.

By even rather ordinary standards, the common feature of the assorted leftists, New-Leftists, and others we confronted, was that their impassioned utterances were frankly ridiculous. These opponent's views might be fanatical, and implicitly dangerous, but they were also ridiculous. Anderson's story, about "The Emperor's New Clothes," illustrates the point.

You probably recall. The emperor had been hoodwinked by a pair of scoundrels, into believing that he was being adorned with a marvelous set of tailored garments, where no garments in fact existed. Since no one dared suggest that the garments did not exist, the point was reached at which an adoring population turned out to admire the emperor's public display of his "new set of clothes," until a small boy in the crowd was heard to say, "But, he has nothing on." The spell was broken.

That is among my favorite stories, and for a reason which should be obvious. The popular opinion of many circles, and even the general public, is filled with such delusions. An instinct to search out the humor of the case, is prerequisite to a healthy mental attitude toward much we encounter in the guise of presumably authoritative, or simply popular opinion. How can one argue with a delusion, except to expose it as a delusion, except to attempt to convey the ridiculousness of a conceit?

By ordinary standards, "membership" in the Labor Committees has always been difficult to define, especially so during the early years. I have been a contributing factor in this loose arrangement, but it developed and continued as a reflection of the way we came together, the way loosely organized forms developed more by happenstance than plan, and the distaste for excessive organization among the group of graduate students who dominated the core of members during the late 1960s and early 1970s. We were, and remain essentially, a collection of exceptionally intelligent and very individualistic individuals. It was an association characterized by a certain mood and style, and by tendency to agree on a few basic ideas held in common.

There are certain difficulties in an effort to define us in terms of ideas, too. I brought to the association a Socratic sort of hatred of fixed ideology. To the extent that someone might wrongly imagine that we represent an ideology, we are far less ideological than the Republican Party or the liberal faction of the Democratic Party. We are committed to a few things, such as scientific progress, to technological progress in an energy-intensive and capital-intensive mode, to the general principles of a current of republican thought we trace to Solon of Athens and St. Augustine's elaboration of the principles of Western European civilization, to the heritage of the American Revolution, and to establishment of a just form of international economic order. We are an international philosophical association, one facet of a broader, loosely organized movement, committed to defense and promotion of what St. Augustine identified as natural law, and to the defense and development of classical and scientific culture. That implicitly covers everything I might think of.

The first development which might be termed a "factional" affray within the Labor Committees, occurred during early 1970. Some associates, centered in Philadelphia and Cornell University, came forward with the suggestion that we were all wrong in our current orientation. They said that the "movement" was moving off into a new direction, and that we were in danger of missing the boat, if we did not adjust to this new direction. This "new direction" was "the ecology movement." The proponents of this orientation added that they had been given inside tips by unnamed banking circles, suggesting that we move in on the ground floor of this emerging venture.

I replied, that if the Labor Committees were going to move off in such a direction, they could let me off at the next stop. Most agreed with my view, and a few weeks later, a couple dozen walked out in a rush to overtake the new "movement." We have had many knock-down, drag-out debates over overtake the new "movement." We have had many knock-down, drag-out debates over policies of evaluation and tactics since, but it was the only internal factional affray we ever experienced. We had walk-outs by organized groups later, but these were each operations organized by Soviet or U.S. intelligence agencies.

That one, brief factional affray was important in two respects.

In general, those who walked out were not hostile to what we represented as a whole. During 1967–1968, the principal figures of the group had been leading figures of a number of brief, but rather large-scale events. They had learned to enjoy the rough-and-tumble of that sort of political warfare. They wanted new action of that sort. Intellectually, most of them were superior personalities, able to think more rigorously than most around them. They liked thinking, but they liked the taste of mass political organizing a bit more. They were like persons smitten with a new infatuation; "getting the girl" obsessed them to the point that all counsel to the contrary was simply brushed aside. The debates helped to clarify some useful points respecting the proper relationship between ideas and action.

The initial voicing of the debated proposal served the useful end of prompting a general flurry of investigative interest in discovering the who, when, where, and how, of the indicated surfacing of such a "some bankers"-sponsored radical project. Both sides of the debate agreed on one point: We should address ourselves tactically to this development. The sponsors of the proposal wished us to dissolve into the leadership of the new movement, and take it over from within. The prevailing view, which I shared, was that we must confront this evil stuff by the same methods employed to confront and destroy SDS.

In a manner of speaking, we had destroyed SDS. We had prevented its being used as the kind of operation its behind-the-scenes sponsors intended it to become, and, we did have the pleasure of putting the nail into its coffin on the occasion it split into several various shrieking and mewling fragments. However, the behind-the-scenes sponsors soon had their fall-back options in place. The "ecology movement" was but one of the leading such fall-back options.

Perhaps the single most influential among the books which steered the New Left into assuming a left-fascist character was Herbert Marcuse's *One Dimensional Man*.

This attack on traditional American values became the most-used text in breaking the will of thoes vacillating between traditional values and the proferred hedonistic delights of the "rock-drug-sex" counterculture. The principal complement to Marcuse's ideology, in this respect, was the proliferation of Tavistock "encounter group" methods of "ego-stripping," used to recruit young men and women to both a "sensitivity" cult, and sundry, subsidiary, lesbian and male-homosexual practices. The anarchosyndicalist leftism of the New Left was replaced by the explicit theme of "The Dawning of the Age of Aquarius," *Oh, Calcutta,* and *Hair*.

So, the New Left of the 1963–1968 interval was replaced by the "Rainbow Coalitions" of 1969 and the 1970s. Once the antinuclear, "environmentalist" movement was established, it became the umbrella organization for the assortments of lesbians, "gays," terrorists, and what-not brewed out of a blending of the relics of the New Left and reprogrammed "Old Left" currents.

So, from the beginning of 1970, our organized activities were centered upon three themes we saw as mutually interdependent: the urgency of international monetary reform, the danger of the "counterculture" generally, and not only defending a high-technology orientation, but accelerating relevant scientific development and investment. Our tactical orientation was like President de Gaulle's Force de Frappe: all azimuths.

I was nearing fifty years of age, and growing tired of simply teaching the same one-semester course over and over again. I enjoyed teaching as much as ever, but there were other projects awaiting my attention, including the completion of work on a series of one-semester courses addressing directly my indebtedness to Cantor and Riemann. I wished to be among a group of intellectual peers, gifted persons generating important original discoveries. Many among my associates had the educational background and exceptional skills needed to undertake and complete such work. I wished a kind of association which was tactically oriented, but at the same time a kind of university. I wished others to take over the teaching of the one-semester class. I had incompleted course preparations and other researches to which I wished to return more of my attention.

My complaints were heard. That was a role a large portion wished to assume in any case. I supplied a tentative agenda of categories of research which might be of general importance to our common efforts. Others modified that tentative agenda.

One large chunk of the researches was devoted to counterintelligence work on matters centered in the history of the socialist movement and Soviet Russia more immediately. Educational policies were another. American history studied in light of primary sources, was another. The history of philosophy was another. Research bearing on courses leading into a general education in Riemannian physics, was a topic I pushed with special emphasis.

Our first encounter with the KGB

This was preliminary to a more systematic organization of such efforts launched during the autumn of 1971, and to the founding of the *Executive Intelligence Review* in March 1974.

There was one other principal development of the 1970–1971 period which was to play a growing role in my life during the later years. It was during the period 1970–1971 that the Soviet KGB first showed an adversary interest in my activities. It started in Europe.

During the fall of 1968, a student organization at the City College of New York had arranged for me to teach a course for one semester. I became increasingly aware of two students of Greek ancestry in that class, Costas Kalimtgis and Criton Zoakos. In due course, they approached me, confiding the nature of their political activities of the moment. Costas was a key figure in a Greek exile movement centered then around the titular figure of Andreas Papandreou. Criton, after completing his military service in Greece, had emigrated to the United States, and had been drawn into Costas' political circle. In due course, they confided more details of their activity, and asked me to advise them.

They did not join the Labor Committees until years later, after a Soviet KGB operation had wrecked their work in Europe, and they returned to the United States. Although I met Costas and Criton together frequently during the 1968–1970 period, I discovered that they were by no means of the same commitments or personal characteristics.

Costas himself came from a KGB family. His father had been an American citizen, caught in Greece during the Nazi occupation, who had become a captain in the Greek resistance, and lost a leg in the fighting which ensued. The KGB side of Costas was his mother, whose first husband had been a top official of the Greek Communist Party, and whose two brothers were high-ranking KGB officials, one operating out of the KGB center in Varna, Bulgaria, the other operating as a control agent in Soviet networks among Greek sailors. Costas had been trained as a KGB operative during studies in Greece, and in Bulgaria. From about 1972, while Costas' father lived, Costas behaved as a loyal part of the Labor Committees in every known respect, even to the point of assisting me in some delicate operations I conducted in U.S. national interests. After his father's death, Costas' loyalties changed. Costas stated that it had been his mother who directed him to shift his loyalties; he ended up, after 1980, as a KGB-linked channel operating under protection of relevant U.S. agencies affording such arrangements, and works as coordinator of a personally directed cell, against my frends and me, coordinating his activities with both KGB and FBI channels today.

The developments around the Greek exile movement

during 1970–1972, overlapped the beginnings of a Labor Committees network as such in Western Europe. Beginning with the KGB operation coordinated in West Germany, Belgium, France, and Britain, in 1970–1971, the network of my friends became increasingly the target of covert operations by assorted intelligence services, Soviet and western, with the two sometimes collaborating in these operations.

By the end of 1971, our efforts ceased to be merely a novel project spun out of my classes. We were becoming a factor in politics, and were being so regarded by the intelligence services of several nations. We were by no means a ponderable factor in our own right, but we were viewed, and treated, by assorted agencies as a "potential danger" to what they viewed as their interests.

Philip S. Ulanowsky

The author at home in Virginia in 1984.

Friends of LaRouche take up economic issues during the Columbia University strike, spring 1968.

(Right) The author (seated, left, with glasses) debates Abba Lerner (at podium), New York City, spring 1971.

(Below) Speaking to a U.S. Labor Party campaign rally in New York City, election night 1974.

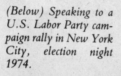

(Right) Campaigning at the Philadelphia Westinghouse plant, October 1976.

(Below)Visting the pyramids at Teotihuacán, Mexico, September 1979.

Fernando Quijano

NSIPS

Virginia Baier

With Helga LaRouche (in white hardhat), tours Seabrook, New Hampshire nuclear power plant, autumn 1979.

WELCOME TO PRINCETON
LYNDON & HELGA LaROUCH

Richard Magraw

Carlos de Hoyos

(Above) In Princeton, Wisconsin with Helga LaRouche in July 1981, where the 1984 campaign for President was announced.

The LaRouches inspect the Goddard Space Center in Greenbelt, Maryland, March 1981.

Addressing the Indian Council of World Affairs, New Delhi, April 1982.

Uwe Parpart

(Above) With Helga LaRouche, Thai military and political party officials during the Fusion Energy Foundation conference on Asian development, Bangkok, October 1983.

Leo Scanlon

(Right) Dining with Peronist leaders, Buenos Aires, June 1984.

Steve Meyer

(Below) Examining the Tristan accelerator at the high-energy physics laboratory, Tsukuba City, Japan, September 1984. Collaborator Uwe Parpart is at left.

Carlos de Hoyos

(Right) Speaking to Pennsylvania television viewers on the crisis in the steel industry, March 1984, one of fifteen network broadcasts that year.

Stuart Lewis

Lyndon H. LaRouche
DEMOCRAT FOR PRESIDENT

Stuart Lewis

Stuart Lewis

(Above) Talking with Dr. Friedwardt Winterberg during the Schiller Institute's memorial conference for space scientist Krafft Ehricke, June 1985.

(Left) A rare return to the classroom, Leesburg, Virginia, summer 1985.

Philip S.
Ulanowsky

Stuart Lewis

Stuart Lewis

(Top of page) Reminding the press that they're liars, National Press Club, April 1986, several weeks after LaRouche Democrats won the Illinois statewide primaries.

(Above) Discussing Democratic Party affairs with a Washington, D.C. talk show host, July 1986.

(Left) In Washington, D.C., October 1986.

(Right) Helga Zepp and Lyndon LaRouche.

(Below) Helga LaRouche displays the Declaration of the Inalienable Rights of Man, signed by representatives of fifty nations, to a Schiller Institute conference, January 1984.

(Bottom of page) Helga Zepp-LaRouche, Patriots for Germany candidate for Chancellor of West Germany, in Dortmund, January 1987.

Philip S. Ulanowsky

Philip S. Ulanowsky

Philip S. Ulanowsky

Who Is Shooting at Us, and Why? 4

The Labor Committees did not begin to dominate my personal life until the autumn of 1971. The 1957–1958 recession had proven to be not merely a turning-point in U.S. postwar history, but a turning-point in postwar history worldwide. The monetary crisis of August 1971 was the second turning-point in postwar history. Those who might have disputed my evaluation of the 1957 recession, could not ignore the immediate and profound impact of the 1971 crisis. Nor could I.

The two developments which best characterize my life during the closing months of 1971 were a memorandum on intelligence organization I presented to my friends at the beginning of September, and a major debate staged between me and Professor Abba Lerner at Queens College.

Those of us familiar with the news media abroad know that the major U.S. news media are the worst in the world, outside the Communist bloc. There is vastly less objective news coverage in the U.S. major media than in any other putatively democratic nation, and a tendency toward coordinated lying which tends to imitate the Moscow radio and press.

There are numerous contributing reasons for this. For example, Americans are far more insular than Europeans. Relative to other democratic countries, our major news media either do not cover important international developments, or report them only in bite-sized gobbets of the current party line dished out to editors by way of such coordination as network conference calls, wire services, and pace-setting opinion of a few major dailies and weeklies. Also, the press of most democratic nations is a partisan press, each publication representing a clearly recognized partisan viewpoint; there is genuine competition, at least to a very considerable degree, among these news media, which tends to prevent any European major newspaper, for example, from daring to lie as consistently as most U.S. media do. We used to have a partisan press, but it has vanished into the bottomless pit of TV audience habits.

When I watch U.S. television news broadcasts, or read the U.S. press, I have an eerie sense that George Orwell's *1984* has already taken over. Not only do I have the advantage of being familiar with most of the world's press; I am one of the best briefed public figures in the world. On important developments, I know enough about the reality involved, to prove that our news media simply lie, over and over again, but appear to get away with it.

In large part, my argument in September 1971 was addressed to this problem of the U.S. news media.

I argued that the August 1971 crisis would unleash new qualities of developments at a rapid pace, inside the United States and in the form of foreign developments which would have major impact on the United States itself. We could not permit ourselves to be influenced by the U.S.

media's fraudulent coverage, and noncoverage, of major breaking developments. We must develop our own news agency, and use our existing national weekly to supply our news agency the needed work-orientation.

The form of organization I proposed was a copy of that of any leading newsweekly. Each regional and topical area of specialization would be defined as a "desk," with one or more persons assigned to the work of each desk. The work of these desks would be coordinated by a person functioning as a "director of intelligence," rather than as an editor. The intelligence organization so constituted under such a director, would act as a resource for the editorial function, rather than as members of an editorial staff.

I stressed that, in our coverage of both foreign nations and the U.S.A. itself, we must free work from the myth of "current events," and view breaking developments as current history, instead. Each nation, and also smaller strata within that nation, represents a distinct culture, both in terms of language, and the cultural heritage transmitted through that language. The work of each "desk" assigned to such a nation, should be not only on knowledge of the language and institutions of the nation. Specialists must not only know, but have a critical understanding of that culture. Culture must not be blindly accepted as a "given." Each culture has characteristic mythologies and other flaws, as well as strong points. Intelligence-gathering must represent an understanding of how these cultural characteristics came into existence over the course of that nation's history.

So, the work of each desk must be twofold. There must be ongoing, in-depth cultural-historical research. Study of breaking developments must be conducted from the vantage-point of that ongoing, in-depth research.

In addition to desks assigned to geographic areas, there were established desks for political-economy, science, counterintelligence, U.S. politics, and culture.

This form of organization was adopted, and put into initial working-order during October and November 1971.

I debate Abba Lerner

According to popular opinion, and also the explicit insistence of university economics professors and textbooks, what had just happened to the international monetary system was something which could not possibly have occurred. Received expert opinion, such as that of Nobel prize-winner Paul Samuelson, was that the "built-in stabilizers" made such developments impossible.

Many students on campuses that autumn regarded the university's economics curriculum as a consumer fraud. Some wag minted the term "quackademics" for the unfortunate members of the economics faculties. We laughed; some of my friends adopted "quackademic" as a kind of verbal stick with which to poke those curious, fuzzy faculty blobs squatting in the pathway of intellectual progress.

Beleaguered economics departments sought spokesmen from their departments, who might debate me. After Professor Abba Lerner's humiliation in his debate before me at Queens College, no one but John von Neumann's former collaborator, Oskar Morgenstern, was willing to take such a risk.

The late Abba Lerner was celebrated, but a very poor university lecturer. His classroom style was that of the academic sadist, whose stock-in-trade is to insult students who might not swallow his assertions whole, rather than a reasoned development of his material. Since the man is dead, I would not mention that fact here, except that it played a key part in shaping the outcome of the debate. In any case, it is not a fault peculiar to Lerner, but a commonplace style among those whose sense of bearing important opinions is not matched by the rudiments of knowing how to actually teach.

The lecture auditorium was packed with both faculty

members and students. Lerner walked confidently into the trap in his initial presentation. It was a laundry list of assertions, without substance, without any definite concept presented. My point was that the reaction to the crisis had been to begin a process of drifting into the kind of austerity which Hjalmar Schacht had imposed on pre-Hitler and Hitler Germany. I added that Professor Lerner's problem in dealing with this question, was that his own leading work had been in advocating Schachtian austerity measures.

The rebuttals, counter-rebuttals, and questions, over-ran the time allotted to the use of the auditorium. Some of the faculty, in particular, wished to continue to debate. Smaller quarters were promptly secured. I persisted in what I had begun upstairs in the auditorium, to induce Lerner to respond directly to the issue of his own Schachtian doctrines. Lerner, cornered, defended Schacht, saying that if Weimar had adopted the measures which Schacht introduced under the Hitler regime, Hitler might have been avoided. At that point, jaws dropped among the faculty members occupying the forward rows; there was a considerable amount of bustling among the students gathered in rows behind the faculty tier.

Professor Sidney Hook, an intimate crony of Lerner's, and then teaching still at New York University, said: "LaRouche defeated Lerner in the debate, but he lost the war." He prophesied, accurately, that no faculty spokesmen would debate me after that.

Lerner was nominally a social democrat, a student of Keynes, with the reputation of being a leading international authority on Keynes' work. Lerner came by his fascist inclinations honestly, as Keynes' German introduction to the 1936 Berlin edition of his *General Theory* leaves no doubt. Keynes argued that he thought the 1936 regime in Germany better suited to his economic policies than other governments.

The problem which popular opinion sees in reports

that leftists are fascists of one sort or another, is the prevalent delusion that politics is based on the somewhat perilous seating arrangements in the French National Assembly of 1792: left, center and right. Granted, people are overheard saying, "I'm part of the Left," or "I'm on the right," or "I sit in the center." One hears about proposals for "unity of the Left," "unity among conservatives," and so forth. I respond to these declarations with two observations. First, if a man insists that he is a giraffe, I do not necessarily believe that he is a giraffe; but, if he persists in insisting upon the assertion, then I do tend to draw relevant conclusions about his mental state.

There are no "leftists" or "right-wingers." There are people who believe that they are "leftists," and those who believe that they are "right-wingers." In both cases, I place little importance on what they claim to be, but attach a great deal of practical political importance that they adhere to such a belief. "Right," "center," and "left," have no practical meaning in history, excepting the practical importance of the fact that many people take such mythologies very seriously.

In the entirety of European history, there are only two persisting polarities: "republican" as typified by the example of Solon's reforms at Athens in 599 B.C., and "oligarchical," as the latter is typified by the Babylonian, Persian, and two Roman empires, and also by the Lycurgan slave-society of Sparta. The first, the republican, is based on the notion of a universal, permanent body of natural law, to which all peoples and individuals are properly equally subject, such that each nation, each person has equal claim to rational dispensation of justice according to the principles of such natural law. The second, rejects such natural law, and insists upon a form of society ruled over by a cartel of powerful families, such as Soviet society, ruled over by a collection of "noble" families of the official *Nomenklatura*.

Over the course of 2,500 years of European civilization in Europe and the Americas, at no point has any nation been wholly dominated by a republican faction. In most cases, either the one dominates, with the other as opposition, or there may be a shift in power from one to the other.

In our own case, our federal Constitution establishes a purely republican form of government. At first, under President Washington, the republicans dominated. Yet, a part of the Tory opposition to U.S. independence had stayed behind during 1775–1783, to emerge as the "Eastern Establishment families" of today. The oligarchical faction of Aaron Burr duped President John Adams, destroying the Federalist party, and used the treasonous Gallatin to gain control over key policies of our government, under Jefferson and Madison. The "warhawk" faction led by Henry Clay, brought power back into the hands of the republican faction, under James Monroe and John Quincy Adams. Jackson and van Buren were outright tools of the Tory faction, as were Pierce and Buchanan. Lincoln was a republican, in addition to being a Republican. Since the passage of the treasonous U.S. Specie Resumption Act, during the 1870s, the oligarchical "families" of the Eastern Establishment have been, collectively, the dominant force in our government and political parties, as well as controlling our banking, currency, credit, and public debt.

Both the republicans and the oligarchs, as pure political types, have usually appeared in the form of influential elites, operating to a large degree from behind the scenes. Political parties, or large fractions of them, are run as covert projects of one or another section of one of these two kinds of elites. Tiny political organizations are usually also operated as special projects by some section of the elite, or by some intelligence agency. The cases of socialist and fascist organizations fall within this sort of complexity.

Except for "neo-Nazi" and like synthetic organizations operated as covert operations of intelligence services during the postwar period, fascist organizations have been consistently creations of groups of wealthy oligarchical families, and socialist organizations usually so. The mother of the socialist organizations of nineteenth- and twentieth-century Europe and the Americas, was the international organization built up around Guiseppe Mazzini, run directly by an international freemasonic organization, including Britain's Lord Palmerston; this freemasonic organization was a front for a network of wealthy oligarchical families centered in Venice. This included Mazzini's Young Europe and Young America organizations, the latter centered in Harvard's "Concord" circles and the South Carolina secessionists. The socialist organizations of nineteenth-century continental Europe, were products of Mazzini's organization, and were run as covert operations of wealthy oligarchical families. British socialism was created under the direction of the Pre-Raphaelite Society of Oxford University's John Ruskin, with cooperation from the Cambridge Apostles.

Around the world, there are nominally socialist organizations, some of significant political power in their nations, which are exceptions to this. Some of them would regard the founders of the United States as socialists of their own persuasion. Such exceptions aside, the socialist and fascist movements are otherwise both tools of wealthy oligarchical families: the fascist entirely so, the socialists usually so.

The only significant difference between socialists and fascists, traditionally, is the difference in their attitude toward the interests and demands of organized labor. The socialists are used by wealthy rentier interests chiefly as political battering-rams against industrial-capitalist interests. The fascists are used as battering-rams against resistance to savage forms of austerity, and are therefore traditionally antilabor. If this is rightly understood, there ought to be nothing astonishing in the fact that a professedly socialist Abba Lerner should be an advocate of Nazi forms of austerity.

Within the left wing of the Socialist International today, there exists a very influential faction which frankly admits itself to be fascist. Many aspects of the socialist reforms in Sweden, for example, are plainly fascist. During one period, during 1974, this faction emerged publicly in New York City, to announce itself as "fascism with a smiling face," thus seeking to convey the idea that theirs was a "nice fascism," not to be confused with the nasty varieties. The case has been argued, with considerable cogency, that the present Soviet state is to be regarded as fascist. The Gregor Strasser wing of the Nazi party, which produced Josef Goebbels, styled itself as "National Bolshevist"; except for racial issues, there were many points of convergence between Nazism and Bolshevism: Adolf Hitler was, in a very meaningful sense, a German-speaking Fyodor Dostoyevsky.

The debate, back and forth, on the similarities and differences among Bolsheviks and fascists, might continue indefinitely, without firm conclusion, unless we situate the analysis within the proper frame of reference. That frame of reference is identified by the cases of Crowley and Nietzsche. Between the opposing values associated, respectively, with the Age of Pisces and Age of Aquarius, where does socialism stand?

Nietzsche defined "Age of Pisces" with the tradition of Socrates and Jesus Christ. This is what Nietzsche resolved to see destroyed during the twentieth century, as did Crowley and his theosophist and Golden Dawn followers. Yet, the root of this is already found in the English Hellfire Clubs of the eighteenth-century British liberals, and in the dogmas of Hegel, Savigny, and Oxford's John Ruskin. Where do the socialists stand with respect to the trial of Socrates? Where, with respect to the doctrines of natural law of St. Augustine, Cardinal Nicholas of Cusa, and Leibniz? On this, "leftist" I.F. Stone stands beside Crowley and Nietzsche; most U.S. "socialist intellectuals" do similarly.

Essentially, I define individuals and organizations not

by what they imagine themselves to believe, but rather by how they think. The republican mind and the oligarchical mind, see God, Creation, and man, from opposing philosophical standpoints; their minds work differently. There are significant differences among republicans, on this account, and among oligarchists; those differences are dwarfed by the fundamental differences between republicans and oligarchists.

The debate between me and Lerner, was a debate between a republican and an oligarchist. With that shamefaced admission which I finally eked out of Lerner that day, this essential difference was brought out into the open. The objective I set myself in that debate, from the outset, was to shift the emphasis away from what Lerner asserted himself to believe, to force Lerner to show the audience how his mind worked. Those "families" which imagine themselves to be like the gods of mythical Olympus, using mere lowly mortals as their whims decree, were most displeased by their report of that debate, not because I defeated Lerner in the debate, but because of the way in which I did it. In those Olympians' curious freemasonic ethic, I had committed the unforgivable sin of speaking out of turn.

I have often spoken out of turn. I have denounced Henry A. Kissinger, supplying proof which the Olympians know to be completely true. I exposed Walter F. Mondale similarly, saying nothing I did not prove, nothing which the Olympians did not know to be true. Horror of horrors, I spoke the documented truth about the leader of their freemasonry, the Queen of England; I had committed not the ultimate crime of speaking out of turn, but one close enough to it (the truth about Capri and the cult of Mithra, is one of the ultimate secrets, forbidden to the public). Observe the strange way in which the news media today, repeats over and over again, the allegation that I have said unbelievable things about Kissinger, Mondale, and the Queen. Why this silly repetition of that, especially since the proof supporting my observations is so thoroughly proven by documentation? Who are they trying to send what message, by means of constant repetition of this symbolic ritual? What else, but to mobilize the lower ranks of institutions controlled by these "families," to rally against this figure who dares to impeach those public figures of whom we currently approve.

Do not imagine that this reaction by the Olympians is some empty cult-ritual of their particular sort of club. Suppose it becomes the rule, that any Johnny-come-lately, armed with nothing more than a set of very damaging facts, can run about the streets making prominent figures unpalatable to the general public. Suppose the general public refuses to tolerate public figures exposed in this way. What is the result? Very simply, once the Olympians are weakened in their power to decree who will be a respected influential figure, and make this stick, their power over our society begins to be very seriously weakened. Once the Olympians' carefully built up system of orchestrating public opinion begins to be undermined in such a way, all the money in the world cannot keep the Olympians in the degree of power they presently represent.

Their policy ever since has been: Since you are unlikely to beat him in debate, don't give him a forum to debate the issues. That debate with Lerner established the view, that I had ceased to be merely an amusing annoyance. In their eyes, I had become potentially dangerous. Professor Sidney Hook had made, at worst, a shrewd guess.

The Soviets start to play rough

Evidently, the Soviets had reached a similar view. At the beginning of 1973, they deployed a series of covert operations against us, reaching out for cooperation from among various circles in the West, including the Boston-based section of the Institute for Policy Studies and the Russian Studies section of the London Tavistock Institute. We had experienced Communist Party hooliganism during

1972, but this was on a grander scale and far, far more serious. The prepared operations were launched during February of 1973. For the next sixteen months, KGB actions in the U.S.A. and Western Europe were closely co-ordinated. The Soviet operations included an optional assassination of me, which they eventually called off, when both the FBI spies in the Communist Party U.S.A. and we got wind of the operation. The Soviets play very rough, but they are also politically cautious in their own way.

The two initial Soviet operations against us that year involved the drugging, abduction, and attempted brain-washing of a friend of mine in West Germany. This operation began in February of 1973, and came to its conclusion during June of that year. The second operation surfaced in the front pages of the Philadelphia news media in mid-March. The U.S. Communist Party was committed to put the Labor Committees out of existence physically.

Local U.S. law enforcement was curiously uncoop-erative, as they had been during prior physical attacks on me and my friends. We knew that a "fix" was in from somewhere, probably the FBI, since the pattern of this seemingly pro-Communist behavior among local law en-forcement was national. We were left to our own resources. Tired of the beatings, we decided we had better prepare to defend ourselves if necessary.

The Communist goons received the surprise of their lives. They were no match for our hastily improvised, but expertly organized defense squads. Naturally, the liberal news media wept tears of sympathy over the poor, abused Communist goons. The SWP led a "united Left" into an alliance with the Communist Party. By June, the "Left" had grown tired of its attempted ambushes. All was quiet on this part of Moscow's western front for the summer and into the autumn.

In June, I made my second of many trips to Europe. I had been to Britain, Germany, and Austria during the summer of 1972. The nucleus of Labor Committees in West Germany, France, and Britain, had been formed over the autumn, winter, and spring. I was assigned to spend two weeks with the leading group of Germans, at a place near Düsseldorf, to conduct an intensive course on method. At the conclusion of this period, our KGB-abducted friend turned up. My visit to Germany took a bit longer than had been planned.

In brief, the facts are these. My friend had been drugged surreptitiously on a series of occasions, all in the vicinity of Cologne, West Germany. Although he was happily married, he was induced to fall in love with a snapshot of the face of a woman in East Berlin. He was induced so, to arrive in East Berlin, to a designated address at a specific time. Subsequently, photographic and other evidence confirmed three key facts about the operation in East Berlin. First, that the woman in East Berlin was a psychiatrist, the sister of a colonel in East Germany military intelligence. Second, that the controller of the operation was a well-known Berger, a second-rank official of the East Germany Ministry for State Security. Third, that the woman in question was part of an East Germany intelligence unit in charge of selling East German medical professionals to West Germany. We also identified one of the West German nationals key to the drugging operation, and found her to be part of an operation run out of the Bulgarian tourist ministry.

This independent confirmation was important to us at the time, for both security and medical reasons. I suggested that my friend be picked up and brought to me at once. He was in a highly disassociated state, barely ambulatory.

He recovered full rational functioning a few months later, but suffered severe psychosomatic side effects leading to some severe illnesses, for years afterward. Fortunately, he was a Greek-American with an exceptionally strong family background, and what is sometimes described as a very high-grade personality of exceptional intelligence. Seeing me there also had a very special effect, obviously not anticipated by the East German intelligence.

He wished to be interrogated, and stuck to it. I conducted a very hard interrogation, but a supportive one. It was like peeling away one layer of an onion after the other. I wished to get him back to the United States for medical attention as quickly as possible, but he needed to be in psychological condition to make the trip, and we needed a working picture of the situation, both for security reasons, and also as clinical information for some psychiatrist with expertise in dealing with drug-hypnosis cases.

For both security and medical reasons, we needed to determine which of the layers of stories told were true. We needed some crucial benchmarks. Those I have listed were the crucial ones we obtained in follow-up investigation. They showed that the final version he provided after two successive sessions over many hours, was accurate, as we have adduced from internal features of the account.

He reported a plan for killing me. That I discounted as a byproduct of what I assumed would have been a normal feature of the conditioning process. He said it was planned for the autumn. I assumed this might refer to a scheduled trip I was invited to make to a conference at Reggio Emilia, in Italy, about that time, but I could not accept the idea that they would have permitted him to pick up indications of any actual assassination plan.

I made the autumn trip from the United States to Reggio Emilia, and then Milan, returning to the United States without incident. In November, the FBI picked up hints in direction of a planned assassination of me from its agent in the leadership of the Communist Party. We were unaware of the FBI's information until it turned up in a about two reams of Freedom of Information Act releases much later. We did pick up independent signs of known assassins conducting a profiling operation in my vicinity.

The group was a Puerto Rican terrorist organization known to be run by the Cuban secret services. This group had military backgrounds, and represented a significant capability in terms of firearms and explosives.

In the midst of this, we had our second case of a covert intelligence services' drugging operation, and later a third. Everything pointed to a possible attack being deployed in the environment of a year-end conference in New York, at which I was to speak. The first of the two druggings occurred in England, an action positively identified as perpetrated by two persons traveling under the names of Paul Walsh and Mrs. Schroeder, the names of two very well known MI-5 operatives. The operation was an elaborate one, involving extensive cooperation with the two perpetrators by New Caledonia Airlines officials. An investigation conducted by a leading British investigative journalist was most helpful in pinning down the essential facts.

The third occurred during the middle of the conference itself. The only significance of targeting of this individual was that he knew certain facts, whose significance he did not then understand, which could have led investigators to uncovering a Soviet asset operating in the environment of this operation.

The New York Police Department came into the picture during these developments. With that development, the Puerto Rican "heavies" folded their tents. What was left, was the residue of an extensive operation of the sort catalogued by spooks under the name of "Chaos." The clear objective was to sow such chaos and paranoia-ridden confusion into the Labor Committees, as to destroy the organization to all intents and purposes.

When that failed, the *New York Times* moved in, to attempt to cover over the pieces. We had blown the story to the press, but the lid had been put on. During the first week of January, to inquirers, the New York news media had reported: "Yes, there is an assassination-plot under investigation, but there is a national security problem involved." The *Times* assigned Paul Montgomery, under whose byline appeared one of the most astonishing masses of outright lies and other lurid fabrications I had yet seen in a major newspaper.

The *Times* does have a very nasty Soviet KGB connection, as it was compelled to admit in a major legal proceeding a few years ago. This connection involves the Moscow Procurator, the KGB, Henry Kissinger, the Anti-Defamation League of B'nai B'rith, the East Germany intelligence services, and former U.S. Representative Elizabeth Holtzman. Currently, at the moment of writing this, this connection involves the special section of the U.S. Department of Justice associated with Mark Richards, the Office of Special Investigation (OSI). The indications are not that the *New York Times'* publishers are dupes of the KGB, but that the *Times* is part of a section of our Eastern Establishment which has special back-door arrangements with the KGB. As part of this arrangement, the *Times* and the Anti-Defamation League assist in targeting selected U.S. personalities whom the KGB selects for special sorts of harassment. January 1974 was one of the occasions the *Times* did the KGB a special favor of that sort.

We intervene in Watergate

In the midst of these cascading developments about us, an ominous terrorist incident occurred at London's Heathrow Airport. Without going into the details of the matter here, we knew that this signaled a very turbulent 1974. We identified the escalating "Watergate" proceedings and the impact of the oil-price crisis as the centerpiece of a complex of probable crisis developments. We took a close, fresh look at Watergate, and observed that the key figures targeting us over the turn of the year included key figures in the Watergate attacks against Nixon.

We had never liked Richard M. Nixon. His economic

and foreign policies had been almost consistently a disaster for the U.S.A. Nonetheless, by the third week in January, we decided that we had to act to defend Nixon, not for personal, but for institutional reasons. A clever and evil piece by Clark Clifford, published earlier on the editorial page of the *New York Times*, had mooted the feasibility of exploiting a crisis around the presidency, to effectively change the form of the U.S. government, from a constitutional presidency, to a parliamentary form. The possibility of such a thing occurring was a highly probable development, if no certainty, of course.

I can imagine myself engaged in assisting my neighbor in putting out a fire at his house. In such a circumstance, I presume that some liberal journalist attended by a TV cameraman, would approach me, and ask "Why are are trying to interfere with your neighbor's fire?"

In the heat of the moment, I can imagine myself retorting, "It might spread to my house, for one thing."

The journalist had me, I could imagine. "Do you have any proof that the fire could actually reach your house?" In her eyes, obviously, my behavior in assisting my neighbor is pure paranoia.

Is my little joke an exaggeration? Not in my experience observing the behavior of liberal journalists, or liberals generally. I believe in picking babies out of the street, even if I cannot first prove that the automobile approaching will run over the child. I believe in acting upon knowledge of the probable consequences of my acts of commission or omission. Better to take what may later appear to have been a superfluous precaution, than to risk not taking the precaution.

This is not only good common sense. It is good philosophy, and good scientific method, too. Events rarely occur in such a way that we can foretell their occurrence in the manner of mechanical cause-and-effect. Events occur because the potential for their occurrence is significant. Shall we concentrate attention on discovering other peo-

ples' intentions in these situations? Most people do not
know in advance exactly what they will actually do; they
respond to the potentialities as those potentialities develop.
It is those potentialities to which we must give special
attention; it is to foster or to counter potentialities, that we
must act. Since most of the detailed features of important
developments, especially those involving governments, are
hidden ones, potentiality is the best evidence one is likely
to have in hand.

So, we decided to intervene on the side of a President
Nixon we disliked. The potential for grave damage to our
constitutional institutions demanded this. My friends and
I have often acted in that way. I hope we shall always do
so. However, we have found, that whenever we act in this
way, to a a purpose of which liberals disapprove, the liberal
objects, insisting, in effect, that one must never shoot a
charging man-eating tiger until that tiger has actually taken
a convincing bite.

On the subject of "Watergate," and the recent spate
of threatened "Reagangate," what did Nixon in was not
any mass of evidence against him. He was done in because
he was unpopular. He was unpopular because of his economic policies. We saw this in the ugly moods around the
long lines of cars waiting to get into gasoline stations. We
saw this in the rage of those suffering the economic recession of 1974, following the slide through the 1974 crisis
into the crisis of August 1971. They voted for Nixon in
1972, because they feared McGovern, and because "vote
Nixon" was the word among their peers on the block.
They didn't like him. Once he became officially unpopular,
their pent-up hostilities against his presidency were unleashed. The same logic is the key to efforts at "Reagangate." The President's, and the Republican Party's policies
on the economy cost the Republicans the Senate, and signaled that the unpopularity of the President's administration was spilling over against the President himself.

Nixon was defeated, less for what he did in connection

with Watergate allegations, than because he did nothing to remedy the true, chiefly economic causes for the unpopularity which erupted against him. President Reagan's folly, in his initial response to the "Irangate" allegations, was to repeat the folly of President Nixon's 1974 State of the Union address, Reagan's arguing: Enough of "Irangate"; let's get on with the great economic recovery under way—when a depressionlike economic collapse, and chains of bank failures were sweeping most of the nation. Of course, in Nixon's case, he more or less sealed his own political doom, when he moved to exonerate the two culprits who had set the events into motion leading into the Watergate burglary, Kissinger and Haig. Once Kissinger and Haig were cleared, those remaining were doomed to shoulder the full blame. Once Nixon covered up for Kissinger and Haig, he was vulnerable to the charge of cover-up.

Nixon lost his fight, but we never regretted our attempts to prevent this undermining of the presidency. In the long run, our efforts did help the course of future developments, and we learned a great deal from our efforts.

During the first weeks of 1974, while I was being shunted from one safehouse to another, my friends pulled together a relatively impressive, functioning international organization. The intelligence function was expanded. The energy and effectiveness of every facet of our activities was qualitatively improved. When a member of the Soviet United Nations delegation conveyed a desire to meet with me to "clear up possible misunderstandings," I judged that there was no longer any immediate danger more serious than some chance piece of exuberance by the rag-tag of the local "Left."

Greg Rose had been sent in to the Labor Committees in 1973 as a mole, after being given intense preparatory training. His background was William F. Buckley's circle, but some of the gobs of intelligence he brought in from "sources" was passably good material. We did a background check on him during the autumn of 1973. It was worrying. I noticed two things during events immediately following our year-end conference, and gave a warning suggestion that he be kept away from anything we would not wish a potential provocateur involved in. We let him roam in areas of activity we deemed relatively nonhazardous, while I supported the view that it might be a good idea to play out the string, better to discover exactly who had deployed him.

On his own initiative, Rose visited the Soviet United Nations mission. At first, when he spoke of such meetings, we wondered if they had occurred at all. He identified his Soviet contact as one Gennady Serebryakov. Then, like a dog with a trophy in his teeth, he announced that Serebryakov wished to meet me at our offices. Several of us were astonished when this proved true. We confirmed that he was an official of the Soviet Embassy. His card said he was such a person, and he did wish to discuss "clearing up misunderstandings." I brought a friend with me who had a background in military intelligence. I placed my cards on the table, listing the cases in question, with emphasis on the problem of the local Communist Party and the East German security services. I judged, that for the time being, our problems from such quarters would be at an ebb.

The founding of EIR

I inspected the progress in the daily print-outs of our in telligence. There was no doubt that our information covered a considerable amount of newsworthy material not generally available, and some of it good quality counterintelligence. In early March, I proposed to the press staff, that they consider producing a weekly publication based on a selection from this flow of material. The habits of the management consultant persist in my sporadic exposure to the business decisions of my friends' activities. Only once in the past dozen years have I assumed an executive function in connection with my friends' business ventures, and that briefly, during a crisis situation, during the period from October 1980 into January 1981. Like any seasoned consultant, I am usually pleased when one of my suggestions is adopted and carried through successfully. So, the weekly *Executive Intelligence Review* was born a few weeks later.

During that period, I began the practice of fairly regular meetings with those heading up intelligence functions associated with the production of what became *EIR*. It began as a regular daily roundup of developments around the 1974 year end. For a while, I was involved almost daily in such meetings with the intelligence heads, either with our European bureau when I was in that vicinity, or in New York City. After my trip to Iraq, West Germany, and Italy, in April and May of 1975, the frequency of my attendance at these meetings tended to trail off, and I relied increasingly on being briefed by telephone, or by someone's dropping by to bring me up to date on matters not adequately covered in the ream of detailed filings I received each evening. Today, reading through such reports, a few selected periodicals, and so forth, consumes an average of between three to four hours each day. Receiving oral briefings on background or on breaking developments, consumes from one to two hours a day. The pattern was set during the first half of 1974.

Over the years from the late-1971 founding of the news agency, through events of 1974, my personal life changed in a very significant degree. More and more, my knowledge and activities were shaped by the intellectual and related work of those associated with me, and proportionately less on my individual work. I became part of a division of labor in such matters. My personal life since, is centered around a series of projects, each dominating my attention for a period of time, in much the same way each consulting assignment dominates one's attention, until it is succeeded by a new one.

I launched two personal projects during 1973, two mutually interconnected projects during 1974, and moved into major international political activity during 1975. So far, in this chapter, I have covered the crucial organizational developments around the Labor Committees over the 1971–1974 interval. Before turning to 1975, let us catch up on my principal personal activities of 1973 and 1974.

At the beginning of 1973, the one sector of our news agency which had not been able to function in any well-organized manner, was a section we then identified as the "science file." This "file" was then headed informally by a person who had graduated in physics from Columbia University, and had gone on to graduate work at Maryland. He was talented, but his scientific method was a poor one, and he was a poor organizer personally. During February, this problem was pointed up to me by various delegations, each complaining about the state of affairs in that "file," and pressing me to intervene with some suggested new directions. The old management consultant in me "took the assignment," resulting in a memorandum and supporting oral argument which I presented during March.

Since the center of our competency was in economic science, I emphasized in that memorandum, the benchmark to be used as reference in organizing the work of the "science file," was the role of Riemannian physics in my original contributions to that science. I argued that two lines of work ought to be adopted as task-oriented points of reference: thermonuclear fusion, and the way in which physical economy interacts with a Riemannian view of the biophysics of the biosphere. Both projects were adopted.

I suggested that Uwe Henke von Parpart be called to New York to give a series of presentations on Riemannian physics, to supply needed additional orientation for the members of the "file." Uwe, then teaching at Swarthmore, had emigrated from West Germany, to do graduate studies in mathematics at Princeton, and had gone on to doctoral work in the philosophy of science at Pennsylvania, taking an assistant professorship at Swarthmore while preparing his doctoral dissertation. In 1970, I had suggested that he rework my own earlier analysis of the connection between the work of Riemann and Cantor, a project he had nearly completed during early 1973. His lectures would be useful for the purpose I indicated to the "science file." I was also being a bit tricky; I thought that Uwe's preparing those presentations would catalyze his already overdue work of putting his results into publishable form.

If any among you ever wish to write a good book on any subject, first qualify yourself to teach the subject effectively in a standard sort of one-semester course. Any really good scientist, is either an exceptionally good univerity lecturer, or could readily become one. I have never observed Dr. Edward Teller teaching, but I am certain of two things: He was an excellent lecturer, and those qualities which made him effective in the classroom bear directly upon his successes as a scientific organizer. I am an old hand in these matters, and I know how to recognize the signs. If you are a conscientious teacher, the sort who constantly doubts the quality of one's own work, and who seeks to simplify the subject for the students by concentrating on the role of underlying assumptions, wrestling with yourself to discover and correct the defects in your teaching, will improve your mastery of the subject, and greatly improve your presentation of the subject. Then, write it down in the manner of speaking to a well-defined sort of audience you wish to address. So, I have pushed people with something important to report, to present the material in lecture-form before presenting a final draft for publication. The written report will be much better, and it will be more likely that it is done on time.

The response to my March 1973 memorandum and accompanying oral argument, was most fruitful in several ways. Most narrowly, it sparked the two proposed projects, which produced two eminently successful results over the following twenty-odd months. The work on thermonuclear fusion took on a life of its own. It led to collaboration with a number of leading scientists, which required that the work be taken out of the news agency's science file and assume an independent life in the form of what became the Fusion Energy Foundation. The work on the interaction between physical economy and biosphere assumed a narrower, task-oriented focus, the functional relationship between a breakdown in physical economy and the emergence of interacting combinations of both animal and human pandemics, and pestilences and diseases of plant life. This was the subject of a report which stands up as remarkably prophetic, in predicting precisely the general timing of the development of patterns of famine and epidemic erupting over the course of the 1980s.

Conventional biological thinking has overstressed the role of genetics, and has moved away from the original approach of Leonardo da Vinci and the point of reference provided by Louis Pasteur's work on optical activity in living processes. The popular view of genetic determination, exaggerates the role of genetics, subordinating biological research all too much to a statistical way of thinking consistent with the fallacious assumptions of statistical gas theory. Inevitably, with the popularization of both "information theory" and the radical influence of an anti-scientific "linguistics" promoted by the 1930s collaboration of Karl Korsch and Rudolf Carnap, a lurid sort of metaphysics has been superimposed on the language of molecular and cell biology.

These sorts of problems were made apparent to me in the course of my wrestling with Rashevsky's biophysics. Certainly, genetics and so forth existed, but this did not account for the way in which they came into existence. One must never lose sight of the elementary fact, that whatever genetic action, for example, does, in the case of healthy processes, this leads always to an harmonic ordering congruent with the Golden Section. If the theory adopted to analyze the phenomena of cell life, were not premised on characteristically negentropic continuous functions, the theory is provably absurd to that degree.

I did not propose that the "science file" forget about genetics. I proposed, that we must rightly assume, that whatever genetic functions do, those functions are subsumed by, and thus ultimately governed by an appropriate sort of Riemannian function. This emphasis must be especially appropriate in the case of processes taken on a very large scale over extended periods of time. This must be most conspicuous in the evolution of species and varieties, and in the general evolution of the biosphere. What laws govern the transformation of genetic material, to such effect that the newly determined species or variety is a successful design? By taking evolution as the crucial event in existence of biological processes, we require ourselves to explain the non-evolutionary sorts of biological behavior from the standpoint of the higher-order biological laws which subsume the relatively stable existence of successful forms of fixed genetic types.

For example, Rashevsky's problems underscored the fact for me, back during the late 1940s, that, instead of starting from the existence of the cell as such, cell biology must be subsumed under a generalized function for mitosis. Rashevsky had worked mightily in the effort to work his way around this fact; his lack of success in this approach, was inevitable. I would hope to see ongoing work lead to a mastery of the correct standpoint during my lifetime.

As I have already indicated, my method is based on the principle of the "hereditary" implications of underlying assumptions. All of what scientists describe as the strongest of really "strong proofs," are obtained only from this vantage-point. No group of experiments based on "less strong" sorts of hypothetical designs, no matter how conclusive that experimental evidence appears to be, can be rightly considered disproof of a truly "strong" hypothesis. This, I emphasized to my friends back in March and April memoranda and discussions of 1973, was the "trick" in scientific work, which we could exploit to our advantage in the matter of the interconnection between physical economy and the biosphere.

Beyond psychoanalysis

My other major project of 1973, was launching an attack upon Freudian psychoanalysis. Three pressing considerations prompted me to take this up. The central role of "sexual liberation" in the rock-drug-sex counterculture, was the broad political consideration. I was also concerned that the psychological impact of battles with Communist goon-squads might have unhealthy side effects, unless my friends were inoculated with awareness of how such side effects might develop. Much closer to my heart than either of these two important considerations, was the matter of the conflict between the erotic impulse and higher, creative functions of mental life.

There has been a significant amount of professional and other gossip, over the centuries, to the effect that erotic impulses are at the root of creative work. The case of the German poet, Goethe, is merely exemplary; he plunged into dark periods of infertility, from which he was rescued in every case but his best period, by some wild sort of amorous interest. Freud is notorious for speculations along such lines. From my own personal experience in my own creative work, and, more importantly, from the standpoint of my attack on "information theory," I knew that such popular myths were not only false, but dangerously so.

In its lower aspect, human nature partakes of the characteristics of beasts: irrational enslavement to hedonistic impulses of seeking pleasure and avoiding pain. In that which distinguishes us as human, our nature is of an opposing character. The only worthy motive of human beings generally, is to subdue the beast within oneself, to become less bestial, and more human. This conflict determines, as I have already referenced this point, the three general categories of human character types, as typified by the "In-ferno," "Purgatory," and "Paradise" of Dante's *Commedia*. This is the pivotal feature of human psychology, the only admissible premise for a science of the human mind.

These conflicting tendencies within the personality are associated with opposing qualities of powerful emotion, each emotion primarily associated with an impulse which the English usage calls "love," and also with an emotion of fear-hate, directly complementing the impulse associated with that distinct type of "love." From the classical Greek, the baser sort of "love" is associated with "eros," and the opposing, human emotion, with "agape." Creative work is highly emotional, in this sense, with the emotion of "agape." It is the cultivation of that latter emotion, which drives the creative personality.

The emotion of "agape" is the emotional aspect of reason, and is associated with love of truth, love of classical forms of beauty, and love of that which distinguishes the human in each of us from the beast. It is also the emotion of Christian love. The Christian acts, not out of fear of God, but of fear of being estranged from a God one loves. The Christian wishes to please God, as we enjoy bringing joyful surprise to friends. It is this quality of love which is the proper basis for a sound marriage, for love of one's spouse, and the loving rearing of one's children. It is the love, close to tears of joy, in observing any child working through what is, for that child, an original discovery of some sort, and witnessing the child's joy in that accomplishment.

We associate God with reason. We know this reason as the Logos, or "Holy Spirit." This is God expressing the lawfulness of a process of continuing creation. By assimilating reason, to the purpose of furthering the objects of our love of beauty and of mankind, we may hope to shape our wills so that we participate in God's work less imperfectly, by acting less imperfectly as agents of His reason. This expression of Christian love is exemplary of what drives and builds the truly accomplished scientist. This is the genius of that Western European Judeo-Christian civilization traced from the Crucifixion, according to principles understood by Philo Judeaus and St. Augustine, and as expressed most profoundly by the *Gospel of St. John* and Paul's *Epistles.* If we love God, we love his sheep; so our proper work in life is ordered.

Dr. Sigmund Freud was a philosophical materialist of that positivist variety of Viennese associated with the influence of Ernst Mach. He was also a gnostic of the variety associated with the heritage of Feuerbach and the theosophical currents of Aleister Crowley. He was, incidentally, a "bisexual," a personal inclination of direct bearing on aspects of his psychoanalytical doctrine. His gnosticism was displayed most nakedly in his *Moses and Monotheism*; his homosexuality was displayed in his projection of his own sexual orientation in a wildly incompetent, and fraudulent treatment of Leonardo da Vinci.

His psychoanalysis could be dispensed with easily, but for the fact that he was a keen observer, and a most effective one relative to most of those varieties of the socalled "new science" of psychology which had emerged out of French positivism during the second half of the nineteenth century. Relative to these psychologists, Freud was right most of the time. In terms of accepted professional psychology of this century, Freud's was the "least bad" by a wide margin. It could not be simply written off after exposing the fallacy of its underlying assumptions. One had to consider the ostensibly positive side of Freud's clinical doctrines, and indicate the proper standpoint from which to reassess those results.

From my specific standpoint, the clinical side of Freud's work was barely more than description. Any person of Socratically self-critical disposition, who applies such knowledge of self to observing the behavior of persons around him, can more or less readily adduce the valid features of Freud's work without qualifying himself in that clinical profession. The valid part of psychoanalysis, as analysis, is merely a searching-out of hidden assumptions. Since most people view other people, and themselves, as having a more or less fixed character, most people do not examine behavior of themselves or others in this Socratic way. Therefore, for them, psychoanalysis is some mysterious mumbo jumbo which seems to help some people to cope with neurotic problems, and even the psychoanalyst's clients come to view the analyst, for this reason, as a kind of witch doctor, a "head-shrinker."

Up to a point, the analysis itself is descriptively accurate, and can often be useful. It does not address the essential issues of psychopathology. These limitations of the practice are expressed both as limitations, and also represent a potential for pure evil whenever psychoanalysis is viewed as the guide to "social engineering."

The evil potential in psychoanalysis began to be sharply focused during the 1930s, as Freud associated himself with the Rockefeller-funded London Tavistock Clinic of Brigadier John Rawlings Rees and Eric Trist. The postwar work of that Tavistock Clinic, as an appendage of the Tavistock Institute, is key to the systematic corruption of international psychological associations of the postwar period to date, and is also key to the methods of "social engineering" by which the "rock-drug-sex counterculture" was developed to the point it was broadly unleashed by Margaret Mead et al. during 1963.

Rees's background had been in treatment of "shell shock" patients during World War I. According to his own account of the matter, this clinical experience led him to explore use of this knowledge as a potential weapon of social control. The Tavistock Clinic became a key institution devoted to development of what we call "brainwashing," parallelling the Soviet development of a method of brainwashing based on the work of Pavlov. Rees and his associates occupied their lives in developing such techniques of psychological warfare, taking control of the United

Nation's World Federation of Mental Health, and infusing these brainwashing doctrines into the practice of the psychology and sociology professions throughout the postwar period to date. During the 1930s, Tavistock adopted Freud's psychoanalysis as a means for expanding such capabilities; Freud spent his last years with Tavistock, bequeathing his psychoanalytical association to their control, and leaving his daughter, Anna, to be associated with the clinic for the remainder of her life's work.

Individual psychoanalysis is an expensive proposition, and thus not suited to mass-brainwashing practice. So, work on so-called "group theory," such as that of Dr. Kurt Lewin and his associates, was called into play, and blended with psychoanalysis, to elaborate a practice of "group analysis." The doctrine was reduced to a few simple principles, to the effect that sociology students and similar "lay therapists" could be deployed to conduct such exercises.

Tavistock concentrated on perfecting techniques for inducing psychotic states, exploring ways in which victims could be molded either as what we call "programmed" agents today, or simply to act in a predictable way when turned loose in society. LSD-25 was developed as a synthetic form of ergotamine, for such purposes. The work of Aldous Huxley in the California-based MK-Ultra, was a large-scale experiment in use of LSD-25 and related agents for potential use as an aid to mass brainwashing. The use of drug-assisted hypnosis generally, was explored vigorously.

The Korean War was a breaking point in the developing of Reesian methods of "social engineering." If U.S. intelligence had correctly assessed the emphasis on Pavlovian methods of political conditioning introduced immediately in the wake of Soviet occupation during the immediate postwar period, we should not have been taken by surprise in Korea. The Soviets had developed a nasty, and relatively cheap method of brainwashing. There was a great flurry of effort in the West, to master the Soviet contributions to these methods. The expertise of North Korean brainwashing specialists has shown up in recent years in Soviet assignment of North Koreans to run the brainwashing programs of the Khomeini dictatorship in Iran. Masses of cheaply brainwashed children running into mine-fields, is the handiwork of these North Koreans. The conditioning of suicide bombers is another handiwork. Studies of Korean brainwashing revolutionized Reesian methods over the course of the 1950s.

My friends had seen the results of this sort of mass programming during the 1960s. Mark Rudd, John Jacobs, and so forth, leaders of the Weathermen terrorist underground, were not only "deeply into" the marijuana-LSD side of the rock-drug-sex counterculture during the 1967–1968 period; this was openly displayed as the controlling sense of personal identity of the Bundy-funded "crazies" around the Columbia developments of 1968.

I was first forced to recognize the connection clearly on one occasion during the late spring of 1968. John Jacobs was addressing an SDS meeting of about 200, a meeting convened to deliberate on opposing proposals for a summer school program. Jacobs appeared to be mentally ill, severely disassociated. I had done studies in the language-behavior of schizophrenics during the late 1940s; Jacobs' behavior conformed to that sort of thing exactly. He was hooting out a series of totally disjointed slogans, with scarcely a verb used anywhere. Yet, a large claque was cheering some among these disassociated expostulations. I had no familiarity with rock lyrics, but some eyewitnesses to that event who did, explained the business to me. Jacobs, who later gave the Weathermen their name, was spouting disjointed fragments of rock lyrics, in a sequence corresponding to some disassociated sort of free association going on within him.

How could a sizable number of university-educated students contrive to support a policy expressed in disassociated babblings with no explicit proposal of any sort contained anywhere within the utterance? Such behavior does occur among schizophrenics in psychiatric wards. They were not supporting any idea; they were cheering his fragmentary allusions to a series of rock lyrics, an association which evoked some sort of pleasurable sensation within them. Jacobs wasn't talking to them; he was, symbolically, stroking them sexually, and they decided they wished to be raped. They were not supporting a policy; they were conveying their desire to go with Jacobs, wherever it was he might decide to lead them. There was a distinct resemblance to Adolf Hitler's style at a Nazi party rally. Jacobs was playing Hitler's role, reduced to its bare, "Reesian" essence.

This was the characteristic feature of the 1968 "New Left," and of the beggars' opera assortment of "Rainbow Coalition" ingredients gathered around the "ecology movement" of the 1970s.

It was during 1969, that "sensitivity groups" replaced a disjointed "leftist" rhetoric as the mode of political organizing activity predominant among the New Left. The precedent was the evolution of the experimental project which produced the "Situationists" in France. For the victims of the rock–drug-sex counterculture, 1968 was a "high," and 1969 was a depressing "bummer," a "bad trip." The jaded, damaged little egos of the 69ers were ready for the garbage-collector, who appeared in the form of Weathermen violence and a proliferation of sensitivity groups.

Women in radical-feminist sensitivity groups, decided to become lesbians! Men decided to become "gays" in a similar way. I had never imagined such a thing; the proliferation of this sort of brainwashing captured my attention. The proliferation of "encounter group"-produced lesbians was popularly explained as a reaction-formation. New Left women of 1967 and 1968 had become a sexual "free lunch counter" for whatever traveling honchos were traveling the New Left circuit. The women so exploited in such unpaid sexual prostitution unleashed their accumulated resentments, and hied off to the companionship of their "lesbian sisters." The guilty males confessed their sins, and established closer ties to their "gay brothers." Some lunatics, carried away by their own rhetoric, spoke of a "women's national liberation movement," a sporadic effluvia which vanished in a cloud of mocking laughter. One had the impression of the "New Left" as a whole, that the psychotics had staged an insurrectionary takeover of a lunatic asylum, and declared the national autonomy of that institution.

By the early 1970s, this madness had spilled over from the demarcated limits of the radical New Left, to be considered respectable among a growing number of liberals. "Sensitivity" became an ethical standard those currents were seeking to impose upon the nation in general, and not without some significant degree of success. The liberal news media picked up the dogma quickly. Such lunacy triumphed at the 1972 Democratic National Convention.

Not only had the New Left gone mad; the *Zeitgeist* was a raving psychotic.

This forward march of the "Reesians" made the exposure of the fraud of psychoanalysis indispensable. It had been the respectability of psychoanalysis, especially among families of suburban liberals, which had contributed significantly to the launching of such mass-brainwashing operations. Psychoanalysis must be politically neutralized, by placing both its competencies and its evil elements in an objective perspective. A sizable fraction of my friends had been conditioned to view psychoanalysis in positive terms of reference, partly through families' peer-group opinion, and also through conditioning in public school and university. To help them, and others escape "beyond psychoanalysis," toward a scientifically valid sort of psychopathology, it was indispensable to do a thorough sort of critique.

The negative side of the matter would have been sufficient motive for the effort I put into this. As I said, the timing of the undertaking was immediately prompted by circumstances of the encounters with Communist goon-squads. Violence against persons, even Communist goon-squads, calls up an unpleasant sort of emotions associated with the striking of the blow. This implication of the un-avoidable small war worried me, and a sizable ratio of others among my associates. To avoid being bestialized oneself by such experiences, it were prudent to be aware of, and in firm control of, the kinds of emotions pulled up in such business. This latter prompting of the timing of my endeavor, bore directly upon my positive concern. To control the bestial side of oneself, one must have a cor-respondingly strong sense of identification with one's hu-man side. This is where the failure, and potential evil of Freud shows up most clearly.

In the main, apart from such negative considerations, my objective was to identify the emotional aspect of cre-ative mental life. Gifted people, once they have reached the degree of comprehension of their subject matter at which a breakthrough is ripe, usually fail to do so. They seem to encounter a barrier, and experience a combined emotional and intellectual state most fairly described as "blocking." I had been put on to a clearer view of this problem through the work of Dr. Lawrence S. Kubie, at the beginning of the 1960s. He referenced the point, that gifted young specialists of great promise during their grad-uate studies, go on to become intellectually sterile, re-specting their early creative potential, sometime after gaining their terminal degrees in university. I understood the problem, and saw signs of what Kubie had described among some of my gifted associates. We had new projects of importance afoot, and I feared that progress would fall far short of what I hoped, if this problem of "blocking" were not understood.

The essential assumptions on which Freudian psycho-analysis is premised, are notions better elaborated, in one part, by Immanuel Kant, and, for the rest, by Ludwig

Feuerbach. The general etiological principle of psycho-analysis was elaborated with Aristotelian rigor in the second part of Kant's *Critique of Practical Reason,* "The Dialectic of Practical Reason." The further elaboration of all the essential assumptions of Freud's system was completed by Feuerbach, beginning with his *The Essence of Christianity.* Dr. Erich Fromm was essentially correct, in showing a systematic convergence of Marx and Freud, a commonality rooted in Feuerbach's influence. Freud is fairly summed up as a C-student in Feuerbach's class, later turned psycho-analyst. I had covered these connections as part of my class in economics; that treatment was the starting-point of reference for my 1973 writings on the subject.

The central fallacy in Freud's work, is most directly addressed by reference to those of his assumptions which are copies of the work of Kant and Feuerbach. The analysis of "hereditary" features of systems again. Formally, the problem is identical to that confronted in my attack on "information theory." Freud denied the existence of creative mental activity, to the same effect Wiener did. Freud was a terrible biologist, in the respect that the negentropic characteristics of living processes did not exist for him. What Freud referred to as his project in "psychophysical parallelism," suffices to prove that that misconception of biology was at the root of Freud's assumptions for psychoanalysis. His absurd constructions under the heading of "metapsychology" are further exhibition of the problem. He denied the existence of negentropic functions in mental life, too.

We can prove, as I have indicated in preceding chapters, that the negentropic characteristics of human brain functions can be conclusively demonstrated, to the effect that Riemannian physics is implicitly a capability which can be developed to describe this. Since the brain functions so, it is the duty of a scientific psychology to premise investigation of human mental life on this crucial distinction between human individuals and beasts. To attempt to base a human psychology upon studies of animal behavior, is axiomatically absurd, and can lead only to results which tend to bestialize human behavior. Freud was instinctively right, up to a point, in posing the question of psychophysical parallelism: Something must occur, in terms of a properly defined physiology of brain processes, which parallels what we recognize as thought, including especially creative mental activity. However, to undertake such inquiry, we must first recognize that this problem should be restated, more precisely, as a question of how the negentropy of living processes has functional correspondence to the negentropy of human creative activity.

This identifies the formal side of the question, as the question might be viewed from the standpoint of mathematics. It was essential to add, that we can recognize emotional states and emotional changes in ourselves, which correspond to creative mental activity, and to the transitions between "blocked" and "creative" states of mental life.

This overview of the matter confronts us immediately with the connection between the assorted activities of which our day is composed and the mental state in which we find ourselves when turning to creative work. To be creative, one must live a healthy emotional life during at least most of the other parts of the day. The point is made most easily, by referring again to my curious discovery, that saturating myself with Beethoven in a certain way, promoted my capacity for concentration and creative productivity during the same general time-frame. I learned, that finding myself seemingly hopelessly blocked, my mind tending to wander away from my work, it were better to walk away for a while, and to steep myself in working through great classical musical compositions. If one's hours are saturated with engagement with those forms of beauty which express the negentropic principle of life, and with agapic social life, one has ordered one's daily life sanely, and creative work comes much more easily. If one, on the contrary, lives most of one's day emotionally involved in bestial impulses, the creative capacity is crippled, even to the degree of nonexistence.

Nearly everyone in our culture can recognize much of this rather readily. For example, we have but to look back to certain among the happiest hours of our childhood, when we experienced an emotion like tears of joy, at effecting what was for us then an original, creative discovery. That childlike joy in one's own creative-mental potentials, is a quality we must preserve and develop throughout our lives. That dedication alone, will tend to guide one to a sanely ordered life. That Freud rejected, and that rejection is the kernel of evil embedded in psychoanalysis.

Creative work, of a sort symbolized by valid scientific discoveries, may be the exceptional experience in society today, but it is nonetheless the state of mind in which every human being deserves to live. On condition that scientific endeavor is coupled with love of reason, love of beauty, and love of mankind—agape, the creative scientific personality exemplifies sanity, exemplifies what should become the normal human condition.

We look at the Tavistock Institute

The sundry Soviet-directed, and Soviet-linked operations which I have identified for the period from February 1973 into 1974, were centered, on the western side, in an overlap between the Institute for Policy Studies and the London Tavistock Institute. The evidence to this latter effect, was clear to us early during 1974. The work done on the theme of "beyond psychoanalysis," and the preceding work leading into that, had proven a significant advantage in our counterintelligence work during early 1974.

Four of the key researchers investigating the Tavistock Clinic and Institute asked to meet with me. We spent an afternoon, as each, in turn, summarized his case and its documentation. We discussed back and forth. The thought occurred to me: Was our documentable case a conclusive one? Another round of discussion followed. None of us had any doubt that we had a conclusive case. We knew it should be published immediately on the basis of the facts in hand. Others agreed. It was.

The Tavistock Institute essentially controls the international psychoanalytical profession directly, and coordinates the "Reesian" sociological and psychological networks of the West through channels including United Nations agencies formerly tied to Rees himself and to Julian Huxley. A major campaign was run against me in Germany, during 1974 and 1975, under an affiliate of the Tavistock Institute, the Frankfurt Sigmund Freud Institute, conducting the operation through its own affiliate at Düsseldorf University. That is but one example. It went the other way, too. By exposing itself in its role against us during the 1973–1975 interval, the Tavistock network had drawn our attention to the nature of its work, including its links to Soviet-linked terrorist organizations. The case of the connection between a Tavistock program at a Heidelberg mental institution, and the key role of this program in producing the so-called "second generation" of the Baader-Meinhof terrorist gang, illustrates the point.

We had been oriented to counterintelligence work since uncovering Bundy and Marcuse's directing role behind the SDS "crazies." The behind-the-scenes launching of the "ecology movement" and Weatherman terrorists, had given us some degree of expertise. Soviet operations against my friends during 1971–1972, had sharpened my faculties for this work significantly. The operations of 1973 and 1974, overlapping our investigation into "Watergate" and Henry A. Kissinger, brought us into the spring of 1974 as a respectable approximation of seasoned counterintelligence professionals.

In June 1974, the Socialist International came into the open with an internationally coordinated operation against us. Was this Soviet-inspired, or perhaps by the circles around

Bundy? It was becoming difficult to separate the roles of the two.

A youthful bastard, born Herbert Frahm, fled Lübeck Germany, to assume an international identity as Willy Brandt. He fell into the hands of British intelligence at some point, and spent the war in first Norway and then Sweden, linked to intelligence operations in support of the British and then the U.S. Strategic Bombing Survey. He appeared in Berlin at the end of the war in Europe, applying for a career with U.S. intelligence to John J. McCloy. McCloy recounted the events to a New York audience, with his arm around "Willy."

According to German sources on the ground at the time, it was the U.S. State Department which arranged Brandt's election as mayor of West Berlin. According to sources on the ground at the relevant time, it was Brandt's advice which caused the tearing-up of a U.S. intelligence report which could have prevented the Berlin Wall from being established. Two years after that, McCloy announced to relevant persons that he was grooming Brandt to become the Chancellor of Germany, a process which required teaching Brandt such things as not wearing brown shoes with a blue suit. Brandt was already better known for his drinking than his thinking talents, but soon the figure of Egon Bahr appeared at Brandt's side.

Konrad Adenauer's influence over the Christian Democratic party of West Germany began to be undermined from within the Christian Democratic Union, and outside, that same 1963, complementing escalating, U.S.-backed operations aimed at toppling France's President Charles de Gaulle. The New Left upsurges in France and Germany were coordinated with the New Left operations in the United States, both in respect to timing, and continuing direct links dating from the late 1950s. They overlapped the formation of a coalition government in Germany, and the destabilization of de Gaulle. Brandt moved from foreign minister, where he synchronized with Kissinger's circles in launching "détente," and moved on to become Chancellor, as McCloy had projected in 1963. Shortly prior to the June 1974 operations against my friends by the Socialist International, Brandt had been ousted from the chancellorship, when a close associate was exposed as a Soviet spy.

The Labor Committees had barely existed in Western Europe in 1973, and began functioning as an organized force only beginning March 1974. The Socialist International was resolved to smother the baby in the cradle. It was not an action by the social democratic party of any one or two countries; it was a tightly coordinated international operation, and it was a very nasty operation, including a mysterious death of a Labor Committee member in Rome that year. If the social democratic parties involved had been what they pretend to be, the campaign against my friends had never happened. Of course, Brandt's social democracy is not what it pretends to be, which is the reason I have mentioned a few highlights of Brandt's career.

Who was behind the Socialist International's dirty operation against my friends? Might it be John J. McCloy's circles, as Brandt's case might suggest? Could it be, rather, the Soviets behind this action of the social democracy? Could it be another case of cooperation against my friends, by a combination of Soviet and certain western agencies, as we had seen in 1971–1972, and again in 1973? Looking back to those events from today, there is no doubt that it was a combination.

It started long before the time the American Friends' Service Committee had attempted to recruit my father to actions of sympathy for the Bolshevik Revolution, but a glance at the listing of the tenants, in the year 1919, in a building at 120 Broadway in Manhattan, is a good place to pick up the trail.

The Secret of the Twentieth Century   5

Around the Vatican today, the present state of the world is referred to as "Apocalyptic." Pope John Paul II, for example, has laid repeated stress on the fact that Satan exists, and that satanism is a very concrete and powerfully evil force afoot in the world. Among those around the Vatican with whom I have discussed this view of the present state of affairs, I have met no millenarian's mystical symbolism of the sort with which I am familiar from revival meetings under tents outside Rochester, New Hampshire decades ago. Their views are very down-to-earth, very precisely reasoned, and very well informed.

Does this view of our period, as apocalyptic, focus upon a ripening of the superpower conflict, and some Armageddon triggered by an attack on Israel by Moscow's Syrian satrap? That danger, a very real one, is a matter of concern, but it is not the way in which I define this period as apocalyptic, nor does it appear to be the view of anyone I know around Rome. The Soviet menace is a very real

167

one, but it is only an aspect of a much deeper, older, and broader threat to the very existence of civilization itself.

AIDS: *the Apocalypse*

In 1974 my friends completed an epidemiological forecast based on my memorandum of March 1973. On the assumption that then-existing trends in international monetary policy persisted, there would be an exponential rise of conditions for famine and pandemics over the period from the mid-1970s. These conditions would become statistically significant during the early 1980s, and would zoom upward beginning about the middle of the 1980s. The first major development of the 1980s, would be famine and cholera in the Sahel region of Africa. These developments in the Sahel, already gruesome in their own right, would be only what medical specialists term a "marker" for a broader eruption of combinations of both old and new varieties of epidemic disease and pandemics. Without knowing that AIDS existed, my friends had forecast the AIDS pandemic of the 1980s.

AIDS is the "marker" for the conditions my Vatican friends view as the apocalyptic character of the present time.

Governments have become increasingly, and justly terrified by this AIDS problem. At the close of 1986, the U.S. National Academy of Sciences issued ominous warnings and a call for dramatic action by governments. The governments of Western Europe are frightened. Near the close of 1986, the leader of the World Health Organization (WHO) announced, in New York City, that WHO's earlier estimates on the menace of AIDS had been a dangerous underestimation. Yet, so far, no effective action has been adopted by any government. Under present research programs in progress, as of this moment of writing, the disease's spread throughout the world's population will never be stopped, and, probably, a vaccine and cure will never be developed.

The best information presently available, indicates that the AIDS infection began to spread in black Africa, at about the same time it began to spread inside the United States. However, because of health conditions in black Africa, especially in the tropical belt, the infection spread much faster than it did in the United States. Today, the nation of Uganda is as good as biologically an extinct nation, and Zambia is not far behind. The present forecast is that AIDS will render black Africa essentially extinct by sometime early during the coming century.

However, the disease's spread is not localized. Cuban troops returning to Cuba included numbers of homosexuals. Castro clapped these fellows into prisons, and dumped them onto boats into Florida at the first opportunity. The U.S. government shipped some of these Cuban homosexuals into major cities of the United States, such as New York City. They became male prostitutes working the bathhouses and kindred locations in those cities.

AIDS is not a sexually transmitted disease. It is better described as a blood-carried disease, although the infection is presented in every imaginable human secretion from carriers of the infection. Once the infection enters parts of human tissue such as the immune system's cells, it spreads into every imaginable part of the body. It becomes part of the genetic material of the body's cells, and is carried by cell reproduction into the new cells formed in the body. The person infected shows no symptoms, usually, for years, but during those years, that person is a carrier, silently transmitting the infection to other persons without warning.

By means which are not yet properly understood, the AIDS infection interacts with other infections and infestations coming into the body or already present in the victims. The infected person becomes the victim of what are called "opportunistic" infections, a condition associated with a breaking-down of the immunological system of the AIDS-infected carrier. AIDS causes eruptions and spread of tuberculosis epidemics, for example. Often, the role of AIDS in promoting opportunistic illnesses, and combinations of such illnesses, is described as "AIDS Related Complex." If the AIDS-infected individual does not die as a result of such "AIDS Related Complex," he or she will die, probably by ten years or so after infection, of a neurological breakdown, the way in which the AIDS virus itself kills its victims directly. The best medical evidence so far, is that AIDS will cause the death of every person it infects, possibly with very rare exceptions, but possibly not.

Naturally, the most rapid spread of the infection, during the initial phase of the epidemic, is through direct transmission of contaminated blood or through trauma caused by homosexual acts. So, inside the United States, the largest concentration of AIDS-infected persons is in metropolitan areas with large populations of homosexuals and drug users. These modes of transmitting the infection, are conveniently described as "fast tracks" for spread of the infection.

However, once a significant percentile of the population becomes infected, the virus is transmitted in more ordinary ways, pretty much like any virus. It is convenient to call these pathways of transmission "slow track" routes. It is a fair guess, that your chances of contracting the infection by such routes is about one percent as great, or perhaps slightly less, than being infected by an ordinary virus along the same routes of transmission.

The fact that the "slow track" transmissions act much more slowly in transmitting the AIDS virus, than ordinary viruses, has been used to promote a dangerous overconfidence in condoms and clean hypodermic needles as ways of containing the spread of the disease.

In the case of an ordinary virus, an infected person comes down with the disease within a matter of weeks.

The victim either dies, or recovers. A person who has died or has recovered, is no longer a carrier. With AIDS, each infected persons remains a carrier, on the average, for more than a hundred times as long the carrier of any ordinary virus. When the percentile of currently infected AIDS carriers builds up to a level more than a hundred times as great as ordinary viruses usually do, your chance of catching the AIDS infection begins to be as great as catching an ordinary virus, in more or less the same way you could be infected by any ordinary virus.

I have assembled the known facts about AIDS into the design for a computer projection. Some of my associates have programmed this projection. Several levels of mathematical sophistication have been used to produce more accurate computer studies. From our work with leading agencies around the world, we know that our computer studies are, at this present moment, the only such studies done anywhere in the world. We are cooperating with some of the world's leading agencies, who are using our work.

AIDS is the first known case of a dangerous form of retrovirus specific to human beings. Even in animals, these kinds of infections were not recognized until about fifty years ago. We know such epidemics as Maedi-Visna in sheep, and in forms of the disease killing cows, horses, and other fauna. AIDS is almost exactly a human variety of Maedi-Visna, and is normally transmitted among human beings in the same way Maedi-Visna is transmitted from infected to other sheep. (Animals do not inject themselves with homosexual needles, or engage in anal homosexual activities.) Sheep crowd more than people do, and so do cows; horses are a better standard of comparison. Known statistics on spread of retrovirus infections among sheep, cows, and horses, are presently the best standard for comparison with spreading of AIDS among human populations.

One of the important facts about Maedi-Visna, is that, after fifty years of attempting to develop a vaccine for this infection, we are not close to developing one. We face a similar problem in using conventional methods of developing a vaccine for AIDS itself, unless someone stumbles across a vaccine by a great piece of pure luck. There is much talk about tricks with chemotherapy, which might prolong an AIDS victim's life briefly, but the press reports of such promising developments are very greatly exaggerated. The problem is, that vaccines work by helping the immune system to cope with an infection; AIDS infects the immune system itself. A vaccine, in the ordinary sense, will not work.

The best computer estimates, using the most conservative estimates based on known statistics, is that AIDS can make the human species extinct within as soon as thirty-five to forty years from now. We can imagine a time, about forty years from now, at which the last surviving human being, dying in the last stage of neurological breakdown, casts one eye toward Heaven, and the other, simultaneously, toward Hell, but seeing neither, expires, murmuring a last gasp of gibberish.

This is Apocalypse.

Can this Apocalypse be avoided? I say a confident, "Yes." Objectively, it can be avoided, but only if we adopt the sweeping changes in policy needed to do so. We can take public health measures which will slow down the spread of the infection, and there are new avenues of, not medical research, but fundamental biological research, which can bring us to a cure for the infection. So far, governments have refused to consider the urgent public-health measures needed to slow the spread of the disease; the very types of biological research which could lead in the direction of a cure, are being shut down for lack of funding.

What will happen, if the government of the United States continues its policies of 1986? Probably, a few years ahead, as the panic spreads, popular hysteria will force homosexuality to be classed, once again, as a capital offense, and the mere use of recreational drugs will be treated in a similar way. Probably, lynchings of homosexuals and drug users will become endemic, and so forth and so on. History warns us that these are soon-to-be-expected responses to the growing fear caused by the spread of the infection to a significant percentile of persons who are neither homosexuals nor drug users.

AIDS is becoming, rapidly, a potential Apocalypse. However, as my friends' 1974 forecast proves the case, the conditions which caused the spread of AIDS are man-made.

Our 1974 forecast was based on two sets of facts. The starting-point of the study, was my March 1973 memorandum on the calculability of the interaction between physical economy and the biosphere. The second was the assumption that a collapse of the levels of physical economy must occur, if existing trends in monetary policy persisted. Let us focus attention on this second factor first.

In my 1958–1959 forecast, I had forecast accurately the course of economic developments for the coming twenty years. Although, as I have already pointed out, I underestimated the Kennedy administration's positive economic-policy actions, the pattern over the entire twenty-year period was, in total, exactly what I had forecast. Kennedy's actions merely delayed my projection of the earliest probable eruption of monetary crisis, about 1965, to my later option, 1967–1968. When the breakdown of the Bretton Woods agreements occurred, in 1971, the U.S. government and international monetary authorities reacted with Schachtian measures, exactly as I had predicted at the end of the 1950s.

Over the period from 1954 to the present time, including the post-Sputnik acceleration of aerospace development, there have been many changes in current economic and monetary policy. Therefore, we cannot blame the developments of the entire thirty-year period on the Eisenhower, Kennedy, Johnson, Nixon, Ford, Carter, or Reagan administrations. Something deeper is involved. Through nearly every change in policy, from one administration to the next, the trend in policy making has remained the same at almost every turn. In nearly every case, the new policies have continued the same long-term trend in economic and monetary practices as the preceding policies.

So, the cause for the long-term trend, is a policy-making structure, controlling the major decision making of both government and banking, an influence more powerful than any elected government. It is that policy-making structure, which is the ultimate, and really efficient cause for the AIDS pandemic.

The responsible policy-making structure is not limited to the United States. It includes the Venetian reinsurance cartel, the Swiss insurance and banking cartel, and the powerful London financial center. These influences, combined with our own Eastern Establishment, shape U.S. government and banking decisions on U.S. economic and monetary policies, and the U.S. government and banking system then play a leading part in shaping the economic and monetary policy decisions of the OECD nations and the international monetary authorities. It is the policy-making structures of the West's so-called industrial powers as a whole, which are to blame.

The Socialist International has played a leading role in enforcing these trends in economic and monetary policy, as is merely typified by the case of Willy Brandt's acting at the direction of World Bank President Robert S. McNamara, in the work of the Brandt Commission. The Soviet press has editorial orgies over the evils imperialism bestows upon developing nations, but I know first hand, from facing the Soviets directly on monetary-policy issues over the period since mid-1975, that it has been Soviet policy to back up enforcement of economic and monetary policies of the West's international bankers.

This policy-structure has created the AIDS pandemic, and as the human race is doomed by continuation of present policies on AIDS, unless we change these policy-structures, the human species will be extinct within a couple of generations. It is that policy-structure which is the true Apocalypse.

Nuclear war is not the Apocalypse. Over the past twenty-five years, the Soviet military general staff has believed that the Soviet empire could win and survive a general nuclear war with the United States, if certain preconditions are met. They believe, that a combination of passive civil defense, of strategic ballistic missile defense, and a devastating first strike, mean a United States knocked out, unable to retaliate effectively, after the first blow, following which Soviet nuclear-armed regular forces overrun those nations of Western Europe which refuse to capitulate peacefully. This Soviet war-plan is called the Ogarkov Plan, and is rightly called the Andropov-Ogarkov Plan.

Nuclear warfare is horrifying beyond the imagination of nations prior to the bombing of Hiroshima. It is not necessarily Apocalypse. The human species, although savagely injured, could survive such a war as a species. AIDS is the Apocalypse.

Nonetheless, the superpower conflict is a major ingredient of the same complex of monstrous developments in which AIDS has now emerged as the ultimate horror. Bolshevism is one of the great horrors of this century, and one of the great secrets of all twentieth-century history to date. The existence and role of Bolshevik power over the past seventy years, is also an integral feature of the same policy-making structure responsible for the trends in economic and monetary policies over the postwar period to date. Bolshevism is not only connected to Apocalypse in terms of global conflicts heating up today; it has been a part of the march toward Apocalypse from the beginning of its existence.

The secret Trust

What is the connection between Bolshevism and the policy-making structures of the West? One point of intersection can be found in New York City, just after the Bolshevik Revolution.

It is the year 1919. Travel in the imagination, down Manhattan's Broadway, and turn into the lobby at 120 Broadway. Read the directory on the lobby's wall. You are not in Lenin's Petrograd or Moscow, but almost there. The firms listed on the directory are linked to powerful law firms, some with the Morgan interests, and, most significantly, with the family of former President Theodore Roosevelt. This is the U.S. headquarters of a branch of Soviet foreign intelligence, known as "The Trust."

One of the law firms into which the Roosevelt family had reached its influence, through dynastic marriages, was that of Milbank, Tweed, the firm of the John J. McCloy who steered Willy Brandt's postwar rise to the chancellorship of Germany, and to leadership of the Socialist International.

Theodore Roosevelt's operations extended directly into the offices of Bolshevik leader Leon Trotsky, who had left his domicile in New York City only two years earlier. One of Trotsky's key aides was a Roosevelt agent, Commander Sergius Riis, son of Teddy's crony, Jacob Riis. Another was a man jointly owned by Teddy Roosevelt's family and Winston Churchill, Odessa-born Sidney Reilly. There was also a Stanley Washburn, and later a Colonel Robins. There was Max Eastman, and John Reed. And so on and so forth. Later, these fellows shifted their backing, from Trotsky, to Bukharin and Stalin.

The recently deceased Averell Harriman cut his first deal with the Bolsheviks, through Trotsky, in 1923, and cut a bigger deal at the beginning of his long friendship with Stalin, in 1927. Harriman also backed Benito Mussolini, and he and his family backed Hitler's rise to power in Germany. Harriman, as I shall indicate, was not really being inconsistent in backing the Bolsheviks, fascists, and Nazis at the same time.

The brains behind the Soviet "Trust" included Soviet

Foreign Minister Chicherin, and the father of present Soviet Prime Minister Mikhail Gorbachov's wife, Raisa. The Armand Hammer who contributed to funding of a major subversion operation against the West, Raisa Gorbachov's Soviet Cultural Fund, has been a Soviet agent since the 1920s, beginning as an integral part of the same "Trust" which included Teddy Roosevelt and Harriman's interests.

The investigation of 120 Broadway nearly seventy years ago, might convince you that you had stumbled upon the greatest secret of the twentieth century, until your investigation went further, and you discovered that this was only one of the pathways leading to much darker secrets.

Peel away another layer of the onion. What is the common root of the connection between Teddy Roosevelt's family and Trotsky? Go back to the Isle of Capri about 1909–1910. In the grotto there, you could have met Trotsky, Lenin, and many other leading Bolsheviks of later years, being indoctrinated in the mysteries of future Bolshevik culture by Maxim Gorky.

Go back to shortly before 30 B.C. We see, in the same places where Gorky later walked, the triumvir Octavian, who called himself later Augustus Caesar. Octavian is negotiating with a delegation of Syrians, priests of the cult of Mithra. Octavian agrees to the priests' terms, establishes Capri as a western holy place of the Mithra cult, and receives the backing of the Syrian military orders for his war against Antony and Cleopatra. He wins the war. The plan to make Alexandria the capital of the new Mediterranean empire is doomed. Antony and Cleopatra commit suicide. The empire of the Roman legions is established, and the cult of Mithra becomes the cult of the legions, although not of the nominal capital of the empire, the City of Rome. Octavian becomes Augustus Caesar, and the sacred Isle of Capri is made the hereditary property of the Caesars.

Go ahead to the time of the Crucifixion of Jesus Christ. Augustus' son and heir Tiberius is pacing in his villa, waiting for the messengers from Judea announcing Christ's death. The soothsayers of the cult of Mithra attend him. The Crucifixion was arranged by Pontius Pilate, the husband of Tiberius' niece. It was the Syrian cult of Mithra which had ordered Christ's death.

Five centuries later, the Byzantine emperor established the Benedictine Order, and donated Capri to the order, like the site of the temple of Zeus on Monte Cassino. During the nineteenth century, Capri reverted to private hands, including the Mithra-cultist Alex Muenthe, who occupied the site of Tiberius' palace, establishing Capri as the world-capital of sodomy, and the cynosure of the followers of theosophist Aleister Crowley, Madame Blavatsky, Fyodor Dostoyevsky, and Friedrich Nietzsche. It became, with Venice and the Torre e Tasso palace at Trieste, the world-center of the cult of the "Age of Aquarius." Gorky manufactured Bolshevik culture, under the patronage of Muenthe, there.

Go ahead about two decades. Muenthe is receiving a visitor, the fat, cocaine-sniffing Nazi, Hermann Goering. Hermann's business is to buy the site of Tiberius' palace for Adolf Hitler, whom Goering swears to be the reincarnation of that emperor. Muenthe refuses to sell, explaining that it is he, Muenthe, who is Tiberius' current reincarnation.

Later, the Benito Mussolini who knew many secrets from such sources as his patron, Count Volpi di Misurata, explained, that Bolshevism and fascism had been created as the two sibling rivals of the twentieth century, and that Mussolini himself prophesied that fascism was about to prevail absolutely. Both siblings are creations of the "New Age" cult established by such as Nietzsche and Crowley, a cult whose insiders know it as a rebirth of the cult of Mithra, and its spiritual capital as Capri. That is the great secret of the twentieth century.

It is 1986. The place is Rome. A young American couple visits the Basilica of San Clemente. They are there to see the reconstructed temple of Mithra, under the church. The guide welcomes them, "We wish Americans to see this." The couple is horrified by the abomination they witness within. They leave. The guide asks them their impression. The woman answers, that it is pure satanism. The discomfitted guide's facial expression darkens, and he scuttles away to await a more susceptible American visitor, perhaps one indoctrinated in one of the books silly Rosalyn Carter donated to the Pope during President Jimmy Carter's visit to Rome, William James' *Varieties of Religious Experience*.

That, too, touches upon an evil secret of the twentieth century.

After leaving the presidency, Theodore Roosevelt summed up his political convictions by founding a radical political movement named the "New Age" movement. This was the movement of Jacob Riis, out of which the Progressive Party was spawned. There was no coincidence in this use of "New Age" and the European use of the same "New Age," as short form for "Age of Aquarius." Roosevelt's association with the gnostic cult-center known as the New York Museum of Natural History, out of which Margaret Mead, clomping her great horned witch's staff through those corridors, played her key coordinating role in the launching of the rock-drug-sex counterculture.

I reemphasize the point I have made elsewhere. The Bolshevik Revolution, as popular legend views it, never happened. What is called the "February Revolution," largely British-financed, and the "October Revolution," largely German-funded, were palace coups, conducted from the inside of the czarist and Kerensky governments, respectively, with the help of what were otherwise merely coordinated, bloody street riots of no greater dimensions than those launched to topple the government of President de Gaulle. The coordination was international, but the role of the czar's minister of war, and the czar's secret police, was crucial. The documentation of the details survives in the West to the present day. My friends have gained possession of much of it. The Okhrana officials who had created and directed the Bolsheviks prior to October 1917, became high-ranking officials of the Bolshevik intelligence services under Dzerzhinsky and Chicherin.

The combination of international forces which directed the revolution from inside and outside Russia, were, barring the lower ranks of British and German intelligence services involved at the time, the same wealthy families which had organized the 1815 Congress of Vienna, and had made Russia "the policeman of Europe" for approximately three decades after 1815. The 1815 Congress of Vienna had had the more limited objective of crushing the influence of the American Revolution in Europe and the Americas. The "New Age" adopted the more ambitious goal of eradicating those forms of nation-state and cultural traditions associated with the heritage of St. Augustine and the Golden Renaissance. Whereas Russia had been, until 1905, the target of spread of the western civilizing influence, the "New Age" crowd intended to reverse that process. Although Czar Nicholas II was a silly man, since Peter the Great, the Romanov dynasty had acted several times as a conveyer-belt for relatively successful efforts to "westernize" Russia. The forces behind the 1815 Congress of Vienna had been committed to preventing such "westernization" since the seventeenth-century plots involving the Orlov brothers and Prince Potemkin. The instrument existing inside Russia repeatedly used for these antiwesternizing ventures, was a mass-based current called the "Old Believers," or "Raskolniki." The Pugachev revolt which threatened to overthrow Catharine the Great had been a "Raskolniki" insurrection. As Lenin himself conceded, the Bolshevik Revolution was also a revolt of the Raskolniki.

Although the peasant masses of the Raskolniki were, and continue to be hostile to technological progress, the antiwesternizers did not object fundamentally to industrial progress in Russia. They objected to industrial progress only insofar as technological progress became the channel through which western cultural values—Augustinian values—were mediated into Russian life. So, Fyodor Dostoyevsky had argued at length. This was key to the crucial role of a Maxim Gorky who has more influence on Soviet Russia today than does Lenin.

The bringing of the Raskolniki to power, guised as Bolsheviks, was merely a critical feature of a broader grand design: to establish a form of what the Trilateral Commission advocates today as "global society," a kind of global parody of the state of European feudalism during the fourteenth-century "New Dark Age." Fascism was another of these battering-rams developed and deployed for this purpose.

The new organization of the Eastern Establishment of the U.S.A., around Morgan and Mark Hanna's National Civic Federation, and the far-flung domestic and foreign intelligence organization centered on the extended family of Theodore Roosevelt, shared in this view of a step-by-step destruction of an Augustinian heritage, for a "New Age" somewhat in the image of European feudalism during the fourteenth century's New Dark Age.

The unfortunate thing has been, that those who have stumbled across the documentation showing a longstanding connection between Bolshevik Russia and some of our prominent Eastern Establishment families, have tried to adduce a "communist" sympathy among those families. Certainly, Teddy Roosevelt's role in the 1905 Russo-Japanese War, and his policy of looting of Central and South America, does not accord with what legend associates with "communistic" proclivities. True, the British upper classes, into the ranks of the British royal household itself, seem to be saturated with Soviet spies and persons of kindred inclinations. However, the Anglo-American establishments as a whole cannot be explained away so simply.

They are not "communists" in the popular sense of the term. They are an oligarchical faction, who view Soviet

Russia as an integral part of a geopolitical grand design, a useful chess piece to be deployed, even granted world-domination for a time, as part of a long, step-by-step process, aimed at bringing out of perhaps a century of bloody chaos, a new kind of world order, which they hope that their families will then dominate and maintain forever. The statements of the Trilateral Commission, on its goal of a step-by-step emergence of "global society," and some of the statements to the same effect by such Trilaterals as Zbigniew Brzezinski and Henry A. Kissinger, are an accurate reflection of the actual motivations of those families for whom they work.

This oligarchical grand design is the Apocalypse. It is the influence of powerful rentier-financier interests committed to some approximation of such a geopoltiical design, which is the crucial element in the policy-making structure which has created the conditions for the apocalyptic peril of AIDS.

Either we free our nations from the grip of such a policy-making structure, or civilization is certainly doomed by our failing to do so. Civilization would be certainly doomed; probably, if not certainly, the human species would be extinct by sometime early during the coming century.

The oligarchical world outlook

However, although there are many layers of conspiracy involved in the antics I have summarily described, it would be a great error to attempt to explain all this in terms of merely some "conspiracy theory." Before one rushes to explain everything by wicked conspiracies, or good ones, a very simple question must be faced: What brings people to conspire so? The conspiracy is not the cause of itself; something else causes it to come into existence.

On this point, we must turn again to the Socratic method. People act as they do because they have motives to do so, and also because their decisions are given concrete form through the guiding influence of certain underlying assumptions. These assumptions define for them what they recognize as their motivating self-interests, on whose behalf they imagine themselves to act. This definition of self-interest is shaped by certain underlying assumptions. Their choices of decision, to act in a way they believe consistent with that self-interest, are also shaped by underlying assumptions, most of these the very same assumptions which shape their notion of self-interest.

In the final analysis, these assumptions are the same ones which confront us as the central issues of theology. What is God? What conception corresponds to the nature of His Being? What is God's Will? Above all, what is the relationship of the being and actions of the human individual to this God and His Will? These are questions posed in that form since Parmenides and Plato. And, so forth and so on.

Today, we can trace the existence of the European oligarchical current from origins in the Harrapan culture of Dravidian India, where this was associated with the cult of Shakti-Siva. This was transmitted into the Middle East through "Harrapan" colonies such as Sumer and Sheba-Ethiopia, into such new names for Shakti as Ishtar, Athtar, Astarte, Venus, Cybele, and Isis, and such new names for Siva as Satan, Beelzebub, Lucifer, Osiris, and Dionysus. The cult of Apollo at Delphi and Rome, and the Mithra cult are forms of this. Gnosticism and modern theosophy are outgrowths, and continuations of this.

These are the religious matrices of the Mesopotamian, Roman, and Byzantine empires. The conception of man and nature reflected in Mesopotamian, Spartan, Roman, and Byzantine codes of law, and political institutions, are forms consistent with and determined by these sorts of pagan theological assumptions.

The oligarchical mind of today retains those assumptions, sometimes in the form of revivals of such ancient cults, or merely in preference for principles of Roman imperial law over law based on Augustine's definition of natural law, such as is expressed by our Declaration of Independence and the arguments for our federal Constitution presented within *The Federalist Papers* which Theodore Roosevelt rejected and abhorred.

To be an effective leader of our civilization, a public figure must understand the apocalyptic character of our times in these terms of reference. It is not sufficient to know what particular measures are objectively sound ones. It is necessary to establish a new combination of policy-making structures, through which means it is possible to implement such desirable actions, and to ensure that the next generation will be able to continue civilization on the upward path out of the apocalyptic horror looming before us now.

During 1973 my friends and I were faced with the fact that there was some strangely efficient collaboration between the Soviet KGB and powerful forces of the West. Merely as a matter of self-defense, the attacks upon us by such combined forces obliged us to discover, as rapidly as possible, how this sort of combination functioned. Beginning the following year, as our efforts came into the center of an international fight for a new international economic order, we began to put the pieces together. Since then, we have walked the trail which leads to "where the monkey sleeps."

The second implication of our 1974 forecast of the 1980s rise of pandemics, is the conflict between the method we employed for that forecast, and the prevailing view of both scientific method in general, and the reductionist method that dominates biology up to the present time. Over the years since then, we have accomplished a great deal of research into the archives of the internal history of modern science. What is presented in classrooms and textbooks as the history of science, we have proven, from primary writings and related work of the leading scientists of the past, to be an entirely fraudulent, as well as absurd view of the matter.

The essence of the internal history of science, since Cusa's *De Docta Ignorantia* most emphatically, has been a back and forth of cultural warfare, not only against frankly irrationalist mysticisms, but, more significantly, between the constructive-geometric and axiomatic-deductive standpoint in method. There is not one, but two distinct historical currents of the development of modern physical science. What is represented as such science, in the classroom, textbook, and most of the papers published in relevant journals, is based on ignorance of the back and forth between the opposing currents within science, with the axiomatic-deductive view generally used today in the effort to explain, fraudulently, what the textbooks borrowed from the work of Leonardo, Kepler, Leibniz, Gauss, Riemann, and so forth.

The internal history of science is a history of political warfare, with occasional outright assassinations, as well as character-assassinations, included. Naturally, once a student has gotten it firmly into his head that the assumptions of the axiomatic-deductive method are the correct ones, he tends to employ and defend those views, whatever his political persuasion might be otherwise. However, when we focus on the figures which steered these political fights within science from the top, we discover that the authors of the axiomatic-deductive forces, are representatives of the same oligarchical faction which opposed the American cause during the eighteenth century, backed the 1815 Treaty of Vienna, and so forth.

Respecting AIDS as such, it is virtually certain that research methods based on the hegemonic, axiomatic-deductive sort of statistical biology, will fail totally to develop the equivalent of vaccines and cures. The known nature of the way mitosis must be defined, spectroscopically, to account for the invasion of chromosomes by the AIDS retrovirus, does suggest a definite approach toward a cure. With use of proper forms of electromagnetic instruments, we must search for proof of principle, to the effect that we discover how, in principle, to "de-tune" those features of the process of mitosis which allow the AIDS infection to persist, and having discovered proof of principle, we must probably develop something which can be swallowed or injected into the bloodstream to catalyze the same sort of "de-tuning" of the undesirable aspect of the mitotic process.

We know that medical clinical research, however useful in other respects, will not bring us an inch closer to successful treatment. The nature of the AIDS infection proves that conclusively, in advance. It must be primarily biological research. It must be biological research freed from reductionist methods in biology.

In this respect, the cultural warfare we must conduct to defeat the political and economic conditions favoring the spread of the pandemic, must be extended also to the domain of scientific practice.

In this Intermezzo, I have described summarily the real adversary we faced. With that in view, the following chapter's accounts are placed in proper focus.

I Keep an Old Promise 6

The idea of standing for election to any sort of public office, is so alien to my personal inclinations, that until the autumn of 1974 even the idea of rejecting such a thought had not occurred to me. During January 1975, I decided to campaign in the 1976 U.S. presidential elections. Naturally, I had no thought of winning a significant vote, but I thought this was the only way to exert a significant influence on behalf of the idea of long-overdue international monetary reforms. In those terms, my 1976 presidential campaign was a very successful one.

Although my proposals for monetary reform were incorporated into the final resolution of the August 1976, Colombo meeting of the Non-Aligned Nations—significantly to the credit of Guyana's foreign minister, Mr. Fred Wills, none of the changes sought were actually implemented during the 1970s. Yet, we had accomplished something of lasting importance, which could not have been accomplished but with aid of my election campaign.

In significant degree, my decision to campaign was a result of our experience with "Watergate." We had collaborated with many among both Democrats and Republicans. We saw the presidency itself savagely weakened. We saw both major parties crumbling, at least to a very significant degree. I think it is fair to say, that up to that time, I had assumed that our constitutional processes of government were so constituted, that if one institution essential to those processes were endangered, the others will rally to its assistance. To this day, there are still some aspects of the way in which "Watergate" began, the which mystify me, but the way in which it unfolded was clear enough to my friends and me even then. On that latter aspect, our views were verified as to key facts by a number of Nixon administration insiders, in connection with the later compilation of a published Kissinger dossier. Nixon's part in protecting Kissinger and Haig, had unleashed a process in which government almost seemed to destroy itself, to the degree that a monstrous evil nearly established its dictatorship over our nation. I was conscience-stricken; we citizens who had taken our government's institutional stability for granted, must be involved in defense of an institutional stability exposed to be a fragile one.

Since that time, I have been emotionally involved with our government and the policy-making structures within and around it. That emotional involvement contributed in a decisive, if marginal way to my decision to campaign. The principal reason was, however, the issue of international monetary reform.

Up to that time, most citizens had viewed the issues of improving the economies of developing nations as a matter of U.S. foreign aid. Speak of such matters, and one was viewed as advocating another round of handouts at the expense of the U.S. taxpayer. We had been conditioned to view such foreign aid as part of the work of containing the spread of Soviet influence. The idea that we had a domestic economic interest in promoting the ability of those economies to import U.S. capital goods, was known to a few, but this was not the prevailing view.

The exceptional view was one which I had maintained since my postwar months in Calcutta. We had a moral commitment to aid those nations. It was our national interest to do so, Soviet threat or no Soviet threat. It was also in the vital interest of our domestic economy, that we do so. I had promised, explicitly and otherwise, back in Calcutta, to represent such a point of view when I returned to the United States. To a certain degree, I had kept that promise. I had proposed an "atoms for peace" policy during an American Veterans' Committee-sponsored debate on nuclear policy, at Northeastern, in 1947. On every occasion it was appropriate to speak of such aspects of U.S. foreign policy, I held true to that same general view. This has been the subject of my first published paper for the group which became the Labor Committees, back in 1967. And, so on and so forth. It was time to organize on behalf of such a policy: My own circumstances, as well as developing circumstances in the world around us, during late 1974, indicated that the time for such an organizing effort had arrived.

By the mid-1970s, the conditions of developing nations were worsening at an accelerating rate. The U.S. economy was contracting. Developing enlarged exports of U.S. capital goods was the most obvious way to reverse the U.S. decline, and also that threatened in Western Europe. There was a convergence of the urgent objective economic interests of both the industrialized and developing nations on this point. To serve that interest, we needed only to return to a gold-reserve monetary system, reorganize the becoming-bankrupt financial structures on a gold-reserve basis, and direct the functioning of a new monetary system to the principal goals of promoting both economic development of developing nations, and increased flows of capital-goods exports from industrialized nations.

My test case was Bangladesh. That nation was tottering on the brink of Hell. The obvious access-point for launching the needed development of the economy as a whole, was a system of water management. The fragile rice-and-jute-growing estuaries were a problem area in which the relatively smallest feasible action would yield the maximum chain-reaction benefit. We had to control the flooding, and improve the stability and yields of the agriculture in that region. A task force of my friends was on the telephone to experts in various parts of the world, locating and cataloguing suitable dredges, other equipment, and engineering capabilities, which might be available immediately.

In the address announcing my candidacy, I referred to this effort on behalf of Bangladesh as the "dredge-end" of a new international economic policy.

At that point, the Labor Committees represented vigorous organizations in the U.S.A., France, West Germany, Italy, and Mexico, and functioning seedlings established in Canada, Belgium, the Netherlands, Denmark, and Sweden, all offices linked by either continuous or daily telecommunications to either Wiesbaden or New York. In each country, Labor Committees associates were partly associated with our international news agency, and otherwise engaged in organizing activities. The Labor Committees as a whole committed themselves to the project of a new international economic policy, while my friends in the United States decided to rally around my electoral campaign as the vehicle for putting this forward.

The United States and imperialism

Although my 1976 presidential campaign might be fairly described as a symbolic gesture, I saw it as virtually indispensable. Up to that time, most among those who demanded economic justice for developing nations, saw their views as "anti-imperialist" ones. The initial postwar hope, that the United States would lead on behalf of such nations, had been replaced by the view that the United States was the leading obstacle to such reforms, and aided such nations only to keep them from "going communist." It was necessary that this "anti-imperialist" view of the matter be changed. It was most important that these nations see workable reforms as a proposal emanating at least from a presidential candidate of the United States, if not yet the U.S. government itself.

For that very reason, as early as 1974–1975, the rumor was spread in many parts of the world that my friends and I were an instrument of the U.S. Central Intelligence Agency. British Fabians peddling the "anti-U.S.-imperialism" line, sections of the Socialist International's leadership and others peddling the same view, as well as outright Soviet tools, spread this from even the mouths of officials of government, during that period.

The standard "anti-imperialist" line against the United States, converged on V.I. Lenin's popularized doctrine of imperialism, that "imperialism" was an inevitable "final stage" of metamorphosis of industrial capitalism. Even professedly stout anti-Bolsheviks among social democrats and others, each shared, or at least parodied Lenin's formulation. My friends and I were seen as a threat to that doctrine's influence. We said, "If you believe that, you do not understand the history of the United States." True, the political faction from which Teddy Roosevelt traced his ancestry was a British colonialist faction within the United States from China opium-trading days; true, this faction had dominated U.S. policy making since Teddy Roosevelt's presidency, but "imperialism" was the product of forces which had been enemies of the U.S. industrial-capitalist system from the beginning. Imperialism was not a product of capitalist development; it was the result of the conquest of power over capitalist nations by a usury-oriented rentier-financier interest older than feudalism.

Industrial-capitalist interest demanded the successful

growth of developing economies, so that the developing nations would be able to purchase larger volumes of high-technology capital goods. This meant improved conditions of life in developing nations, and increased productivity and emphasis on better-quality forms of employment of operatives in the industrialized nations. Although the U.S. Eastern Establishment might be fairly viewed as "imperialist," the vital interests of U.S. industrial capitalism were anti-imperialist. My friends and I had to deliver this message to the patriotic currents within the United States, and seek allies for such patriotic currents abroad. Meanwhile, the only way in which developing nations could secure justice for the foreseeable future, given the correlation of power internationally, was to promote such a self-interested change in policy-outlook within the U.S.A., primarily, and seek out allies for the same enlightened view of the matter in Western Europe and Japan.

For this reason, enemies of our proposals decided to portray our efforts as the sort of thing which might be expected from the CIA. I imagined that the CIA itself must have found this very funny at the time.

I had been invited to Iraq, to participate in the annual Ba'ath Party celebration. I was interested in Iraq and other Arab nations as developing nations. I like every nation I have known, and, take advantage of being on the scene to become acquainted with the culture, government, economy, and as much of the history as can be assembled. The old habits of the management consultant linger on in such matters; I view each nation with something close to the commitment I used feel toward the well-being of each client. Influential visitors from many nations would be there. With all, I put forward my proposals for monetary reform. With Iraq's National Command, and also with some special Arab representatives from other nations, I stated my proposals for seeking to develop Arab-Israeli economic cooperation.

My return flight took me from from Baghdad and

Beirut to Geneva, Switzerland. At Geneva, I telephoned the Wiesbaden office, to inform tham I was flying in to Frankfurt. A few days later, I presented my proposals to a packed press conference at the conventional Tulpenfeld in Bonn. Not a word was published, but the impact was like that of an earthquake. Most of the developing nations' governments, and many business and governmental figures in France, West Germany, and Italy, were in an uproar over my proposals. Secretary of State Henry A. Kissinger heard the repercussions, and soon enough expressed his displeasure in the manner customary to him.

Another development overlapped. As if to show how totally unimportant matters may turn up in important business, Greg Rose, of all people, popped up again.

Greg had a problem respecting other people's property. We judged this a psychological quirk not unrelated to his pathological problem of overweight. He confessed and made restitution in one case, and later confessed and promised to make restitution in a second. Then, he disappeared for a while, to almost everyone's relief. He turned up later, as a paid informant for the New York offices of the FBI, and while on the FBI payroll, ghost-wrote a piece of lurid political science-fiction for the Communist Party's *Daily World.*

We expose Hilex '75

The Hamburg newsweekly, *Der Spiegel,* had published a leaked detail of a NATO Command and Control exercise, "Hilex '75," to be run in the autumn of 1975. As Hilex '75 unfolded, it seemed to us that a number of the hypothetical events listed by *Spiegel* were actually operational. We cross-gridded the patterns. I was in the Wiesbaden office at the time; my response was, that this was insane. The whole business smelled of James R. Schlesinger's "theater-limited nuclear option" policy.

The idea, supported by Schlesinger at that time, that

Moscow would "accept" a nuclear war limited to the European theater, was not only the clear significance of Hilex '75, but the exercise was being run under actual, rather than the standard hypothetical conditions. My suspicions were forwarded to the head of the Senate Armed Services Committee and other relevant Washington points. The only war which Moscow would consider, was a war directly fought chiefly as a nuclear war against the United States. Any idiot, such as Schlesinger, playing around with nuclear games based on different ideas, must be put into the looney-bin as quickly as possible. We obtained a declassified, sanitized handout on draft NATO doctrine MC 14/4, which confirmed my suspicions.

We were naturally delighted with President Gerald Ford's 1975 "Hallowe'en Massacre," in which Schlesinger was dumped from the Defense Department, and Kissinger's direction of both State and of the National Security Council was curbed slightly. Kissinger struck back personally against my friends and me. The FBI was assigned to run a top-secret operation against me and my friends. The operation, code named "Kwarterbak," focused upon Costas Kalimtgis' mother's KGB connections, as the leading pretext for the operation. It was alleged that we had spied on NATO, securing Cosmic-classified secret documents as the basis for our reports. The allegation was based, allegedly, on the unsupported statements of Greg Rose. The operation ran until early 1976, until the FBI officially wrote off Rose as a fantasy-ridden spewer of false tales.

Meanwhile, during the autumn of 1975, a group of ambassadors in Paris decided to organize a week-long seminar, at which I was to present my theses on monetary reform, and then consult with smaller groups and representatives of individual nations. A group of African nations asked the Iraqi ambassador to host the meeting, which he did, with the backing of the Iraqi foreign minister, who stayed in Paris to be able to participate. Leaders of the

Gaullist party of France would attend. The Saudi government, hearing of the festivities, announced it would send a delegation.

I arrived in Paris from the United States in the middle of the week. The seminar was to begin on Saturday, and last through the following week. It was to occur at the residence of the ambassador. I met with the Iraqi ambassador at his residence on Friday evening. The final details were arranged. An hour later, I received a call from the ambassador. He seemed slightly agitated, as he told me that a car which had been watching the residence while we were inside, had tailed us as we left. Hours later, there was a second call. Would I please develop a diplomatic illness, rather than attending? I understood, and enjoyed my first diplomatic illness during a weekend of excellent personal health.

We learned later, from the office of Interior Minister Poniatowski, that the harassment against me in Paris was directed via the U.S. Embassy. From our Iraqi friends, we learned that the highest level of threat of reprisals against Iraq itself had been used to abort the seminar. We learned later, that the operation was entirely Kissinger, personally.

My proposal was also well-received by circles within the government of Israel. I had a delightful meeting with Abba Eban, in New York City. He has a first-class mind, and he taught me something I have often remembered. He said, "You are forgetting that some heads of governments are clinically insane." The observation has served me well on a number of occasions since. Out of this came my off-again, on-again contact with circles associated with Shimon Peres, leading naturally to my full support for his 1986 resurfacing of his longstanding views, as his proposal for a Middle East "New Marshall Plan." Peres' circles and I had been converging on agreement to such a solution since 1975. If we would bring Arabs to discuss the matter on some neutral ground, we were told by an Israeli official, a meeting would occur; but, we must hurry, since developments in Israel indicated there was not much time to act.

Soon after that, the Israeli official had his legs broken in New York City. Years later, our key PLO contact was murdered at a Socialist International conference in Lisbon. It was not the first time that a PLO friend had suffered physical violence at Kissinger's direction. People who cross Kissinger, usually suffer violence, sooner or later.

For the purpose of the 1976 presidential campaign, my friends and I organized a political party, the U.S. Labor Party, a party based constitutionally on the tradition of Henry Clay's Whig party. There was a typical bit of happenstance in the name. The name had been used by a group of my friends as an "electoral trade-style" for a 1973 New York municipal election. It had been used again in several local elections in 1974. In 1975, we adopted this trade-style as the name of a political party, and formalized the constitution along Whig lines at the end of 1976. My friends and I have often done things that way.

At the last minute, in October 1976, my friends scraped together something in excess of $100,000, as the price of a half-hour nationwide NBC-TV broadcast on election-eve. Jimmy Carter never forgave me for that broadcast. I blew the policy of James R. Schlesinger, for an early nuclear confrontation with Moscow, and exposed the genocidal policies which key Carter backers, such as George Ball, had publicly demanded as measures for drastic population reduction of nations such as Mexico. More broadly, I presented a policy of international monetary reform, as alternative to a deepening crisis in the developing sector, which would lead us toward a thermonuclear showdown, whether anyone actually desired it or not. Carter launched an FBI Cointelpro operation against my friends, which went into operation during spring 1977, an operation which continues in various forms to the present day. It was run then under the acronyms of FIST and SWEEP. The most important other effect of that broadcast was that it put me on the Washington political map.

During the spring of 1976, I sponsored a new counterintelligence project, a continuation of our earlier study of the Tavistock networks. Since our experience with Bundy's backing of SDS "crazies" at Columbia in 1968, we had tracked Eastern Establishment and kindred covert direction of various radical projects. We had accumulated proof that even various terrorist projects in Europe and North America had been brought into being through a supporting role by such covert interests. We had also tracked the effort to promote "fascism with a smiling face," launched publicly in 1974. We cross-gridded our facts, publishing the result in a special report called *Carter and the Party of International Terrorism*. That report stands up as a unique, and indispensable source for use by investigators today.

Actually Carter did not win the 1976 presidential election. We had solid proof of massive vote fraud in three states, New York, Ohio, and Wisconsin. We later showed proof that the fraud in New York City alone was nearly sufficient to overturn Carter's election in that state. Late election night, we were on the telephone with the White House, and with relevant figures around the nation. In the wee hours of the following morning, we had word that the President had gone to bed, resolved not to concede the election.

As of ten o'clock the following morning, our current information was that the President was sticking to this resolution. Then, we watched the President, standing by his daughter, quiet tears shown, while his wife, Betty, read a statement conceding the election to Carter. Ford, whatever his weaknesses, was a decent human being; Carter, we already knew in detail, was not. I knew that the United States was in deep trouble; I was very, very right.

The President might have conceded, but we had not. The magnitude of the vote fraud in three key states was so great that it made the very idea of the citizen's ballot a sham. We could prove over 200,000 fraudulent ballots in New York State, alone. I shared the view, with a diverse assortment of other concerned political figures, that the very idea of electoral democracy was in jeopardy. No one had the right to do this to the U.S. Constitution and get by with it. Otherwise, what did future elections really mean? I traveled quite a bit, to Milwaukee, to Ohio, and elsewhere, discussing the implications with concerned political figures. We lost in the federal courts, essentially by decisions which echoed Justice Holmes' irrationalist innovations in law. We learned that there is no legal protection for ballot integrity in the courts of the United States.

In the spring, I went to Europe, for what was originally intended as a few weeks' continued work on the project of monetary reform. I became involved in writing a book attacking the influence of Walter Lippmann's 1943–1944 writings on the continuing policies of the United States. The draft completed, I turned for relief, back to Beethoven, and did what I had put off doing for too long, analyzing his Ninth Symphony. My summary description of my findings on the fourth movement of that symphony, transformed our "culture file's" work in promoting work on study of classical music, and set into motion a study of the deep principles of classical polyphony, including the physics principles underlying classical polyphony, which has gained increasing significance among the activities of my friends over the years since.

A new assassination threat

About that time, my personal situation in the United States had changed. I had work still to do in Europe, and remained there until news of a turn in my mother's illness brought me back in mid-1978. In the meantime, I narrowly escaped assassination by the Baader-Meinhof gang of terrorists.

During 1977, our favorite banker was Jürgen Ponto, head of Germany's Dresdner Bank. My friends and I had rather frequent contact with the relevant offices of that bank, especially in connection with projects in which Ponto's and our own approach to development converged. A meeting between Ponto and me was being arranged for early August. He was murdered by the Baader-Meinhof gang just a few days before the arrangements for our meeting were to have been negotiated. A few days later, I was awakened during the night by an urgent telephone message. It was a message from a source of the highest authority in such matters. Ponto was but the first of several targets selected for a series of such assassinations. I was the next target. Certain recommendations for my immediate action were included in the message.

I was forewarned that I should expect no cooperation from official channels. The targeting of me was known at the highest relevant levels of the Carter administration, but there was no interest in keeping me alive, in those circles. I would have to rely upon unofficial channels. It was strongly recommended that I retain a specialist, Colonel Mitchell Livingston WerBell, as a security consultant. My friends asked if I approved if they retained Mitch WerBell. I did.

We had relevant friends in security services of several European governments. Some of them confirmed the report. Mitch confirmed the report through his sources. Unofficially, a very substantial armed screen was placed around me by collaborating security forces of four nations. For about a month and a half after that, that screen remained up.

Mercedes-Benz's Hans-Martin Schleyer was also warned, as I had been. He was provided with a screen, and a professional armed security force was secured for him. Later, he was abducted in a highly professional assault on his convoy, and was later murdered by his captors. I wondered why Schleyer had been taken, while I survived. Several factors were obvious. He was a more prominent figure, such that the psychological sort of political advantage to the terrorists in seizing him was greater than in seizing me.

My real importance was not understood by the general public at that time. Politically, the terrorists could afford to take greater risks in going after Schleyer. Also, he moved about in a fairly predictable way, so providing numerous opportunities for a well-planned professional attack. I stayed put, as I was advised to do. With the "steel shield" in place around me, the terrorists were faced with an element of incalculability. An attempted attack on me which failed to reach its objective, would have political consequences of a sort which the backers of Baader-Meinhof definitely did not desire.

Among my key personal projects during the spring of 1977, was my increasing role in antiterrorist intelligence. During that period, I had limited knowledge of how terrorism was run from the Soviet side, but I knew much of the infrastructure in place on the western side. I had issued an alert on something major brewing immediately prior to the Entebbe incident, for example, by tracking a curious pattern of developments around the movements of a known terrorist, Wilfrid Boese. My friends and I had a particularly close watch on the terrorists' political infrastructure within the antinuclear movement. I had picked up a clear indication of some major terrorist action brewing in West Germany during weeks prior to Ponto's assassination. The first warnings signs had come from France, from a series of meetings among representatives of various terrorist support networks inside the antinuclear movement. A kind of international conference of these types from various European nations had been convened. Out of this conference, the slogan emerged "nuclear energy is fascism," "death to the nuclear fascists." During July, the greatest degree of activity around this slogan was in West Germany. Willy Brandt was induced to issue a letter, warning against underestimation of the "fascist" danger within West Germany.

Through my news agency, during 1976 and early 1977 I had developed channels for back and forth review of antiterrorist intelligence concerns with relevant functions of various governments and other suitable sorts of expertise. I benefited significantly, from counsel relayed to me and my friends on what to publish and what must be withheld to protect ongoing antiterrorist operations. Although I had no direct contact with the U.S. CIA, I knew with certainty that I was in rather efficient indirect contact with officials there. I would usually pass my information on terrorist-related developments to those and European channels before recommending reporting on these matters to our news agency. I was not a member of the news agency personally, but the consultation was more or less daily, either directly or indirectly. My function among my friends, was chiefly my work on international monetary reform and my sundry private projects, which I would dump into someone's lap once I had done my part.

Apart from my projects, my chief activity was being trotted about to meet with various governmental and other officials which one or another among my friends arranged for me to meet. Except as a *primus inter pares* on economic science philosophical matters, I had no specific authority or function in the activities of my friends. In December 1976, I had been elected chairman of the U.S. Labor Party, an essentially honorary position I held through 1978. As a courtesy, I was placed on the masthead of the *Executive Intelligence Review,* and later coopted to a nonpaid advisory function with the board of directors of the Fusion Energy Foundation; my function there consists chiefly of participating in scientific seminars and working as advisor to some particular research projects. Only briefly, during the interval from November 1980 through January 1981, did I assume any executive responsibilities for any of my friends' activities, and my functioning during that interval was essentially that of a special consultant called in to straighten out a particular problem. Within those general parameters, I have no particular function except my personal projects, but manage to keep very busy.

Why should Ponto and I be on the same array of

selected targets during the July–September period of 1977? The two of us were prominently associated with nuclear energy at the time, and among the few whose activities were significant ones internationally, as distinct from the internal nuclear-energy programs of a particular nation. Schleyer did not fit this category. Among Ponto, Schleyer, and me, there was only one common denominator: economic cooperation in the development of the southern region of Africa. Ponto and Schleyer were the only paid-in backers of a pilot-project known as the Southern Africa Development Fund. This involved a network of white South Africa reformers, backed by the Rembrandt interests, and centered on the University of Pretoria. This had been a project my friends and I had backed, as a concrete element consistent with our campaign for international monetary reform, and as part of a major project of long-range economic planning, for the economic development of the Middle East and the African continent.

If we know that most of the "neo-Nazi" groups of West Germany are run through the Czech intelligence service, and, that Czech intelligence, as well as East German, Hungarian, and Bulgarian, is heavily involved in left-wing terrorist and proterrorist groups there, the South Africa common denominator among Ponto, Schleyer, and me, makes the most sense.

Presently, the world's monopoly on production of the bulk of what are called strategic minerals, is concentrated in the Soviet Union and among the nations of the southern African shield. All the logistics of the black nations of southern Africa's strategic minerals production, are centered in the Republic of South Africa. The leadership of SWAPO and of the African National Congress was already controlled by Soviet intelligence during 1977, as it is today. Also, the Cape of Good Hope is the keystone of one of the world's principal strategic maritime choke-points. If Moscow could effect destruction of the strategic minerals flow from southern Africa, it could collapse the industrial strength of the West. If Moscow could also establish military land bases near the coasts of southern Africa, such as in Angola and Mozambique, Moscow's growing naval capability could control the Indian Ocean and the South Atlantic.

If racial peace is established in southern Africa, through reforms in South Africa like those presently existing under the multi-racial and multi-tribal provisional government of Namibia, Soviet strategic objectives would be set back in a major degree. Ponto's approach, expressed by the Southern Africa Development Fund, was therefore a major threat to Soviet strategic interests. Since Kissinger's great gift to Moscow, in his Africa policy actions of 1975, policies such as Ponto's were the only serious threat to Soviet plans for the region.

Moscow had excellent motives for killing off a passel of those significantly involved in such kinds of reforms for southern Africa. To the extent that Moscow controls terrorists such as Baader-Meinhof in the West, these would be used by Moscow for precisely such actions.

After discounting complicit agencies in the West, who operate with a certain kind of understanding with Moscow in such matters, all international terrorism is coordinated by Moscow, and an increasing portion of operations associated with illegal narcotics traffic. Generally, operations involving terrorism, political strikes, antinuclear violence, and so forth, are run by the Fifth Directorate of the Soviet KGB, and are coordinated with the "active measures" programs of Soviet military intelligence, the GRU. International terrorism is coordinated chiefly through Syrian intelligence, with heavy reliance on families formerly associated with Nazi intelligence operations. North Korean, Cuban, East German, Czech, Hungarian, Bulgarian, KGB-controlled sections of Polish intelligence, and Anna Pauker's network inside Romania, are coordinated, together with Syrian intelligence, by the Soviet intelligence services, with East Germany's intelligence services having the highest degree of relative autonomy among Soviet-controlled services.

The slaying of Ponto and Schleyer, and the terrorist targeting of me in 1977, were political assassinations run on the initiative of the Fifth Directorate of the KGB.

Terrorist assassinations seem to come in waves, like changes in the weather. There is nothing mystical in this. Terrorism is a form of irregular warfare, whose actions are planned and coordinated in a manner resembling military campaigns. This character is enhanced by the fact that the Soviets are ultra-methodical, in calculating out irregular warfare as well as regular warfare campaigns. Activities, even covert ones, cannot help but reflect the characteristics of the agencies which direct them. So, after the taking and death of Schleyer, the probability of a new Soviet assassination-attempt against me dropped from about eight or nine on a scale of ten, to about four or five. If I did nothing foolish, to facilitate a purely opportunistic attack from such agencies, I could move about, provided I took certain precautions and moved about with the greatest relative degree of unpredictability.

The threat-level has fluctuated from about three to eight, on a scale of ten, ever since. I am a bad choice of target for the enemy. I have learned the rules, much better than most assassination-targets have. The chief rule, is worry about the potential for successful planning and deployment of attacks, more than the details of a possible attack. Keep the potential for a successfully planned attack at a minimum. It is the best general rule. Above all, do not over-plan deployments and related activities.

Anyone can be killed, if a major power insists on doing this at all political risks. I keep the political risks high, by close attention to factors of potential. The physical protection provided me has chiefly that purpose. It is adequate to ensure the probable failure of a lower level of attack, and thus forces the enemy either to abandon the venture, or commit himself to forms of action sufficient to overwhelm that security protection. The political penalty for most among the optional forms of a professional attack on me is high, and the several known assassination-projects so far have been aborted before they went into action, although two completely verified actual assassination attempts against my wife have occurred, and one of them came very close to being a successful one.

It has been a deadly game of chess between me and the Soviets' terrorist assets since July 1977. I might lose, but I might just possibly win.

Moscow and the ADL

Approximately May 1978, the Soviets and their friends adopted a new approach to dealing with me. That month, two nominally U.S.-based organizations, the Heritage Foundation and the Anti-Defamation League (ADL), launched coordinated campaigns against me which are continuing to the present moment.

Former Reagan White House Chief of Staff Michael Deaver was very helpful to us in tracking down the origins of the Heritage Foundation's campaign against me. The Reagan campaign-newsletter which Deaver edited up to the 1980 presidential campaign, had published a blip attacking me. Deaver indicated that the blip had been conduited from the Heritage Foundation, and gave us additional leads leading us to the Mont Pelerin Society as the author of the Heritage campaign. Subsequently, journalists cooperating with our news agency secured tape-recorded interviews with Heritage Foundation officials, through which we were able to back-track the Soviet connections into the British-import leadership of the Heritage Foundation. Incidentally, the Heritage Foundation's program for manipulating the Reagan administration, as told to the tape recorder back in 1980, has worked out pretty much as Ed Feulner et al. bragged back during the 1980 "transition" into the Reagan administration.

Most of the Heritage members and supporters are merely rather typical "conservatives," simplistically "ideological" in the extreme, and therefore easily duped. The influence and money at Heritage's disposal have helped in attracting such dupes. The foreign control over Heritage, is run under the cover of the Mont Pelerin Society and London's International Institute for Strategic Studies (IISS), the left wing of the strategic think tank circuits. The ideology of Heritage's British-import controllers is a mixture of "conservative" ideological rhetoric on the outside, and British Fabian Society assumptions on the inside. During the 1980 "transition" period, Feulner and others explained this with shameless frankness.

Nominally, the ADL is an intelligence arm for the Jewish freemasonic association, B'nai B'rith. However, less than one percent of the members of B'nai B'rith, or ADL contributors knows actually what ADL is, or what it does. For example, ADL runs most of the Ku Klux Klan and self-styled neo-Nazi groups inside the United States. Check stubs of ADL payroll disbursements to one Jimmy Rosenberg, a key organizer and coordinator of such groups, is merely one example of this.

The Anti-Defamation League was founded in 1908 as the B'nai B'rith Public Relations Committee, in Chicago, by an avowed fascist, Sigmund Livingston, and renamed the Anti-Defamation League in 1913. It was created under the sponsorship of Morgan's close collaborator, William Moore, the ancestor of Bishop Paul Moore, presently head of the New York Episcopal Diocese, who cofunded the establishment of a cult which came to a celebrated end in Jonestown, Guyana, and whose diocese has been a principal backer of satanic cult-projects coordinated through a Lindisfarne operation run by that diocese. It was established as an offshoot of Teddy Roosevelt's "New Age" projects, and served initially as part of the effort to promote hatred of Germany among the substantial German-Jewish immigrant population of the Midwest.

It is closely coordinated through the U.S. branch of

the British Fabian Society, the League for Industrial Democracy, and has been closely associated with Soviet intelligence operations in New York City since the 1930s. It was an active opponent of the anti-Nazi, boycott movement among American Jews during the 1930s. Since the 1930s, the ADL has been closely associated with what are often described, euphemistically, as "former organized crime" circles centered around the lately deceased Meyer Lansky. Through its leadership, the ADL is closely tied to drug-trafficking operations coordinated through Bulgaria and Cuba, as typified by the business relationship between Fidel Castro's Robert Vesco and Kenneth Bialkin, former ADL national chairman, who was Vesco's attorney.

Although all the dirty side of the ADL but its Soviet-intelligence connections, are frankly acknowledged in and around the Executive Branch of the U.S. government, the ADL enjoys the advantages one might imagine ought to be afforded only to actually respectable organizations. It is "highly protected" by those Eastern Establishment circles which make use of ADL's "dirty tricks" capabilities, and is also highly protected in the Executive Branch of government as well, especially by the dirtier sides of the U.S. Department of Justice and the FBI.

Although the Heritage Foundation and ADL were deployed against me simultaneously, and by the same agencies, their propaganda-tirades against me differed significantly. Since the Heritage Foundation must sell its output to politically simple-minded among the self-styled "conservatives," Heritage, using ADL and Soviet-linked advisors, characterized me as "Soviet-linked." In due course, it adopted the Greg Rose written off by the FBI, as the authority for its charges. Since ADL's standard activity is creating "neo-Nazi" and Ku Klux Klan grouplets, as fund-raising stunts addressed to the purses of folk such as Miami Jewish communities, ADL denounced me as a "neo-Nazi anti-Semite," both the wildest of lies, but a good fund-raising tactic.

The sponsorship and motive for the simultaneous attack launched that May was, in very large degree, our work against the international drug traffic. During 1978, the international side of the drug traffic was not less than $200 billion. Today, it is three to four times that volume. Drugs are second only to international weapons-trafficking in volume of business, and the two overlap as a single complex of business transactions at many points. Today, the largest single cash-flow through the western banking system is generated by this traffic. Any attack on the drug-trafficking is a threat not only to those directly engaged in the business. It is also a threat to those banks and other financial institutions which had come to depend upon "laundered" drug money as a growing portion of their cash-flow.

I suggested that my friends' researches into the drug traffic be assembled in the form of a book. The book covered the general history of the drug traffic, from the British East India Company during the eighteenth century, through to 1978. The book featured four special investigations. The general background on the history of drug-trafficking in the United States was assembled from the archives of the old Federal Bureau of Narcotics. Research traced the way in which the launching of the rock-drug-sex counterculture, under the auspices of MK-Ultra, had become entangled with the founding of a curious entity called the Mary Carter Paint Company, a project in which David Rockefeller and Meyer Lansky had been prominently involved. We received help from former CIA agents who had been assigned to in-depth investigations. We studied the mechanisms by which drug funds were laundered through the banking system. It was this last feature of the work which made us a major threat to what both drug runners and certain financial institutions linked to personalities of the Mont Pelerin Society might tend to view as their vital interests.

The connections of the ADL's leadership to the drug traffic are major ones. The Soviet connections to the ADL come up prominently here.

The targeting of U.S. youth by the drug traffic was first used as a weapon of irregular warfare by Mao-tse Tung. The epidemic of drug usage in the United States during the early 1950s and the early 1960s, was the work of the Peoples Republic of China. Perhaps Mao thought turn-about was fair play; after all, the most respected among today's Eastern Establishment "blue blood" families accumulated a major part of their initial wealth as partners of the British East India Company (and government) in the China opium trade of the late eighteenth and nineteenth centuries.

Soviet involvement in drug-trafficking as a weapon of irregular warfare against the United States began approximately 1962. In a secret speech dating from that year, Khrushchev praised Mao-tse Tung for developing the drug-weapon against the United States. Major Soviet entry into both narcotics and terrorism dates from Yuri Andropov's rise to power as head of the Soviet KGB during the late 1960s. Although China continues to exploit the drug traffic, supplying drugs from the traditional "Golden Triangle" areas, the Soviets are the major factor in the world's production of drugs for international trafficking today.

The production of marijuana and cocaine from Mexico, from other parts of Central America, and South America, is almost entirely Soviet-controlled. The same is true in East Africa and the Middle East. The Soviets direct most of this traffic into Western Europe, and the principal portions of the supplies into the United States are produced and exported under control of Soviet assets. Much of the control of production for export from these parts of the world, involves Lausanne, Switzerland centered networks of the modern Nazi International, who work under the control and protection of Soviet agencies. This is true in Mexico, in Central and South America generally, and in Syrian-controlled Lebanon, to name key examples.

In the Caribbean area, the Cuban intelligence service is the general coordinator of the Soviet side of the traf-

ficking. The principal other Soviet connection is through
Bulgaria, and the Bulgarian trading organization, Kintex.
The direct Bulgarian role became active during 1979. According to confessions obtained from leading drug traffickers, and according to relevant admissions by Fidel Castro
himself, one of the key figures in the center of this is
Castro's protégé, Robert Vesco. Vesco is the key to the
ADL's links to the Soviet-directed side of the drug traffic
into the United States.

The ADL is also a part of the drug lobby inside the
United States. The greater part of its operations against
me and my friends since 1978, has been done in collaboration with the organized drug lobby. This has featured
the circles centered around the official, gutter-level prodrug
periodical, *High Times,* the circles of Dennis King. The
prodrug *Playboy* magazine generated the Playboy Foundation, the conduit used to back the organizers of the 1968
Chicago riots, the Yippies, in establishing the prodrug *High
Times*.

These attacks launched against me in May of 1978
were part of the background to new threats of assassination
awaiting me after my trip to my mother's hospital bedside.
Assassination threats were delivered from the circles of the
Michigan-based Communist Labor Party, one punctuated
by a knife-assault against a friend of mine. I had one near-
miss in Detroit. One must never discount the factor of
comedy of errors even in execution of a well-planned assassination attack. At the time I was to arrive at a meeting
hall, to deliver a scheduled address, three vehicles moved
into positions well-suited for launching an attack on the
automobile bringing me to the entrance. It happened, that
I was delayed for the better part of an hour, which made
the three waiting vehicles obvious to security forces. Police
moved in to check the situation, and the vehicles took off,
leading a wild chase. A check of the suspicious vehicles'
license plate numbers and descriptions showed that the
threat had been a very serious one.

The level of active threats remained about the same until the autumn of 1979. Once I had announced as a candidate for the 1980 Democratic presidential nomination, in September 1979, the level of threat escalated rapidly.

More comedies of errors intervened. Through incitement by the ADL's Dennis King, two violence-prone groups decided to effect my demise, the Yippies and the Jewish Defense League. Elements recruited from each deployed against the same address, at which I was no longer residing, and stumbled across one another in the process.

The security problems during the New Hampshire primary campaign were serious ones, but were neutralized. After the New Hampshire primary, the threat-level lowered, until it zoomed upward during the period of the New York City Democratic National Convention of 1980. A new, major effort at eliminating me was deployed at the close of 1981. Israeli intelligence assisted me and my friends in dealing with the problem. Private security and a deployment of several law enforcement agencies contained the diversionary operations, and prevented the deployment of a professional assassin awaiting his opportunity at the premises where I was to speak.

An East German was the perpetrator in an attempt to kill my wife, in West Germany, in 1981, and would have succeeded had her driver not been one of the best trained in the security business. She escaped with an injury from which she continued to suffer for several years. The next clear attempt to kill her was by a very sophisticated technique, the firing of a special type of flechette into the tire of her vehicle, a technique generally known only to specialists. Circumstances of the latter case proved that a team had been involved in the operation as a whole.

So, for the past dozen years, I have lived under unusual circumstances. Without the security problem, I would certainly have drifted either into marginally paid employment with one of the business ventures operated by friends, or perhaps functioned as a consultant to some of these. Under the circumstances, the only employed position for which I am qualified, is President of the United States.

Before the events of 1973, I was accustomed to walking about a dozen miles a day. If time allowed, I preferred not to ride if I could walk the distance. By 1973, I was in excellent physical condition, about that of a healthy specimen ten years younger. Body and mind rebelled against my confinement within "safehouses." I had learned to enjoy cooking for myself; planning a meal while shopping for ingredients, was more than half the pleasure. That, and a great deal of privacy, I gave up, and most of the other things which one takes for granted as part of being personally independent. When my mother died, a few weeks after my return to her hospital bedside, I was unable to attend the funeral—for security reasons; that really hurt. There were some moments of relative freedom between January 1974 and August 1977, but since then virtually none. I worked, and so I adjusted myself to these circumstances.

An interesting trip to Mexico

My wife and I were invited to be guests of the governing party of Mexico, at the party's fiftieth anniversary. The Mexican government provided us a top-flight security team, and the meetings themselves were covered by excellent security arrangements; we were out of the hole for a few days. I did not meet with President José Lopez Portillo, except to shake hands, that trip. We were already in occasional contact through mutual friends, but I was already a highly controversial international figure, so we did not meet directly until a severe emergency required this, four years later. There were other Mexican dignitaries we did meet with, part of a group we refer to automatically as "our friends" to the present day.

I thought of Joe LaRouche, who had planned to retire to Mexico, before cancer overtook him, and wondered how many of the things I saw were things he had seen during his trips there. During that visit, we took a side-trip to one place I am certain he had visited, to the site of the famous pyramids, just outside Mexico City. I had a special interest in matters overlooked by the usual tourist visiting that place.

My interest in archaeology began before I entered first grade. The Reverend George Weir had been very strong on what is classed as Biblical archaeology; the household at 3 Coxeter Square had echoed this. I learned to correlate Biblical events with maps, drawings, and photographs of relevant places before I could read. Like everything important to me during childhood, the assumptions I was taught in connection with Biblical archaeology, were matters I reexamined with some thoroughness as I grew older. I had picked this up again during the 1950s, looking at Sumer and its Mesopotamian successors, this time from the vantage-point of my discoveries and related work in economic science. This set me working along a trail, leading to the point of view with which I studied the Mexican site.

From my standpoint in economic science, a remarkably precise picture of some ancient societies can be constructed with what might appear to the amateur as an assortment of odd facts. For example, if we know the general size of an urban site, we can estimate the urban population. If we also know the kind and level of technology employed in typical agriculture during that time, we can estimate the total agricultural population and inhabited land-area of the culture as a multiple of the urban population. That is only the simplest part of the reconstruction possible. These economic and other evidences taken into account, the evidence was conclusive, that "civilization did not begin at Sumer," and that the Sumerians were not Semites. They were the "black-headed people," in fact, black Dravidians. Sumer had been developed as a colony of what we call the "Harrapan" culture of pre-Vedic India.

Skipping over much intervening material, I reached the view that the "pre-Columbian cultures" of Mexico, Guatemala, and Peru, were offshoots of the influence of trans-Atlantic and trans-Pacific maritime cultures, and the culture which Cortez found in Mexico was the net result of a long process of cultural decay extending over not less than 2,500 years. There are evidences of both trans-Pacific roots in the Quiche Maya culture centered in Guatemala, and trans-Atlantic ones for Mexico more generally. The evidence of an included trans-Atlantic cultural ancestry for Mexico, includes such matters as crucial bits of philological evidence, and an array of evidence correlatable with what we know as Homer's *Odyssey*.

If we assume that Ulysses traveled in an ocean-going craft of the type generally used by the "People of the Sea" in the Mediterranean, since not later than the middle of the second millennium B.C., and know a few crucial tidbits of ocean navigation applicable to use of such craft, we can reconstruct Ulysses' voyage with fair precision, from the text of the *Odyssey* itself. He sailed through the "Pillars of Hercules" (the Gibraltar passage into the Atlantic), across the Atlantic, and into the Caribbean. The calculations of route and estimated lapsed time for the outward voyage, are straightforward.

Later, Ulysses traveled up along the Atlantic coast of North America, across the North Atlantic to Europe, by land across Europe to the Adriatic, and down the Adriatic to his home.

The implication is, that Ulysses was exploring parts of the world which had been known to Peoples of the Sea during some earlier period. One is reminded of the false opinions taught to children respecting Christopher Columbus' voyage, or the child's false impression that the Pilgrims stumbled across New England accidentally while intending to reach Virginia. On the first, Columbus had maps, part of a collection assembled during the 1439–1440 Council of Florence. On the Pilgrims, one overlooks the quality of navigational skills of English shipmasters, as demonstrated by Elizabeth's captains during the preceding century. Their first landfall, was Cape Cod, a fishing settlement of Portuguese fishermen; the Pilgrims sailed to precisely where they had intended to go, despite the tale of deception that they had been obliged to tell, to secure permission for the colonization.

There is even a hint, in the *Odyssey*'s reference to the "spirit of the ship," that Ulysses used a form of magnetic compass, and certainly used celestial navigation. We find solar astronomical calendar values for the magnetic pole's cycle in ancient Vedic sources, so we must not be surprised to imagine some form of magnetic compasses were in use by People of the Sea during the second millennium B.C. Poor Thor Heyerdahl, using a reed craft to sail across the Atlantic; sensible Egyptians would have used a boat rather similar to that used by the Vikings, as Ulysses' craft was. Heyerdahl should have remembered the Vikings, and studied the drawings of such ships in ancient Egyptian records.

I never accepted the assumption that the wheel was unknown to "pre-Columbian" America. On the other hand, I never accepted the argument, that the existence of pyramids in both Egypt and the Americas was any sort of proof that American cultures had had an Egyptian origin. The pyramid is a proposition in physics, and the design of the Egyptian pyramids was essentially the design of an astronomical observatory, well suited to line-of-eyesight astronomy, very much like those megalithic sites, such as England's Stonehenge, which are also sensible designs for solar astronomical observatories.

With such points in mind, I explored the Mexican site with more interest than tourists generally. For one thing, the oldest part of the site displayed showed the handiwork of some thalassiarch, or at least a putative admirer: This inland site had been developed at one stage in celebration of a maritime culture. The children's toys were interesting, too. They included small four-wheeled carts.

Cortez's handful of men had conquered Aztecs dominating a Mexico with a population of approximately 20 million persons. He was able to do so, because the Aztecs were bitterly, and most justly hated. Granted, the Spanish Hapsburgs had committed one of the greatest genocides in history, reducing the population of Mexico down to about 2 million, during a period of approximately fifty years, during the later part of the sixteenth century. The Hapsburgs had an excuse; Charles V owed the Venetians a vast sum of money, loaned to him to buy the post of Emperor of the Holy Roman Empire. For the sake of the Hapsburg government's budget-balancing efforts, the Hapsburgs conquered and looted Rome, and the Mexicans owed to the Hapsburgs to die in slavery to whatever extent the international bankers required. One might say, "Of course, such things could never be repeated today," but such were the rules of international banking in the sixteenth century. During the same time-frame, about the same exact degree of genocide was carried out in Peru.

Unquestionably, the Hapsburgs were an international disaster, and did things to Mexico and Peru for which they should have been hung at Nuremberg. That scarcely makes the Aztecs heroes. A culture which cuts out thousands of living hearts of helpless captives, simply for a religious ritual, represents a satanic sort of religion which ought to be stamped out of existence, and never permitted to reappear in any form again. Granted, the Aztecs did not come close to exterminating the population of Mexico; they were evil enough to have done that job before Cortez arrived, but they just weren't as well organized as the Venetian and Genoese debt-collectors.

I wouldn't put the Incas into the same moral category as those damned Aztecs. They represented a step up for local humanity, over a nasty regime which had dominated much of the locality earlier. I would suggest that we might know ancient cultures a lot better than we do today, if anthropology had not been invented during the middle of the last century.

A new U.S. strategic doctrine

By 1978, we had a pretty good squabble—a friendly one—under way with places such as Lawrence Livermore laboratories. Dr. Edward Teller had a number of very good scientists out there, but that computer of theirs seemed to reject many of the best experimental ideas circulating among them. They simply would not accept the physics of Gauss and Riemann; that rejection was holding back important work toward the development of commercial fusion-energy production. We had hints that some Soviet work did reflect reference to relevant aspects of Riemannian physics. I wished to gain access to Soviet papers of a sort which would be of relevance to our squabble with Livermore and a few other places. In the autumn of 1978, we had the opportunity to follow up this line of inquiry.

The Soviets say that they hate me, but they don't necessarily dislike me. Over years, their publications have classed me as a "principled adversary," which, in their vocabulary, sometimes means a fellow for whom they have a sneaking admiration while they are shooting him down. On the level of sentiment, they hate my guts. However, they also respect me as both a "principled adversary" and a person of accomplishments; the trouble is, that the more they admire my accomplishments, the greater a potential danger I represent, and the more they are motivated to have me exterminated. Keep that curious Soviet logic in mind, when I report that two representatives of the Fusion Energy Foundation were invited to attend a Soviet-sponsored, 1978 international conference on laser fusion. The Fusion Energy Foundation asked for my suggestions, to which I responded with the relevant references to Soviet work on Riemannian physics of fusion.

Soviet hospitality sometimes takes curious forms. In

the course of the visit, the KGB drugged one of the two delegates and took the second off for a profiling and conditioning trip to Siberian laboratories. The drugging was of a routine sort. I never had the full story of Steve Bardwell's trip eastward. Apart from that, the conference itself was a success, and the two brought back pretty much what I desired. Soviet scientists admitted in unclassified papers what the United States cloaked under official secrecy. Precisely who is being kept in the dark by U.S. security classifications of that sort? The returning visitors, and others, dropped by the place at which I was being safehoused, for an afternoon's debriefing session. It was then and there that the *Executive Intelligence Review*'s regular quarterly economic forecast was born.

Actually, that quarterly economic forecast was launched as a tactic for attempting to bring people like those at Lawrence Livermore to their senses. The key physical principle in causing laser fusion to work, is isoentropic compression. They way this is accomplished, is defined in germ-form by Riemann's 1859 paper "On The Propagation of Plane Air Waves of Finite Magnitude," the same paper which identified the possibility of transonic and supersonic flight. This also bears on designing a workable H-bomb, as the relevant Soviet papers identified this. The same physical principle is key for solving the kinds of nonlinear functions defined by my discoveries in economic science. I suggested: We have the capability for generating a computer-assisted quarterly economic forecast based on the LaRouche-Riemann method. It will be the only accurate forecast generated. Why not do that, which we ought to be doing in any case, and stress the fact of the connection to crucial principles of laser fusion?

"How shall we organize this?" was the question which followed discussion of my proposal. I suggested that the Fusion Energy Foundation approach the *Executive Intelligence Review*. The foundation would own the physics side of the common product, and *EIR* would own the use of the program for use in constructing its published forecasts. I would supply the parameters for the economic modeling. *EIR* and the foundation worked out the arrangements. There was a request for my memorandum on the specifications of the forecasting model, which I fulfilled with a few days' work.

A preliminary form of the program was developed during the first eleven months of 1979. The first quarterly report was produced at the end of that year.

During 1978, I was becoming more deeply involved in problems of U.S. strategy. During the summer of 1977, Major General George Keegan, just retired, was put into contact with the Fusion Energy Foundation. As former head of Air Force Intelligence, he had shown commendable resourcefulness in compiling information bearing upon what he believed to be Soviet development of a new kind of system of strategic ballistic missile defense. Apparently, he had run afoul of the crowd of Schlesinger, General Daniel Graham, and CIA Director William Colby, according to our subsequent study of the matter; Keegan's valuable, and essentially accurate assessment and proposals had been squelched.

I reviewed my friends' estimate of the evidence. There was nothing in Keegan's assessment which did not correspond to a known Soviet scientific and production capability. Every fact added up to either a Soviet, ground-based particle-beam form of strategic ballistic missile defense weapon, or something so similar as to defy conjecture. My work in physical economy qualifies me to assess the practical implications of physics discoveries, provided that the physics side of those discoveries is supplied by the relevant sort of professional. From the standpoint of the LaRouche-Riemann method, coherent beams of sufficiently high energy–density cross-section on target, represent orders of magnitude greater firepower and mobility than any mechanical sort of kinetic-energy system. In my view, Keegan's concern was more than justified.

Some weeks later, we came to a parting of the ways with Keegan, for reasons never adequately explained. My occupation with the subject of what "arms control" jargon terms "strategic ballistic missile defense based on new physical principles," grew over the months and years following.

The immediate problem of military policy, as I saw the matter during 1978, was that the policy of reliance upon "nuclear deterrence," was becoming increasingly a form of thermonuclear lunacy. Schlesinger's insanity concerning NATO MC 14/4 was an aberration, but the fact that such aberrations were tolerated to the degree they were, showed that the deterrence doctrine was reaching a point of breakdown. The end of the possibility of retaliatory strikes, following a full-scale first-strike assault, was in sight. Deterrence was becoming a hair-trigger for total thermonuclear warfare. Those who insisted we must not change a deterrence doctrine which had kept the peace for so many years, seemed to me to be like the fellow who canoed down the Great Lakes, and saw no reason not to continue his course as he went over Niagara Falls. There had to be a better way.

Suppose we did base Pershing II's, Cruise missiles, and "neutron bombs" in forward positions in the European theater, what good would that actually do? Under the right doctrine, I am in full support of the use of neutron bombs as weapons against advancing tanks, and against flotillas of aircraft and naval-surface vessels. The problem was the doctrine under which these improvements in NATO posture were proposed. The Soviets would never engage in a "conventional" assault, or a theater-limited use of nuclear weapons, unless they were assured in advance that they could get by with such a limited-warfare tactic. For limited warfare, they needed to be assured that the United States would not commit itself to defense of Western Europe, otherwise, their option would be to begin war with a full first-strike assault on the United States. If they were developing a new quality of strategic ballistic missile defense, and we did not develop such a defense, then we were surely headed soon into a state of affairs at which such a first-strike would be operational Soviet doctrine for any general warfare contingency involving U.S. forces.

By relying upon forward-based defense adapted to an option of theater-limited warfare, we were simply lowering the threshold for general nuclear warfare. The key word is "rely." The direction of reasoning in manifest U.S. military policy seemed to be an echo of the folly of the war in Indochina, a reversion to the eighteenth-century "cabinet warfare" doctrine shattered on the fields of Jena and Auerstadt.

The United States needed a new strategic doctrine.

As I emphasized repeatedly during the late 1970s, even before the exchange with General Keegan, "strategy" does not mean simply a military strategy. It means the sort of doctrine I had carried away from my immediate postwar months in Calcutta. A strategy for war must be based on a strategy for winning the peace. If that strategy failed to prevent war, then it becomes the strategy under which war should be fought. The general strategy was already generally clear to me, in a way expressed by my efforts for international monetary reform. We needed a military strategy consistent with that general strategy.

It would be 1981 before I began to be certain I knew what the general lines of the new military strategy should be, and February 1982 before I surfaced my proposals publicly. My thoughts were ticking in such directions since Hilex '75, and were pushed into a useful direction by General Keegan's work. No important development of a major conception is ever produced except by an extended period of concentration beforehand.

My 1980 campaign

At the close of 1978, I had virtually settled on running for the presidency in 1980. A second Carter administration might tend to seal the doom of western civilization. This mood grew, as my friends pieced together the evidence, that the Carter administration was committed to toppling a key U.S. ally, the Shah of Iran, and bringing to power a group of murderous lunatics around Ayatollah Ruhollah Khomeini. By the end of August 1979, I had decided to enter the 1980 Democratic presidential primaries.

The *New York Times* had wind of my plans. A former associate tipped us off to the fact that the *Times* was running a special operation, a private Cointelpro operation. My friends consulted with me. I approved laying some bait in the *Times'* trail, but insisted on being on top of the operation, and it's being agreed that we would pull the string on our operation at any point I judged it time to do so. The *Times* took the bait. Not only did the *Times'* Paul Montgomery and Howard Blum (later caught red-handed and witting in a KGB operation against a U.S. citizen) take the bait; they bragged into a concealed tape recorder.

They bragged as follows. The *New York Times* was out to get me, and Representative Elizabeth Holtzman was in on the plotting. The object was to orchestrate a national news-media libel against me, which would either put numbers of my friends into prison, or bleed us dry in about five years of fighting off false accusations by the U.S. attorney. At that point, I said, "Pull the string on the operation." Press conferences presented the tape-recorded evidence in New York City and Washington, D.C.

As a result of our exposing the *Times'* plotting, the *Times* farmed the initial attack on me out to a New York weekly throwaway publication, *Our Town,* a front operation for Roy M. Cohn, edited by a convicted embezzler, Ed Kayatt. Dennis King was given the script and the byline. Once *Our Town's* series had run for a few weeks, the *Times* produced a slightly milder edition of the same script handed to Dennis King. It started in the Sunday edition, continued into Monday's, and was followed by an editorial which did all but demand illegal measures against me, on Tuesday.

King was used as point man, to assemble a rag-tag of terrorists and mere hoodlums into a mayhem-bent coalition against me. The full resources of the ADL were deployed nationally, in support of this operation. The initial concentration of ADL effort was an operation run through the Boston ADL office, into the New Hampshire primary campaign. The ADL bought the editors of every daily newspaper in the state of New Hampshire, and induced them to run copies of the Dennis King line. Elements of the New Hampshire campaign organizations of Jerry Brown, Ted Kennedy, Jimmy Carter, and George Bush, were caught red-handed in these ADL-run operations. There were major physical threats as well; some experts expressed surprise that I came out of the New Hampshire primary alive.

Despite these New Hampshire operations, launched in October of 1979, I was among the frontrunners at about Christmas time. Even on election day, exit polls showed my vote running about 20 percent of the Democratic total statewide, and carrying wards in parts of the state. These were the estimates of exit pollers for rival Democratic campaigns, as well as our own. Then, the news services' computer had a "malfunction." That evening, poll watchers saw LaRouche ballots tucked in large numbers in other candidate's piles. They couldn't steal all of the vote, but they did reduce it to a few percent. I beat John Connally's score, ran ahead of Brown in Connecticut, and collected over 20 percent in Michigan. However, after the New Hampshire primary, I was out of serious contention, as large numbers of voters inclined to me went over to support Ronald Reagan.

The Carter-Mondale nomination was rammed through the 1980 convention. Dennis King's terrorist cronies threatened to do me in during the period of the convention, but never progressed beyond some nasty street exercises. A gathering of disgruntled Democrats met in the closing hours of the convention, and agreed on the founding of new political action committee, dedicated to cleaning up the Democratic Party. I made some TV spots for the newly formed National Democratic Policy Committee, and flew to Europe to pick up on postponed work there.

The Computron affair

Something was very wrong. Uwe Friesecke informed me that he had been unable to conduct a rational conversation with Costas Kalimtgis. My wife went to the phone to speak with Costas. He cursed her out vilely. I got Costas on the telephone. I was convinced he was having a nervous break-down. I flew back to New York City. Costas had calmed down, it seemed. One thing was clear; my friends had a financial mess on their hands. The problem seemed to center around a firm in which Costas' wife was a principal, Andy Typaldos' software firm, Computron. I met with Costas and Andy for an oral briefing. My friends supplied me with some accounting worksheets. The figures made no sense.

Then, Costas had what must be fairly described as a psychotic episode, and made noises about resigning from his functions. There was another episode. I advised my friends that Costas must be suspended from his functions, at least until he had recovered from a serious mental con-dition. I agreed to take charge of the situation until the mess was cleaned up.

Since this is my biography, rather than an account of the full details of each development, I condense the report. I had met Typaldos during the early 1970s, when he had been working as an engineer for the New York Telephone Company. He pulled Costas into a new computer-sales venture he started, with Costas somehow acquiring a ma-jority interest. Andy was around until 1974, dropped out of sight, and appeared again in 1978. Somewhere near the end of 1977, Andy and Costas had rearranged the part-nership, and Andy had reorganized his firm, Computron,

in a revised legal form. Costas recruited some Labor Committees members to work for Computron as programmers.
By 1979, about forty members were working there, at
about half the scale of pay for their skills in the trade
generally.

Computron's sales were booming, until October 1979,
when the ADL organized a campaign to pressure the firm's
clients into canceling their contracts. But the firm was in
deep financial trouble. Andy was a salesman, in the best
and also the worst sense. He lived in a fantasy-world, a
state of mind which he required to be able to sell effectively.
Any reality which might spoil that fantasy-life, he brushed
aside, explaining, "If I think about that, I won't be able to
sell." Before the ADL's campaign, Computron was already
deep into a looming bankruptcy. The ADL's campaign
merely brought it on earlier than it would have come to
the surface in any case. Andy sued Dennis King and Ed
Kayatt's *Our Town*, the publication which had targeted
Computron for the ADL's operations. It was not until late
1980, that I had any facts about Computron's actual situation. Once I pieced the data together, I recognized the
general nature of the situation immediately.

Since 1978, Costas had been helping Typaldos to bleed
a number of business enterprises, trying to keep Computron propped up. During 1980, the looting became a
torrent. Costas had done this, with no discernible financial
advantage to himself, by arrogating to himself the position
of virtual czar over sundry aspects of business operations
operated by various groups of Labor Committees members. At the same time, as we discovered during 1981,
Costas had also been helping a second major looting operation, run by a group linked to organized crime circles
in Detroit. By the summer of 1980, Costas saw an early
end to his efforts to prevent the grand illusion from being
discovered, and suffered an apparent physical breakdown,
which proved to be essentially psychosomatic and significantly feigned as well. By October, desperation had given
way to psychotic episodes.

Costas had secured advance payments on Computron services to be delivered in the future, had negotiated large loans from various firms, and similar tricks to supply Computron with both cash and leverage for Computron's securing of flows of credit. The operation had been scaled up in late 1979 and 1980, with aid of emphasis on the ADL's politically motivated efforts to bankrupt Computron. Computron could have extricated itself by proceeding to reorganization in bankruptcy, as it was obliged to do, in any case, at the beginning of 1981. Andy Typaldos' ego would not hear of bankruptcy. Costas poured more and more effort into his slogan, "We must save Computron at all costs."

Andy fled the country, putatively on a business trip which was going to solve all his problems. I had in my hands the evidence that Computron was bankrupt. I attempted to reach Andy. Neither Andy's business partners, nor his wife, were willing to face a simple reality. I had assumed a responsibility. I had to act. I pulled the relevant people together, and stated that the string must be pulled on the Computron bail-out operation. Costas went way off the deep end with that development. I had a moral responsibility to all of the Labor Committees members involved, especially those to whom Costas had falsely asserted my endorsement of things of which I had not been informed, and would never have endorsed. Andy's partners went wild.

I saw Costas once again after that, at a meeting arranged by Criton Zoakos. For all that he had done, Costas was mentally ill. He needed help. Punish the sin, and save the sinner. During the dinner, Costas was mild, rational. As he was about to leave, a psychotic fit overtook him. It was the last time I saw him.

I constructed a management accounting chart of accounts, and with that resigned my temporary executive functions, instructing the affected parties to secure professional accounting help and also legal expertise. Typaldos would be going into bankruptcy very soon, and, although I had seen nothing unlawful in anything these businesses had done, I could not be certain of what Costas might have done or tolerated. I concentrated on assembling an investigative dossier on the history of Costas' conduct.

The heart of the affair was KGB. Costas had stated during the rational part of his role in our last meeting, that the whole business had been started on the instruction of his mother, who had ordered him to commit himself to Andy, and he had followed out that instruction. By the end of 1981, the more complete story came out. Costas had worked not only to bleed a number of enterprises on Computron's behalf; he had known of and had condoned massive looting of these same enterprises by an organized-crime-linked operation tied to the ADL. The aggregate looting accomplished by both operations totaled to several millions over approximately a two-year period.

Costas went on to become a protected asset of the FBI, and at last report was organizing perjury from a group of persons under his direction, to the stated purpose of fabricating evidence to assist U.S. Attorney William Weld's ADL-backed efforts to falsely imprison friends of mine. The leading figures organizing this group are linked to the Soviet intelligence services.

While this mess was being sorted out, I traveled to Washington, on more serious business, including a series of meetings with the Reagan transition team.

The SDI Is Born 7

From December into about June of 1981, my relations with the Reagan administration were excellent on the whole. In a curious way, my 1980 candidacy had helped Reagan to be elected, as an unplanned side effect of my part in the New Hampshire primary campaign. On everything but economic policy, my friends tended to agree with many among the Reaganites. We became helpful in a few somewhat important matters. I worked in an effort to bring about a bipartisan cooperation between nonradical Democrats and the new administration, and had some liaison with Democratic Chairman Charles Manatt on this subject.

The closeness ended in June, and relations were greatly strained in November of that year, but certain channels of collaboration remained open into 1984.

My outstanding role during these four years, was to develop a new strategic policy, later named the U.S. Strategic Defense Initiative (SDI). I presented the conception to the administration first during the early part of 1981, and presented it publicly for the first time at a two-day Washington, D.C. seminar convened for this purpose, during February 1982. During the remainder of that year, into early 1983, my friends and I campaigned for the adoption of this policy-option internationally, including my meetings with French and German military bodies. According to representatives of several nations, their decision to support the SDI was influenced significantly by my missionary work.

The first strain between me and the administration came as a result of the President's rejection of the offer by a group of Democratic senators, to back him against Federal Reserve Chairman Paul A. Volcker and Volcker's policies. The President replied, "If you attack Volcker, you're attacking me." The President was committed to renominating Volcker, and backing the existing Federal Reserve policies. Essentially, the chances of serious bipartisan collaboration died on the White House carpet, as the senators prepared their retreat. I was still committed to bipartisan work, because it was the right policy, but not because I saw much hope of success. I resolved to attempt to help the administration, despite the President's ultimately self-defeating economic policy.

The second strain in my relations with the administration came in November. Two dirty operations against me and my friends converged, as a group linked to organized-crime circles attempted to destroy the Midwest organization of the Labor Committees during October of that year.

Houston, Texas' Madame de Menil is a professed Sufi mystic, a backer of the Paris radical publication, *Liberation,* and a long-time backer of the political efforts of France's Socialist President François Mitterrand. She is a member of the super-wealthy Schlumberger family, and thus part of a Swiss-based financial empire, de Neuflize, Mallet, and Schlumberger, dating from the middle of the eighteenth century. She is the widow of a once-famous figure of Russian extraction, Jean de Menil, and has extremely important Soviet connections. She is a power factor in Houston politics, and runs international political operations out of two Texas-based institutions, the camp at Marfa, Texas, and Houston's Rothko Chapel. The later is named for a mystical, "New Age" painter of the Russian genre, a cult-figure of the sort associated with the tradition of Bulgarian (Bogomil) mysticism. During October 1981, she convened representatives of political spokesmen for international terrorism at her Rothko Chapel.

Through our counterintelligence tracking of Khomeini agents, we picked up the threads of this conference at Rothko, and blew the information publicly in a number of relevant locations, including Washington, D.C. and Houston. In this circumstance, Madame de Menil flew to Washington, for the nominal purpose of attending a dinner at the White House, but also to demand action against me and my friends. The ongoing government investigation of the proterrorist festivities at Rothko was dropped. An organized-crime-linked operation against my circles, already in place, was accelerated, coming to a head in October.

Jean de Menil has a long pedigree in intelligence files. Our tracking of him dates back to military intelligence files at the beginning of the 1940s. Back then, he shows up as an associate of synarchist networks operating in the Caribbean region. The military intelligence files classify this synarchist network under the heading "Synarchism: Nazi/Communist." He appears as a backer of Fidel Castro during the second half of the 1950s, and also appears as an associate of circles which Lee Harvey Oswald intersected in the New Orleans/Dallas/Houston circuit. This is the general drift of the dossier, which makes an interesting companion to the dossier of the Sufi mystic, Madame de Menil herself.

Those are the general lineaments of what we rightly viewed as Ye Olde Dirtie Double-Crosse from elements within the Reagan administration. There is much more depth to this case, but until a pending major legal case against one of our key enemies is concluded, it would be unsuitable to tell that part, and other parts must wait until certain things are declassified. I shall merely say that assurances were pledged to us, that no more of this would occur, if we refrained from mentioning certain details of that October caper. When professionals were hired to assassinate me during a conference at the end of that year, the actions of relevant law enforcement agencies did seem a signal that the administration preferred to treat us much more fairly than it had in October.

The discussion of what became known as the SDI began a short time after the resignation of National Security Adviser Richard Allen. I was asked to list orally my agenda of possible actions for recommendation to the administration. One of these items was a summary identification of the urgency and feasibility of such a form of strategic ballistic missile defense. From that point on, my collaboration with the administration on this subject was continuous into the summer of 1983. Some aspects of this work, I am not at liberty to report up to this time; but the technical side of my proposals would involve no breach of secrecy.

At this point, I should state plainly, that I have never been a paid agent of any intelligence service, nor have I functioned in any way as a controlled asset of such a service. I have done things which could be construed as running errands for our government. Rarely, it has been necessary that I know certain information, which I have sworn not to reveal, to the same effect in practice as if I had taken a formal oath officially. In delicate matters, it has always been understood that I am acting simply as a citizen, and as I believe a citizen in my position should. I have never received payment or compensation for expenses on account of such activities.

I have no objection to people being paid agents of our government's intelligence services, but my situation is such that I should not do that. It would spoil everything, including those activities which are my most useful service to our nation.

The charge that either I, or my association, are agents of any secret service, shows either that the person who makes the allegation is a liar, or that he understands very little of the way secret services "handle" their agents. Worse contempt must be shown those who allege, variously, that I am "KGB-linked," an anti-Semite, or any sort of "political extremist" in the conventional usage of "extremist." To anyone who tells you the contrary, you would be perfectly justified in retorting, "Are you a liar, or just one of those people who save energy by turning off their brains before turning on their mouths?"

The Soviet view of strategic defense

As I presented my case to one European military planning group during the months prior to the President's announcement of the SDI on March 23, 1983, the essential military significance of my view of strategic ballistic missile defense, is that it puts nations back into "the strategy business." It defines a general war as a clearly fightable, winnable, and survivable form of warfare once again. The Soviet military general staff was the first to adopt this doctrine, which surfaced publicly in a 1962 edition of Marshall V.D. Sokolovskii's book, *Military Strategy*.

The argument, whether nuclear weapons made future general wars unthinkable, or not, was first argued out in 1938. In 1938, Admiral Canaris, head of Germany's military intelligence, told the British that scientist Otto Hahn had discovered the principle of building nuclear weapons. Canaris was the center of the German military plotters who were desperate to rid Germany of Hitler, and to avoid a new general war like World War I. Had the allies acted as Canaris asked, rather than betraying the German anti-Hitler resistance repeatedly, as they did, the German military was prepared and able to rid the scene of Hitler. Canaris' actions in reporting Otto Hahn's progress must be understood in that light. The British government arranged to have President Franklin Roosevelt informed. Stalin also knew and launched an effort to construct a Soviet nuclear arsenal in 1940. During 1938–1940, there was already a heated debate, although among very restricted circles, on military policy for an age of nuclear arsenals.

The "Atom Project" which Josef Stalin set up in 1940, was headed by one of the world's leading nuclear specialists, the Pasteur Institute-trained academician Vernadsky, who had been promoting Soviet nuclear-energy projects as early as the mid-1920s. Soviet military doctrine for the coming years, was already taking the implications of nuclear arsenals into account prior to the Nazi invasion of Russia. Although Moscow's Pugwash Conference discussion-partners were insisting on outlawing of anti-ballistic-missile systems, as early as 1958 the Soviets were already studying strategic ballistic missile defense as an indispensable part of fighting, winning, and surviving a general war in the age of thermonuclear missiles. The 1962 edition of Sokolovskii's book was the first known location in which we had indications of a definite strategic decision by Moscow on this matter. Essentially, Sokolovskii's doctrine is the kernel of Soviet strategic doctrine today.

Although lasers were a new device during the early 1960s, Sokolovskii already grasped the significance of such devices for active measures of strategic defense. He emphasized that the high-speed interceptor rocket defenses being developed in the West were an inadequate approach to antimissile defense. Only the superior firepower and mobility becoming available in the form of advanced physics principles, could provide an adequate defense. He stated, that it is sufficient that such a defense system be capable of destroying a significant number of ballistic warheads before these reached their targets, to make nuclear war survivable and winnable.

By the late 1970s, our laboratories had proven the

relevant scientific principles, ensuring that we could develop an array of effective such defenses within a relatively short time. General Keegan's findings were just one among an array of evidence showing that the Soviets, were progressing in the actual development of such systems, begun at the close of the 1960s.

Naturally, since such technical possibilities were not understood either by the general population, among politicians, and even among large sections of military professionals, my own and my friends' educational work over the 1981–1983 period had to devote a large ration of effort to explaining technical matters which should have been generally known already. Under those circumstances, it is understandable that this unavoidable feature of our expositions should tend to draw attention away from the original features of my contributions to a military policy of strategic defense. When the Heritage Foundation's General Daniel P. Graham reacted to my own and Dr. Teller's proposals, beginning late 1982, by cluttering the discussion with his "Rube Goldberg" alternative, the so-called High Frontier, the debate which should never have been started distracted public and governments' attention from the sensible issues even more.

There was originality in the way my collaborators and I pieced together the design for an initial SDI system, although each of the ingredients we used was already well-known to scientists at the time. The actual originality lay in the way we proposed to change military doctrine by means of introducing such designs.

What was original in my design, was the application of my discoveries in economic science, to solve the crucial problems posed by the attempt to build war-planning around such systems of strategic defense. I shall focus on that part of SDI a few moments ahead. First, some other military matters must be mentioned, to situate the problem as a whole.

Naturally, the first item of discussion which arises in

discussing active strategic defense is the technology for neutralizing missile bodies and their warheads, before those objects can reach their targets. In a full-scale Soviet launch, we must be prepared to hit relevant targets among as much as 30,000 pieces of material roaming in the trajectories of Soviet intercontinental ballistic weapons. The shorter-range nuclear carriers and their warheads, such as we must defeat in the European theater or in missiles launched off our coasts by Soviet submarines, totals hundreds of thousands of objects. However, what is proven to work for the case of intercontinental trajectories will work as the basis for designing systems to deal with the lower trajectories. So, concentrating attention on the intercontinental trajectories was sound practice, even though many misinterpreted this to signify that we were concerned only with intercontinental missiles.

I viewed strategic defense as the keystone of an entire system of war-planning, with great emphasis on new methods of antisubmarine warfare, and down to the tactical means placed at the disposal of regimental commanders.

I began with the maximum case. The Soviets launch their entire loaded thermonuclear arsenal simultaneously against assigned targets in North America, Western Europe, and against prime military targets elsewhere. Since missiles launched from Soviet submarines off our coasts will reach their targets within minutes, our response must be immediate. Strategic defense must react immediately, and all missiles we intend to launch from ground-based launchers, must be flying within a couple of minutes—or we might never be able to fire them at all. The Soviet heavy nuclear assault against targets in the United States is for maximum effect, but more limited, more carefully selective in the Western Europe Moscow intends to have overrun some days later.

In general, in such a case, there will be no visible prewar shifts of Soviet forces, which might warn us of probable launching of their attack. This drill has been heavily rehearsed by the Soviet commanders and their troops over the recent years. The Soviet commanders must rely upon either knocking out or pinning down most of our thermonuclear response within the first twenty-five minutes after the start of the attack, and must have a combination of active and passive measures sufficient to ensure that the level of Soviet losses is kept within approximately the limits of total Soviet losses during World War II.

In the worst case, if we do not launch immediately, and if we do not have a strategic defense sufficient to destroy a strategically significant ratio of Soviet warheads, the United States is a gone bunny within twenty-five minutes. After the initial barrage, Soviet, nuclear-armed conventional forces are already moving across Western Europe, occupying Bristol, England within less than two weeks.

In the case we have a strategically significant active defense against Soviet thermonuclear barrages, we survive the initial assault as an effective fighting force and nation. In that case, continuing naval warfare and defeating the Soviet air and ground assault in Western Europe becomes the new feature of the war to be emphasized. In that case, the required military objectives are, to halt the Soviet westward assault through East Germany and Czechoslovakia with monstrous losses inflicted on those and deeper-echelon Soviet forces, and to launch a counteroffensive, carrying the fight to Warsaw Pact territory, with the key included objective the liberation of Poland, aided by mass defection of Polish military forces from the Warsaw Pact command.

The crucial other factor to be emphasized, is a system of antisubmarine warfare aided by a total prewar detection and tracking of all Soviet submersibles, especially nuclear-armed types.

If we develop such a capability, and if the Soviets know we have done so, the Soviet commanders will not initiate a general war. If we do not develop such a capability, then the Soviets will launch such a war at some point during the years ahead, and our only option for avoiding such war would be surrender.

The economic advantage of SDI

Such a war-fighting plan requires new technological means in every aspect of our integrated war-fighting capabilities. It might seem that the array of improved technologies of strategic and tactical defense, is a very diversified collection of military objects. Superficially, that picture is an accurate one. From a different standpoint, that of manufacturing such objects, most of the new technologies are like so many puppies in a mongrel's litter: they look different, but the mother and father are the same. All that is really new technology in these objects, is an application of a few general scientific principles. From the standpoint of national industrial mobilization, the manufacturing capacity required is based on diversified applications of a handful of new production technologies: controlled plasmas of high energy-density cross-section, coherent pulses of electromagnetic radiation, optical biophysics, and advanced computer-systems designs. The rest of production is improved auxiliary technologies to support the revolutionary components of the weapons.

At that point, the fun begins. Suppose we take this approach, creating the situation in which the Soviets dare not launch war? What kind of a strategic situation have we created? Second, can the western economies afford the costs of such new systems of defense? The second bears directly on the portion of my work which was truly original.

The highest rate of growth of U.S. productivity during the postwar period, was achieved under the combined influence of the pre-1967 aerospace program of the 1960s, and the investment tax-credit program adopted during the Kennedy administration. The annual average increase of productivity of operatives reached levels above 5 percent.

As a result, the U.S. economy has been paid back, in increased wealth, more than ten cents for each penny our government spent on aerospace research and development.

I considered four other cases roughly comparable to the Apollo-centered aerospace work of that period. I concentrated personally on sources' analysis of the wartime Manhattan Project, the German Peenemünde project, and the work of Carnot and Monge over the period 1792–1814. Collaborators focused, in a later portion of the 1981–1983 period, on the 1940–1943 period of the U.S. wartime agro-industrial mobilization in general. A number of other important case histories could have been included, including that of 1861–1863 under President Lincoln. The most basic model of reference was the Carnot-Monge program, as viewed retrospectively from the vantage-point of the LaRouche-Riemann method. The Manhattan, Peenemünde, and Apollo cases were needed also, to focus upon certain of the problems of rapid technological-industrial mobilization, under conditions of modern industrial economies, and scarcity of qualified key personnel and qualified production capacities.

The LaRouche-Riemann method was directly applied to the classes of primary new technologies involved in SDI, to translate the relevant physics characteristics into the needed parameters used to estimate the impact of these technologies upon civilian productivity.

Over the period 1981–1982, I reduced the initial requirements for a system of defense against intercontinental missiles and their warheads to a minimum of six layers of active defense: 1) Hit the missiles at launch; 2) Hit the missiles during their boost phase; 3-4) Hit the warheads at at least two successive points of mid-trajectory; 5) Hit the warheads in their initial descent through the atmosphere; 6) Provide last-ditch point-defense for military and population targets of surviving warheads. One could add more layers, but these six appeared to me to be the minimum number required. I set as a requirement for design, that each successive layer of defense must be intended to destroy

50 percent of the surviving missiles or warheads coming into its target-area. I proposed that, for purposes of discussion of policy, we must imagine that we seek to ensure that only an ideal 5 percent of all Soviet warheads launched would reach their targets.

In 1982, I projected an eighteen- to twenty-year interval of successively improved systems of SDI. I broke this down into four successive systems of SDI: Mark I, Mark II, Mark III, and Mark IV. The first system must be launched within five years under a "crash program" resembling the Apollo program. Each successive improvement in the system would be launched a few years apart. At the end of 1982, in my presentation to French military circles, I projected a cost to the United States and its allies, of about $200 billion (in 1982 dollars) for Mark I, and a total of approximately $1 trillion, also in 1982 dollars, for the combined Mark I, Mark II, Mark III, and Mark IV.

The Mark I could not be projected to take out 95 percent of Soviet warheads. We would suffer unimaginable death-rates and loss of our economic capacity in the initial assault, obviously. However, two things could be gained. We would survive as a nation, although in ruinous condition, and the Soviets would suffer a degree of destruction way beyond anything they would be willing to risk. In other words, Mark I's net immediate effect is to restore an otherwise lost "credibility" to our strategic deterrent. It would delay the point at which general war is to be feared. Mark I, if combined with improved missiles, at least comparable to the MX, would buy us a few years of war-avoidance.

Mark I also served another, indispensable purpose. It brings into being the new productive capacities needed for developing Mark II, Mark III, and Mark IV.

We would still be walking a thermonuclear tightrope for ten or more years to come, but the only alternative to SDI is either to become Soviet slaves, or suffer thermonuclear holocaust.

Two hundred billion dollars added to defense budgets

over five years, and $1 trillion over twenty, may seem like a staggering added expense, to some. Let us be very pessimistic about this. Let us assume, that over the coming twenty years, SDI causes the average productivity of the United States, Western Europe, and Japan, to increase by a mere 5 percent a year, on the average. In that case, the increased national tax-revenues gained, at 1982 tax-rates, would be far greater than $1 trillion. It turns out to be the most profitable investment we might imagine at the moment. In other words, in the long run, the cost would be less than zero. I called this economic gain the "economic spill-over," a term popularized, with the initial efforts of the National Security Council's Dr. Norman Bailey, during the spring of 1983.

Broadly speaking, relevant circles in our own and allied governments, saw the argument about "spill-over" to be a valid one. The most fundamental points in my analysis of the process of "spill-over" was rarely grasped; most lack the general sense of economic science needed to understand the practical implications of the LaRouche-Riemann Method. They did understand the comparison to the Apollo program, and, for most of them, that was sufficient proof of my general point.

Economics came into play in another crucial aspect of SDI. Could these measures of strategic defense destroy a warhead at less expense, than the combined costs of building and deploying the missile-system? Imagine the ratio, K/C. K represents the value of missile-systems destroyed; C the cost of destroying them. It might appear that the breakeven point, where it is equally advantageous to build either missiles or antimissile systems, is $K/C = 1.00$. This is not strictly true, on two counts. First of all, we must consider the value of the damage to our nation for each warhead which gets through; so we might set the breakeven point for K/C at as high as 100.00, ideally. Second, the choice between building only missile systems or defense-systems does not exist, unless our Defense Department or Congress were certifiably insane. For the foreseeable future, we are going to invest in a balanced mix of missiles and defensive systems. However, the ratio K/C comes into play in another aspect of policy making.

Imagine two economies of equal capacity. Obviously, if it is cheaper to build missile-systems than the cost of killing one with a defensive system, over the medium to long term, the nation which improves its assault capability would tend to win the arms race. Livermore's Dr. Lowell Wood has estimated that it should require about ten cents' worth of my sort of SDI system to kill a dollar's worth of missile-system. That estimate is not a wild guess. The firepower and mobility of the new technologies is several orders of magnitude greater than the firepower and mobility represented by the in-flight missile or warhead which the defensive weaponry must destroy.

Lasers propagate at the speed of light. Missiles fly at no more than several times the speed of the Concorde passenger airliner. We already have Mach 6 aircraft nearing the potential point of actual development, with aircraft at Mach 15 speeds coming up down the line. So, missile and warhead speeds are not really very impressive these days. Why so little progress has been made in rocket-systems over the past thirty years, is a subject in itself.

Then, compare the amount of energy which a coherent beam of suitable frequency requires to destroy a missile or warhead, with the amount of energy required to deploy that missile system. Imagine the energy packed into the bullet that kills the elephant, with the amount of energy represented by that charging elephant.

Such defensive systems can outrun missiles and warheads by a margin nearing the ratio of the speed of light to the speed of sound. The defensive weapon can kill the missile with a tiny fraction of the energy represented by the deployment of the missile itself.

By translating these inherent physical advantages of defensive technologies into proper designs of produced objects, a ten-to-one cost-advantage of defense over offense, is really a pessimistic estimate of the potential of the defensive weapons.

Naturally, if we produce just one prototype of such a defensive weapon, or fail to use mass-production methods, then the costs of the weapon zoom. A good comparison, is the cost of production of a U.S. combat aircraft in 1940 in terms of labor costs of direct labor and of materials and tools, with the average cost of the same quality of aircraft three years later. Any industrial manager who is familiar with standards of management of production during the 1940s and early 1950s, understands immediately exactly what I am talking about. Most specialists in our defense industries are painfully aware of the outright insanity of governmental procurement regulations and related policies today. If you wish to cause a five dollar toilet seat to cost forty or fifty, try operating under the insane features in our stretch-out procurement policies and legal requirements today. Go back to the philosophy of industrial management and defense procurement we used during the 1950s, and with all the defects admittedly in those former practices, the greatest part of the excess cost is brought essentially under control. If one has forgotten how that used to work, go learn from Japan's industrial firms, who had more sense than to ruin the system we used to use, by hiring Harvard Business School graduates. (Instead of boycotting Japan, we were wiser and much fairer to boycott Harvard Business School and similar institutions.)

Instead of investigating the Defense Department every time a military coffeepot costs too much, the Congress ought to investigate itself, for some of the insane rules and procedures the Congress and Justice Department have imposed, to cause such oddities.

Another fact about SDI, which most newspaper editors, and so forth, have so far failed to grasp, is that we are not speaking of some Egyptian pyramid, to stand unchanged, except for decay, over thousands of years. SDI is an evolving "organism," which is becoming more powerful in design each year, as fresh improvements are continually added. People trained to think in the language of constructive geometry can grasp the point quickest. We start from a handful of fundamental scientific principles, involving the addition of recent fundamental scientific discoveries and related advances. The principles will remain essentially the same over about twenty years, but the constructions based on these principles will become wonderfully richer as the process unfolds.

Folk such as members of the Union of Unconscious Scientists, mewl and scold, telling wicked fairy-tales about Soviet countermeasures, which they are confident will neutralize the best possible SDI, including designs which they have never even imagined, for almost the price of a copy of Moscow's famous daily newspaper, *Pravda*. Let the Freudians deal with such fantasies of the Unconscious. The fact is, that there is no weapon ever to be built, which cannot be beaten by a better one. No one can design a system, for which someone will not develop a countermeasure sooner or later. The Unconscious fears of Soviet countermeasures against SDI are meaningless drivel to any scientist who knows the least about the history of technological attrition, military or otherwise.

The point is, that it takes time for the other side to deploy an effective sort of countermeasure, on condition that our weapon is based on the most advanced sort of scientific principle. By the time the Soviets deploy effective countermeasures against Mark I, we have deployed Mark II. By they time they overtake Mark II, we are at Mark III or Mark IV. Any discussion of possible countermeasures not stated in those terms of a continuing technology race, is downright silly.

As the fellow wearing a knight's armor and weapons to modern warfare seems to have overlooked: As technology progresses, old technologies become obsolete ones. In military science, this factor is identified by the term "technological attrition." Assuming that two opposing powers are otherwise equally matched in economic capacity and military capabilities at some point in time, the object of the smarter one is to cause the highest relative rate of technological attrition in the other power's firepower and mobility, by choosing the right pathway of long-term commitment to technological progress for one's own nation.

If we take the combined scientific and industrial base of North America, Western Europe, and Japan, we have a much greater economic potential than the Soviets command. Soviet scientists on the average, are competitively good, and outnumber our own today. We have an additional advantage; because of cultural differences, the labor force of the United States and our allies has a proven superior potential for assimilating technological progress than the Soviet labor force generally.

Our general problem, building up over the past twenty years of "postindustrial" drift, is that we have been destroying our economic capacity and labor force's potential, while the Soviets have progressed significantly in many respects, or, at worst, remained stagnant in others. If we resume a policy of technological progress in an energy-intensive, capital-intensive mode, they cannot match the technological attrition they suffer, without changing their cultural values.

My design of military policy is based on our culture's crucial advantages over the Russian. In a competition based on technological attrition, we must gain increasing security, up to the point that they would give up Khrushchev's prophecy of "burying" us. My military doctrine is a classical nineteenth-century military-science doctrine, adapted to modern technological realities, and subordinated to a strategy which maximizes the likelihood of avoiding general war, and winning the peace in the longer run. We must force Moscow to accept "peaceful competition," and win that peace.

We must not attempt to conquer them. Nicolo Machiavelli rightly emphasized this principle of military doctrine. Always afford a defeated adversary an escape to safety. Make peaceful acceptance of our supremacy tolerable to him; otherwise he were likely to fight to the last man, or nearly so. We should wish the independence of Poland, for example. We must mobilize to such ends, as things to be gained through winning the peace-race.

I stressed to those with whom I reviewed matters during 1981, that we must recognize the risk of any sneak effort to deploy strategic defense. True, the Soviets were trying to sneak their development and deployment of strategic defense, but we must not imitate that. The objective, or probably perceived effect, of one's side having a credible strategic defense deployed, when the other superpower did not, is that the power without may see this as a potential for a first-strike assault, and strike in desperation before our SDI, for example, were fully deployed. Strategic defense must be presented as an offer to deploy capabilities more or less synchronously. In tactical defense, this problem either does not arise, or does not arise in anything like the same degree. Whether or not Moscow accepted such an offer, as President Reagan has made and reaffirmed such an offer, the fact that we offered it would largely neutralize the element of miscalculation on both sides.

For this reason, I withheld presenting my proposal, until it could be arranged that the Soviet representatives would be present to hear me include this offer as a key feature of my own design. As soon I was prepared to make my initial presentation, at the end of 1981, I asked my friends to set up a two-day public session in Washington, D.C., and ensure that a significant Soviet representation was in attendance. The two-day presentation occurred as planned, on February 18–19, and was followed, the next day, by a presentation to a large number of members of the National Democratic Policy Committee, in an adjoining location.

Dr. Steven Bardwell had been drawn close to Costas Kalimtgis and Andy Typaldos during 1979–1980. Part of Steve's problem was his refusal to come to grips with his flaws in scientific method; that was the key factor estranging him from his two chief intellectual paragons of the Labor Committees, his former professor, Uwe Parpart, and me. He had done some good work on the LaRouche-Riemann method's application to computer-based forecasting, but he had never understood, or was unwilling to consider, the importance of the methodological differences absolutely separating LaPlace, Cauchy, Kelvin, and Maxwell, from Leibniz, Gauss, and Riemann, for example. He had a good mind, and a saving experimental sense of his field. He had a number of accomplishments under his belt, but the issues of method had estranged him, and oriented his loyalties toward Costas and Andy, or at least very strong sympathies.

The significance of reporting this, is that Steve, who was pretty much on the way out by the end of 1981, was excited by my Washington presentation and written discussion of the new strategic doctrine. Beginning about March, he worked through June of 1982, piecing together an excellent assembly of known technologies, as an immediately feasible design for a strategic defense against intercontinental missiles. It was a useful contribution to the process, matched by Steve's excellent work during much of the rest of the time, in confronting opponents of the conception on various campus locations around the United States. During the summer, the quality of his continued work fell off; a supplementary section of his original, June report, was mercifully omitted by the editors from the published version of his study. During spring 1983, he was captured by a network of KGB operatives, and broke with a defense of Soviet actions in shooting down KAL 007. Quite naturally, he resumed collaboration with Costas Kalimtgis, and is part of Costas' cell organization today.

Various organizations around the United States endorsed my proposed doctrine. There were those at Livermore, for example, who found the idea sound. Dr. Edward Teller was reluctantly persuaded to campaign for such a military doctrine, balancing his enthusiasm for the approach against his wish not to become the center of yet another scientific brawl at his age. I believe that there were less famous scientific figures who had a better grasp of my approach than did Teller, but, politically, he made the difference, once he came out in support of such a policy during October of 1982. Whatever his shortcomings, which I think are less than those of most persons these days, the United States owes Edward Teller a few major debts; his actions in pushing the SDI are near the top of the list.

At a January 1983 conference, I situated my proposed doctrine within the larger scheme of developments, and indicated that I thought that Reagan must adopt the policy publicly by about March, or the possibility of implementing it would probably be lost irreversibly. I had a relevant sort of experience at a Munich, Germany meeting. Several of the local science establishment raised the objection, that the majority of the U.S. media and many politicians seemed opposed to my proposed doctrine; how could I possibly suggest that its adoption had a chance? I replied: "I have to convince only one man, Ronald Reagan." As replies to questions at such a gathering go, my answer was a precise and prophetic one.

The Soviets were supremely confident that my strategic doctrine would never reach the President's desk. They had been assured by leading Democratic Party circles, that it had been fixed to block the proposal in the echelons of the Executive bureaucracy. For all their penetration of the U.S. political establishment, the Soviets do not yet really understand how our system of government works. Many things of great importance, do not proceed through customary channels; intelligent people around Washington never entrust a really important matter to regular channels. The main road was thoroughly booby-trapped, as the Soviets believed, but . . .

The President's scheduled nationwide TV address

promised to be more or less routine, the press corps assumed, as they gathered in the White House that afternoon to receive the embargoed advance texts of the broadcast that evening. As they read through to the concluding portion of the text, panic struck. Only one reporter in the room knew what that part of the text meant; she went to the telephone to alert her New York office. The information was relayed to me, in Europe, within minutes of her call.

The news media scrambled. What was this all about? They were told that the experts were the Fusion Energy Foundation. The European news media searched me out. I received congratulations from across the United States and from many in Europe. The Soviets were stunned, sullen, depressed. That night on U.S. television, Richard Allen aptly described the President's announced doctrine as "Mutually Assured Survival," to replace Mutually Assured Destruction. Senator Ted Kennedy called it "Star Wars," and since he is perhaps among the leading scientific minds in the United States today, the liberal news media has been calling it "Star Wars" ever since.

A Communist official in Rome whined, that I was to blame for it all, and that I had destroyed Yuri Andropov's life's work.

Back in the United States, I delivered an address on the status of the matter to packed conference hall in Washington, D.C. That April weekend, the Soviet government at the highest level, officially declared war on me. A top KGB official close to Walter F. Mondale, Fyodor Burlatski, opened the Moscow propaganda-war against me in the KGB's *Literaturnaya Gazeta* a few weeks later. I traveled around Europe and elsewhere, delivering addresses on SDI, into spring of 1984.

Moscow's mobilization for war

The Soviet reaction to the President's SDI offer, seen in the light of the particular way Moscow chose to launch and develop the new, escalated public attacks upon me, was conclusive proof that Moscow was operating on the basis of a commitment to a prewar form of mobilization against the United States. In a way, this was no change; this had been long-range Soviet doctrine since Stalin's rule, and implicitly earlier. Yet, it was also a change, and a very significant one.

The Soviet mind is a blend of Russian mysticism and Romantic "historicity" (western-like individual rationality). The Soviets call this standpoint "objectivity," which they counterpose to what their lexicon identifies as "voluntarism." There is a bit of the famous Russian fictional character Oblomov in the Soviets, a mystical fatalism. He lacks any rational approach to history in general. History for him, is a matter of "periods." There is a "period" for one sort of perspective and actions, and then there are "periods" for different sorts of perspective and actions. The Raskolniks, most emphatically, believe that the "Russian people" are an expression of the sacred soil of Holy Mother Russia, Cybele operating under her Russian stage name, Matushka Rus. Matushka Rus expresses her will as the collective will of the Russian People. In one "period" her expressed will is thus and so, and in another, such and such. There are exceptions to this personality type among Soviet leading circles. Lenin was to a large degree an exception, but also not. If one does not recognize and understand this mysticism as the kernel of the Soviet personality, one's evaluation of their behavior will usually be profoundly mistaken.

The transition from Brezhnev to Andropov was not a change in long-term Soviet strategic policy, but it was an abrupt change from one "period" to "another." In reporting my assessments on approaches to the Soviets to the administration, during 1981 and early 1982, I had projected their response-patterns on the characteristic mindset of the "Brezhnev détente period." Over the interval from about March 1982 into the summer of that year, a shift in line had been established in Moscow. It was no longer necessary to prolong Leonid Brezhnev's life indefinitely; the Brezhnev period had ended, and the Andropov period had begun. It was a transition from a period of using détente as a mask behind which to prepare for the next period to follow, to a period of transforming the previous build-up into a prewar economic mobilization against the United States.

During the Brezhnev period, Moscow would have taken the President's SDI offer up as an agenda-item. It could not be said that Andropov's sharp rejection of the offer reflected a suspicion that the President's offer was not sincere. I had made the same offer earlier, publicly, in terms the Soviets could understand very clearly. My personal role was an extremely important factor; the Soviets hate me as one known to be dedicated to his principles. They understood very clearly that my formulation of the offer was a direct outgrowth of my principles. The President's offer had been phrased to conform in all essentials to my own version. In their minds, to the degree that I could trust the President's sincerity, they would have trusted his sincerity, too. If they had wished to probe the President's sincerity, the one thing they would not have done at that time, was launch an escalating public attack on me. Rather, they would have probed me, and watched to see if there were a relevant reaction from the President.

With the spring 1982 agreement to proceed with the transition from "the Brezhnev period," to the "Andropov period," something in preparation since 1956 had been unleashed. This could mean only one thing; Moscow was in a prewar mobilization, preparatory to securing world-domination, by general war if necessary.

I had a sinking feeling. I realized that I had had the clues in my possession months earlier. I had let these crucial facts slide by me. I had missed a crucial turn in Soviet policy by the better part of a year. I felt that my oversight might have lulled the President's circle into a state of unpreparedness for the developments now erupting. By the beginning of May, I had fitted the loose pieces together. I understood exactly what the new "Andropov dynasty" represented; there was not the slightest doubt of the accuracy of my estimation.

During the rest of 1983, I knew that I was not getting this picture through to any part of the administration. I tried in August, in a meeting at the National Security Council. I warned that we must expect an escalation of Soviet aggressive action against the United States within as early as the next thirty days.

Moscow shot down the KAL 007 airliner, with full knowledge that this was a civilian airliner; the maneuvers the Soviet pilot reported, prior to shooting down the plane, made clear in the pilot's own voice, not only that he had positively identified the characteristics of a civilian airliner, but that the pilot's military superiors had heard this report, immediately relayed all the way back to command center in Moscow. The operation was a deliberate shooting-down of a civilian airliner, personally ordered by the authority of Marshal Nikolai Ogarkov himself. This is the same Ogarkov who had worked out the Soviet Ogarkov Plan with Andropov's backing, the current Soviet war-plan for general nuclear attack against the United States.

I was certain that I was still not getting through to the relevant circles in the administration. It grew worse than that.

At the beginning of summer, my wife and I had made a series of stops for scheduled meetings, flying from Frankfurt, to New Delhi, to Bangkok, to Tokyo. My principal reason for the stopover in New Delhi, was for a meeting with Prime Minister Indira Gandhi. In Delhi, an angry buzz-saw was waiting for me. Indian insider circles were in a furious uproar over an article on the current Soviet policy which I had written for the *EIR*. It was to be my last meeting with *New Wave* editor Ganesh Shukla, who had come under devastating pressure from the Indian net-

work of Soviet Politburo member Geydar Alyiev. The
Soviet agents, and those whose circumstances depended
upon not being on the Soviet political hit-list, were having
the kinds of fits which most foreigners would imagine most
un-Indian, most un-Brahmin.

Mrs. Gandhi was her brilliant self. We had been in
personal contact for a number of years, and had met with
her on our last trip to India, a year earlier. We had been
privileged to collaborate with her on several matters of
some importance. Just more than a year later, she was killed
by a terrorist gang which was, and is politically supported
by the Anti-Defamation League and the Heritage Foundation, and by Senator Jesse Helms's Washington office.
When she died, the last living head of state or government
of genuinely personal world-stature died. The day she was
murdered, I was sitting in an Alexandria, Virginia federal
courtroom, looking at the attorneys for and an official of
the ADL which were backers of her murderers, listening
to a piece of human scum, NBC-TV's litigator, make obscene jokes about her death in open court, without rebuke
from Judge James C. Cacheris, presiding.

In front of others, Ganesh was having a public fit.
Alone with me, in private, he was still angered, but rational
and objective. He was furious at my warnings that the
Soviets were committed to destabilizing India, and setting
into motion a gameplan for the dismemberment of Paki-
stan. Granted, I emphasized, that western figures such as
Lord Bethell were involved in the Khalistan terrorist drug-
traffickers, but the Soviets were behind it. If Ganesh is
anything, he is, above all else an India nationalist and a
Brahmin of the Vedantist current. I touched him cruelly
on this point; was he going to be so fearful of Soviet and
Soviet agents' pressures, that he would blind himself to a
Soviet operation building toward the destabilization of India? He was furious. I regretted that, but it was my duty
to confront him with the truth, whether he liked it or not.

When Mrs. Gandhi was killed, he hated me, because he knew I had been right.

Tracking the Soviets is like hunting an unseen beast in the forest. Bits of spoor, here and there, in various parts of the forest, are the most reliable indicators of what is currently on the critter's mind. I did not review the list of names, connections, and operations of the Soviets which I had picked up in Delhi, when I summarized my case at the National Security Council a few weeks later; the odd bits of spoor picked up there, and in other parts of the world over the preceding months, were more important to the certainty of the assessment I summarized than any of the so-called "hard documentation" I had also taken into account. Out there in the jungle, tracking the beast by its spoor, is the place where the certainties of intelligence work are to be found, rather than in purloined documents, loquacious defectors, or the usual other stuff the desk-jockeys prefer. One must travel widely enough, so that one picks up a general pattern of the beast's activities, rather than merely localized stuff.

A meeting in Paris, another around Bonn, a day or two in Rome, followed by other stops: That is the way to pick up the right collection of spoor. Through circumstances beyond my control, I live like a desk-jockey most of the time, but I receive my reports from various parts of the world as if I were on the scene there. I avoid the desk-jockey's state of mind.

Asia: *the new economic frontier*

For a man of my specialized assortment of skills and interests, Bangkok has special attractions. My relevant project of the moment was putting together a long-overdue policy study on a long-range policy of economic development of the combined Pacific and Indian Ocean littoral. There is a group which meets occasionally on the subject of Pacific development, but the reports never seem to get down to any specific proposals except those listed under the topic of tourism. No study of the prospects for serious economic development of the basin existed; the United States urgently needed such a policy option. One of the key items on the agenda of my Bangkok visit, was the revival of one of the projects key to such a basin policy.

The idea of cutting a sea-level canal through the Isthmus of Thailand is almost two centuries old. It was proposed initially as a military policy, of the period of the Thailand-Burma wars, when a canal would have enabled the Thai navy to move from the Gulf of Thailand, to the Andaman sea, and back again. The idea had been put into a modern form, virtually waiting for beginning of construction, by 1973, when one of Henry Kissinger's destabilization projects had struck down the government, and put the project on the shelf. Involved in developing the design had been an American construction firm, and Edward Teller's work on the use of peaceful nuclear explosives for clearing through a high ridge.

Especially in the case, that Indonesia proceeds with an overdue development of efficient maritime transport among its islands, the Gulf of Thailand becomes a center of trade of one of the great population concentrations of the world, a region second only to China and the Indian subcontinent in human potential, and with vast primary resources. The present passage from East Asia into India, is through the constricted Straits of Malacca, including the most constricted Singapore Strait. One modern supertanker sunk at a key point, a not unlikely scenario from several standpoints, and this choke-point is out of business. A sea-level canal through the Songhla region of the Thailand isthmus, near the Malaysia border, is the ideal cut, providing not only a needed sea-level canal with a long-term future, but a natural basis for two valuable development sites at either extremity of the canal passage.

It had been proposed that I lend my moral support

to reviving this project. Before I could put my nose publicly into such an internal affair of Thailand, I must discuss the matter with my friends among influential Thais, and take soundings of the views of relevant functions of the government. The visit for this purpose, provided the occasion for overdue meetings on other accounts. Emotionally, I adopted Thailand as one of the countries taken to my heart; all the signs were, that I should proceed to help bring the idea of reviving the canal project up to the political threshold needed for the government to move toward a more serious commitment in the matter. I put some of the necessary next action on this matter high on my agenda for Tokyo.

It was my first visit to Tokyo, the capital of a nation which has not destroyed its own economy, as we Americans have destroyed ours, and as Western Europeans have been doing. One of my memorable meetings was with the Mr. Shigeo Nagano, long associated with Nippon Steel, and the founder of the effort to set a Pacific Basin development zone into operation more than twenty years earlier. Most unfortunately, he died before our next opportunity for meeting. Mr. Nagano had developed a friendship with Panama's Omar Torjillo, who named a mountain after Mr. Nagano, and they had worked out a plan for building a sea-level canal through the Panama isthmus. I wished to discuss this with my host, and also to sound him out on the possibility of economizing on the costs of constructing both the new Panama and the Songhla canal as coordinated construction efforts, as a way of reducing the costs of constructing each.

The Carter administration's negotiations of a Panama Canal treaty with the government of Panama, can only be described as clinically insane from the standpoint of either Panama's interests or those of the United States. For both military reasons, and also for the future of the Caribbean and U.S. Gulf and Atlantic seaboard regions, we require a sea-level canal through the Central American isthmus, urgently. The present lock canal was designed only to serve as a temporary canal when it was built, and is hopelessly inadequate for many major functions today. To make the construction of a sea-level canal reasonably economical on all counts, peaceful nuclear explosives technology is indispensable. It would open our eastern seaboards to maritime commerce in the Pacific, and also provide related benefits to Europe, Atlantic South America, and so forth. Neither U.S. naval interests nor the U.S. economy were important to Jimmy Carter or his administration; other things, some related to advancing the interests of drug trafficking and related money laundering, were.

If we define our national interests rightly, Japan's vital long-term interests and ours dovetail in a unique way. Japan must develop long-term, stable export markets, especially for capital goods, to ensure a stable supply of required imports. We ought to have an essentially common policy toward China, although there are significant differences in emphasis, and our long-range interests in the stability and development of what is called the Asiatic Rim are functionally consistent.

Poorly informed people may complain of Japan's commercial invasion of our domestic market, forgetting that Japan has been funding a large chunk of our federal debt, and that we, not Japan, have created the conditions which impel Japan to fill up some of the gaping and growing holes we are creating in our productive capacity with our "postindustrial" drift. If we cooperate with Japan, to develop third markets, through promoting development in relevant developing regions, we both benefit fairly, and to great advantage, especially over the long term.

I was not surprised by the technology of Japan's fusion energy research center; it is approximately on the level of Princeton's. What stunned me, most pleasurably, was the way in which Japan had organized its tokamak reactor program. The site was planned perfectly, in a way we no longer do in the United States. The execution of the installations would stir envy in most U.S. industrial managers who can still remember how things should be done. I was stunned by the new cyclotron at the entire city devoted to scientific research, shaking my head with shame for us at the optical fibers used and the way in which the test sites were organized. I was affected similarly, on my next trip to Japan, visiting the Laser Engineering Laboratory at Osaka university. Livermore people would have trouble concealing their envy: contractors who finish ahead of schedule, with quality standards above those specified, and price targets met. Japan is a very well organized society. My wife and I fed the giant carp in the hotel pool, sensing the way in which traditional Japan fits into industrial Japan; in my limited experience I have always sensed the two equally present, and sometimes I have had my sense of this confirmed in a more direct way.

Operation Juárez

I must turn back the clock now, to pick up the threads of developments leading into the Reagan administration's officially distancing itself from me during early 1984.

During early 1982, Britain's foreign minister, Lord Carrington, and U.S. Secretary of State Alexander Haig, were engaged in very devious undertakings. Carrington had been among Kissinger's controllers for such matters as Kissinger's Africa policy, when Henry had been secretary of state. Kissinger confessed to this, in a public address at London's Chatham House, during May 1982. Kissinger Associates was formed shortly after that Chatham House address, and Lord Carrington was prominent among the original set of associates. During early 1982, one of Carrington's devious undertakings was conniving with Haig to set up a war between Britain and Argentina over the Malvinas Islands.

One of Haig's projects was luring the Argentine government into supplying military forces for Central America. General Vernon Walters is familiar with the details. U.S. representatives promised the Argentina government that the U.S. government was so filled with love for Buenos Aires over the prospect of troops supplied to Central America, that the Reagan administration would back Buenos Aires against Britain, over the issue of Britain's return of the Malvinas Islands which Britain had stolen from Argentina in violation of the Monroe Doctrine, and renamed the Falkland Islands.

In that setting, Carrington aborted the negotiations between London and Buenos Aires. Buenos Aires, assuming that the U.S. promise would be kept, deployed its troops to occupy the islands in question. The junta had no intention of any shooting confrontation with Britain. The war happened because Haig double-crossed them. If the United States permitted a war between Argentina and Britain, the U.S. position in the entirety of Hispanic America would be placed at risk, to Soviet advantage. I proposed that the President must invoke the Monroe Doctrine.

Legally, the Malvinas had been the terrority of Buenos Aires at the time the 1823 Monroe Doctrine was promulgated. Britain had seized the islands by military force, in violation of the Monroe Doctrine, during the 1830s, and had deported the inhabitants of the islands in a particularly savage proceeding. Under U.S. law, the islands belonged to Argentina. For the same reason, the U.S. obligation to uphold Argentina's claim to title was clearly implicit, and partly explicit, in the terms of the Treaty of Rio de Janeiro, and several kindred treaties written into U.S. law during the preceding years. Thus, the U.S. promise to back the junta against Britain, on the issue of Argentina's legal claim, was simply an acknowledgement of the Reagan administration's intent to uphold U.S. law.

This crisis was set within another looming crisis, about to engulf Hispanic America as a whole. Actions by international agencies, with U.S. government backing, at the beginning of 1982, had plunged Hispanic America into a looming debt crisis.

The U.S. government's posture, in the course of the Malvinas war and later, that it regretted the character of the junta, was sheer hypocrisy on two other notable accounts related to the looming debt crisis. First, the administration had solicited the military assistance of the junta in Central America. Second, the junta had been placed in power and ordered to suppress youthful protests by Martinez de Hoz, a follower of one Raúl Prebisch. Martinez de Hoz, identified by the Argentina military as the author of the order to effect the "disappearances" of political dissidents, had done this in support of the monetary policy which the U.S. government, as well as Swiss bankers, had demanded. Kissinger was the relevant U.S. official most directly responsible for the establishment of the junta, and for insisting on the policy under which Martinez de Hoz had demanded the actions leading to the "disappearances."

In short, U.S. policy in the matter, stunk all the way from Kissinger, to Carrington, to Haig.

By one honorable deed, the United States could have saved its honor, and respected its own law. Instruct Britain that she shall not send forces of war against sovereign republics of the Americas, as the Monroe Doctrine and other relevant treaty law obliged the President to do. I stated the case in policy, interest, and law, most clearly, most emphatically, most accurately, and with the most accurate prophecy to boot.

The President bent to pressures, and did not act so. Now we have the Soviets taking over continental shelf rights in the region, and sundry complications which could have been avoided with a bit of respect for law and simple prudence.

Whatever of my warnings the Reagan administration preferred to disregard, one observation I made during that period captured the attention of people around the world.

To describe the strategic situation of Argentina, I announced the existence of a ticking "debt bomb" throughout Hispanic America. In the hustle and bustle over other matters, Washington and New York City appeared to overlook the fact that a tidal wave was about to sweep over the continent, sufficient to bring down the international banking system. My term, "debt bomb" entered the vocabulary during the summer of 1982, and has remained in use to the present time. Well it might remain; the debt bomb is bigger and more menacing than ever before.

I flew once again into Mexico City. This time, President Lopez Portillo and I met. The President arranged a press conference for me to address at the end of our meeting.

I briefed the President on the situation his country faced, and the general situation throughout the continent. The international bankers were going to move to take Mexico apart piece by piece, and he must expect the crisis to hit not later than September. I summarized the policy alternatives. In August, the crisis exploded. For a matter of several hours, the world banking system teetered on the edge of collapse. The crisis was stabilized by a telephone conversation between Reagan and Lopez Portillo. The collapse of the international banking system was avoided, but the problem which had nearly set off the crisis was growing worse day by day.

Later, during that same brief visit to Mexico, I met for breakfast with an old friend of ours. He spoke for various relevant interests in this matter, as well as concerned circles in Mexico itself. He put it this way. True, I had written many pieces on the subject of the debt crisis and its solution. The time had come to restate the analysis and policy options in a single book, which could be used by a wide assortment of concerned influentials of Hispanic America. I agreed, and when I returned to New York, pretty much locked myself away to write a book-length report which I entitled *Operation Juárez*. I delivered the document at the beginning of August. When the crisis struck, President Lopez Portillo's government moved to implement the key among the policy options I had identified.

Had President Reagan acted upon *Operation Juárez,* there would be no crisis in Central and South America today, and there would not have been four more years of collapse of the physical economy of the United States hanging in ruins around our necks today. Kissinger was deployed to Mexico. Amid other threats of bloody events, Kissinger demanded that no president of Mexico ever again meet with me personally. Argentina and Brazil dropped out of the alliance with Mexico. The looting of Mexico resumed at an accelerated tempo. The currency has been inflated by about 3,000 percent at my last count, and there is a process of ongoing collapse which brings up images of Hapsburg looting during the sixteenth century, and the murderous looting by the Hapsburg Emperor Maximilian during the 1860s.

The actions of the Reagan administration, in response to the "debt bomb" crisis, have crushed and looted a nation of approximately 70 million persons, Mexico, directly bordering the United States. These measures have savagely increased Mexico's debt, while lowering Mexico's ability to pay debt in an approximately equal degree. The United States put Mexico into national bankruptcy, and used brute force to oblige Mexico to adopt a "recovery" program whose effect has been to make Mexico vastly more bankrupt in 1986 than it was in autumn 1982.

The manufacturing and agriculture of Mexico have been collapsed massively as a direct result of the measures to which the U.S. government has forced Mexico to submit, time and time again, during this period. A relatively strong peso of the early 1980s has been turned into toilet paper, on orders of the New York banks, and with backing of persisting threats from the Reagan administration. The living standards have been savagely depressed, turning much of Mexico's population into a breeding culture for whatever epidemic diseases may choose to take advantage of this situation. Once any such epidemics have taken root in Mexico, they will pour across the northern border into the United States, carried not only by a massive back-and-forth of tourists across the Texas and California borders, but also by wealthy U.S. vacationers in Acapulco and Cuernavaca. Inside Mexico, the conditions for spreading pockets of famine and epidemic disease have now been established. More Mexicans could die because of the policies imposed by the Reagan administration, than the number of people who died in Hitler's concentration camps.

As for the Mexico debt crisis, the New York banks and Reagan administration (or, should we say the Regan-Kissinger administration?), the debt crisis throughout Central and South America is far worse today than it was in 1982. It has been made worse by the policies dictated to these nations by the Reagan administration. What is holding up some of the key banks in the United States, which are otherwise bankrupt, is the flow of debits originating in the combined flows of the international drug and weapons traffic; otherwise, the U.S. banking system as a whole, is itself bankrupt. The Reagan administration is responding to this internal crisis, by choosing which banks it will prop up, and which, larger portion of our nation's banks will simply be allowed to collapse, and be looted by the New York banks being propped up temporarily.

In 1982, I gave the Reagan administration a master plan for solving the debt crisis of the Americas. This master plan took the form of *Operation Juárez* plus a number of confidential, supplementary communications as background on some relevant matters internal to the United States, and military and other global-strategic implications of the choice between adopting the proposed measures, or rejecting them. The governments of the key Ibero-American nations were prepared to accept these measures immediately, and to act with our government in these matters.

Today, there is no doubt that this plan would have succeeded. There is no doubt that the opposing policies, which the administration adopted, have been such a monstrous failure that the word "incompetence" does not even begin to describe the U.S. policies involved. More broadly, the policies which were adopted have such a depressing effect upon the economies of the Americas, and of Western Europe, that the western allies are now approaching a point of no return in our capacity to resist the strategic expansion by the Soviet empire.

The myth of economic recovery

The most frightening aspect of this and similar cases, is not that the Reagan administration has made major blunders, but that it refuses to recognize that these policies were blunders, even when the evidence is so massive.

My own forecasts, especially those of the 1970s and 1980s, are well known to international banking circles and to the U.S. government. Although the government insists that GNP data show a monetary expansion of the U.S. economy, the government knows that to call such a monetary expansion an "economic recovery" is to ignore the accelerating collapse of the physical economy of not only the United States, and the entirety of the Americas, but of Western Europe and other places as well.

It knows that the budgetary crisis is a result of nothing but a collapse of the U.S. internal economy, to a degree that in more than thirty of the fifty states today, the relative degree of collapse of agriculture, industry, infrastructure, and the relative extent and degree of poverty, are as bad as or worse than conditions during the 1930s.

Excepting two categories, after adjusting for inflation, the levels of federal spending per capita are below those of the 1970s. If we use a 1968 market-basket standard to measure inflation, defense spending under President Reagan has been below levels under Carter-Mondale. The only two categories in which net federal spending has been rising per capita, is in debt service and what are called entitlements, the latter typified by federal pensions. The trends in levels of state and local expenditures echo those in federal expenditures. Yet, the prevailing argument in the administration and Congress, has been that skyrocketing levels of federal budgetary deficits are caused by excessive governmental spending.

There are two causes for the rise of per capita cost of entitlements. The first cause is demographic. The drop in the birthrate over the past twenty years, plus the shift out of higher-paying to much-lower-paying employment, and unemployment, have increased the ratio of persons who are past retirement age, to the number of persons employed in production of physical output. The growth in debt service accounts for about two-thirds of the margin of federal budget deficit. The chief cause for this, is continuation of the policies which President Carter and Federal Reserve Chairman Paul Volcker introduced in October 1979.

The administration and Congress have concentrated considerable efforts on the attempt to slash payments for entitlements. Since bipartisanship died on the White House carpet, during mid-1981, no effort has been made to attack the more massive problem of growth of terms of payment of debt service. Most of the cuts made under Gramm-Rudman-Hollings, and similar philosophy of practice, have had the net effect of lowering the revenues of the federal government, by large cuts into areas which stimulate higher levels of activity in the physical economy.

After we deduct the amount of the deficit caused entirely by refinancing U.S. debt under the terms established by Jimmy Carter and Paul Volcker, the rest of the federal deficit is entirely the result of a deepening decline in the taxable income of businesses and family households. Under the Reagan administration, from January 1981 to December 1986, the U.S. federal debt has zoomed, from about $800 billion under Carter, to more than $2 trillion. At least half of the $1.2 trillion increase of federal debt under Reagan, was caused by Reagan continuing the Volcker policies introduced by Carter. The remaining portion of the federal deficits, and increased federal debt, must be blamed entirely on President Reagan and his administration. Under Reagan economic policies, the U.S. tax-revenue base has been falling, as the physical foundation of the economy has continued to collapse.

Take a typical $30,000 family income, a low-moderate income for a family of four, by 1986 standards. Examine what this $30,000 buys, by comparison with 1968. Break total purchases into three groups. The first group, is made up of basic physical goods: food, housing, home furnishings, public utilities payments, clothing, and transportation. The second group is made up of certain classes of essential services: education and medical care chiefly. Do not include in either the financial charges for use of consumer credit, or mortgages, in making these purchases, but only the amount paid to the seller of such goods and services. Do not include sales taxes or taxes generally. The third group is "other": anything, including taxes, spent for anything but the first two categories of purchases.

Then, taking a $30,000 annual income for such a family of four as a standard for comparison, look at household-income trends over the period 1969–1986. For both 1968 and 1986, break income-levels down into a few classes. For example: 1) Below absolute minimum subsistence standards of nutrition, housing, and medical care; 2) Very poor; 3) Poor; 4) Low-moderate; 5) Moderate (about $40,000 for a family of four in 1986); 6) High-moderate (about $50,000–60,000 in 1986); 7) High; 8) Very wealthy. What percentile of total households falls into each classification in 1968, and in 1986? Now, compare the breakdown for 1938 with that of 1968.

In more than thirty of the fifty states, the United States is in an economic depression. Under Reagan, the United States slid into a depression at about 5 percent a year during 1983–1984, at a slightly higher rate during 1985, and by about 15 percent or more during 1986.

The situation is much worse than household purchases

of the two primary groups of physical goods and services suggest. How much of total households' purchases represents purchases made with borrowed money, rather than purchases out of income? What would the average purchases be, if there were no large-scale use of credit-card "money" and similar forms of credit?

About 60 percent or slightly more of the world's total debt is indebtedness of the United States' public and private institutions and households. Taking only the portion of debt which is linked to the international monetary system, the indebtedness of the United States is about ten times greater than the indebtedness of all developing nations combined. That illusion of "prosperity" in President Reagan's speeches, over the years 1983 through the end of 1986, is based entirely on the growth of U.S. debt, under conditions of a collapse of real income levels.

So, the portion of after-inflation-adjustment income which is the tax-revenue base for federal, state, and local government, has been shrinking rapidly over the 1980–1986 period. The chief cause of this has been the combined effect of what are called Volcker's policies inside the United States, combined with U.S. support of the policies of the International Monetary Fund.

The first regular Quarterly Economic Forecast issued by the *Executive Intelligence Review*, was issued in December 1979. This first forecast calculated the effects of the policies which Carter and Volcker had introduced during October of that year. When would a recession come to the surface as a direct result of those policy changes? *EIR* said February 1980; it happened so. How deep would the first wave of recession be? *EIR* saw it continuing through the summer. In September 1983, *EIR* completed a comparison of *EIR*'s quarterly forecasts with both U.S. government forecasts and those published by *EIR*'s leading private competitors. The forecasts of the U.S. government and the private competitors were wildly off the mark, missing both the direction of trends, and levels of economic activity, even by the crude standard of U.S. government National Income Accounting data. *EIR* had called every shift in trends, and had been remarkably close to the mark in forecasting volumes.

The same comparative performance has continued since. If some well-known leading experts have been consistently right, and the government's and competing private experts consistently wrong, but government continues to base its policies on the methods of forecasting used by experts who have been consistently wrong, how do government's policy makers stand up? On economic policy, award the Reagan administration a straight "F" grade.

The cause of the federal deficits, is the collapse of the physical economy of the United States. Did the President or the Congress do anything to attack that cause of the problem? They proposed to cut the federal budget, instead, but the cuts in the budget could not keep up with the rate at which the tax revenue base was collapsing. For the sake of defending the Reagan economic policies, which had consistently failed, the administration and Congress increase the misery of growing numbers of Americans, in order to "save the President's economic agenda"!

Of course, the Reagan administration did not invent the policies of looting imposed on Central and South America over the 1982–1986 period. It was the international bankers who demanded those policies. The Reagan administration merely acted under orders from those bankers, through channels of such bankers' agents in the administration as former treasury secretary and White House Chief of Staff Donald T. Regan. To understand what happened, to cause the Reagan administration to reject my *Operation Juárez* option in 1982, and bring in Kissinger Associates to shape U.S. policy instead, we must not assume that the motives of the bankers and the motives of the Reagan administration were identical. The bankers and the administration combined their efforts to produce a single result, but the motives of each were different.

Circumstances permit me to identify the Reagan administration's own motives precisely. During most of 1982 into about March 1983, there was a raging policy fight within the administration, with Treasury's Donald Regan the point man for the bankers' policies. Some thought that my analysis of the "debt bomb," during the spring of 1982, had been brilliant thinking; I had recognized a major development which most in government had missed. My *Operation Juárez* was recognized as a workable solution to the crisis, and leading forces in Central and South America trusted me, at a time when they had lost confidence in the good will of Washington generally. It was clear that Central and South America were ready to enter immediately into the kinds of new agreements set forth in *Operation Juárez*.

There were two pressures on the administration, through which the faction of Kissinger and Donald Regan won out. The first, was the pressure from the bankers, and from those Eastern Establishment forces with which Reagan had cut a preelection deal during 1980. I remembered Costas Kalimtgis' slogan of "We must save Computron at all costs." The word around the administration was, "We must save the bankers at all costs." The second pressure was the President's own simplistically ideological thinking on economic matters. The argument which seemed to persuade the President, was that my solution was clearly workable, but "dirigistic," inconsistent with Adam Smith's dogma of the "Invisible Hand."

The President capitulated in October 1982; but the policy fight within the administration continued. The fight ended about April 1983. What turned the President completely against the kinds of policies I proposed, was his belief that the new figures showed the U.S. economy in a recovery. Donald Regan and Henry Kissinger were "in" solidly.

Kissinger wanted desperately to be appointed to the President's Foreign Intelligence Advisory Board (PFIAB). Kissinger needed this, not only because he needed the prestigious position as sales promotion for his private firm, Kissinger Associates. Members of PFIAB have access to top secrets of all branches of government, and a substantial, if intangible influence on functions of government. Kissinger wanted to detect and crush out of existence every channel of influence I might have had around Washington. PFIAB would give him the information and influence to launch such an effort.

Putting Kissinger into any corner of the administration was politically delicate. Reagan had once promised loudly never to allow Kissinger anywhere near an administration of his. The President waited until a long quiet summer's weekend to make the appointment. Kissinger promptly organized his cronies on PFIAB to back up his effort, and demanded that the FBI launch a covert operation against me and my friends that same summer. The Kissinger channels of Soviet influence were officially positioned within U.S. policy shaping, and my influence was presumably on the way out.

So, although the President announced the Strategic Defense Initiative on March 23, 1983, by early during the following month of April, the initial commitment to immediately implementing SDI was weakened, my influence was greatly weakened, and Kissinger was coming back in rapidly. The SDI was kept out of the 1984 Reagan reelection campaign, up until the second of the President's televised "debates" with Walter Mondale, and the SDI lost political momentum greatly as a result of this election-campaign policy's influence on the administration and Congress.

As of about April 1983, or shortly after that, the President decided to base his reelection campaign on the assumption that the appearance of an "economic recovery" could be sold as a prevailing popular perception at least until after the November 1984 general election. Deals were cut with Donald Regan and Paul Volcker's Wall Street friends, to ensure that the financial centers did nothing which would tend to undermine popular belief in an "economic recovery" during the span of the election campaign. For these deals, the President paid a political price.

Two almost simultaneous actions were launched during April 1983, in an effort to undermine and kill the SDI. The most publicized was the report of the Scowcroft Commission. Less publicized, but more important for the long run, was Paul Volcker's launching a demand for what became the Gramm-Rudman-Hollings legislation.

Brent Scowcroft is known around Washington as "a Kissinger clone." During the fag-end of the U.S. war in Indochina, Kissinger had used his position at the National Security Council to recruit faithful servants from among U.S. military professionals. Alexander Haig, Kissinger's deputy at NSC, was helpful in this effort. So was Kissinger's old sponsor, Fritz Kraemer, seated in a key position over at the Pentagon. In addition to the "career management" opportunities which Kissinger could arrange for military professionals around Washington, through his patrons in the Eastern Establishment, Kissinger has the ability to buy people with such accommodations as well-paid lecture tours, and other forms of manna not exactly from Heaven bestowed on the material well-being and social status of professionals, and the family's members. The practice reached beyond professionals on duty in Vietnam. Brent Scowcroft's present career is typical of those military "Faustians" who have more or less sold their souls to Kissinger's circles. The Scowcroft Commission itself was typical of the sort of political plum handed to those in Kissinger's good graces.

The presentation of the Scowcroft Commission's April 1983 report was tailored in its last weeks of preparation to serve as a propaganda attack on the flanks of the just-stated SDI policy. The proposed substitution of the Midgetman missile, for the capable, much-needed MX, was a real favor to the Soviets, and must be seen as the original purpose of the commission's report. However, the propaganda output associated with the submission of the report, was directed at destroying political momentum for the SDI, specifically to fostering misguided resistance to SDI among the Pentagon's military branches and civilian bureaucracy.

Just prior to Volcker's April initiative, my friends' news agency had picked up on Soviet deployments against SDI into Western Europe. The Soviets were discovered advising influentials among western opponents of the SDI, that, rather than limiting efforts to taking on the SDI directly, politically, more reliance should be placed on destroying the SDI by chopping away the U.S. military budget. Within a week of our completing a preliminary gridding of such Soviet efforts, Paul Volcker was lobbying for a campaign in the direction of what became Gramm-Rudman-Hollings.

Paul Volcker's views on the Soviets I do not know to this day. Volcker has a long track record of association with Secretary of State George Shultz in launching and managing the new monetary system brought into being during August 1971. Shultz's autobiography claims that Shultz was the chief architect of the 1972 Azores and 1975 Rambouillet monetary summits, where the "floating exchange-rate system" was consolidated. Shultz exaggerates, although he played an important bureaucrat's role from the U.S. side. Volcker's role was also significant. In more recent years in public life, Volcker's principal function has been to implement a set of policies designed for the Carter administration by a special 1975–1976 commission of the New York Council on Foreign Relations, a set of policies later published as a series of volumes under the rubric *Project 1980s*. Volcker's role since he campaigned for appointment to the Federal Reserve chairmanship, in the spring and summer of 1979, has emphasized the monetary and economic policies set forth in the report of that commission, policies which that commission, and Volcker, have identified by the label "controlled disintegration of the economy."

Whether a taint of direct Soviet influence played a part

in Volcker's actions of April 1983, I do not know. What he proposed, in his lobbying campaign that month, might also be fully explained as consistent with Volcker's continuing commitment to "controlled disintegration of the economy." Volcker's actions may, therefore, have been a coincidence. There is no coincidence in the Eastern Establishment's pushing and continued backing of Gramm-Rudman: The defense budget, and especially the SDI, have been the consistent target of Gramm-Rudman advocates from the beginning.

In February and March of 1983, we collaborated with the office of Prime Minister Indira Gandhi, and other relevant leading figures of the Non-Aligned Nations, to launch a new effort for international monetary reforms. Two factions sought to sabotage the efforts at the New Delhi Non-Aligned conference: a large section of the British Commonwealth representation, and the Soviet agents. Fidel Castro, always a maverick by instinct, and sensitive to the moods of Hispanic America as a whole, was inclined to adopt our proposals, but the Soviets agents, including those in Cuba, vetoed that in the strongest terms.

Sooner or later, the United States government must come around to my policies on this matter, or we shall have the worst world depression in modern centuries. I keep working to bring that needed change in policy about.

Mrs. Gandhi and President Reagan had begun to discuss these matters earlier, during the summit at Cancun, Mexico, but the White House and State Department bureaucracy, passionately anti-Gandhi, were determined that Mrs. Gandhi and the President would not become involved in serious discussions of any sort.

Any head of state, especially those of major nations, leads a very isolated life. In every case, the head of state is surrounded by a Byzantine sort of palace guard, bureaucrats whose minds function on about the same level as the concubines and eunuchs of an oriental palace's harem. What the President is allowed to read, and precisely what words, what turns of phrase, what emphases, and which not, shall reach the President's eyes and ears, reach such extremes, that a faction fight in the bureaucracy can erupt over the including of not merely a single paragraph or sentence, but the inclusion and placing of a noun, adjective, or adverb. Who is permitted to meet the President, even whose name shall be mentioned in his presence, is very high on the list of means by which palace guards seek to brainwash the chief executive. What bureaucrat shall sit in whose meeting with the chief executive, sometimes even to censor the President's line of conversation, to change the subject of conversation, to "gently remind," and to sabotage under-standings reached, by bureaucratic means applied after-ward, is very, very high on the list of manipulative arrangements. There is very little in the President's social surroundings which is sincere, or even real.

For that reason, I place great importance on direct meetings, one to one, between heads of states and their governments. Bypass the foreign ministers and diplomats as much as possible. Among the statesmen of the world during her time, Mrs. Gandhi had the highest rank in personal qualities of intellect and knowledge, in addition to being the leader of the second largest nation in the world, a nation which is a superpower in the Indian Ocean region. Unlike most leaders of governments today, who are largely figureheads outside of a very narrow area of decision mak-ing, Mrs. Gandhi actually governed, shaping her own pol-icies, and able to formulate a policy coherently, as almost no elected heads of government today even attempt to, or could do. Were she alive, and I President, that extraordi-nary little woman was one with whom I would have wished to review the formulation of crucial aspects of U.S. foreign policy in most areas of the world.

If President Reagan could achieve an accurate sense of what this woman was, what she actually represented, in world outlook, commitments, and capabilities, he and the U.S. presidency would have been strengthened in a very considerable degree. Years before she succeeded her father, Pandit Jawaharlal Nehru, Mrs. Gandhi had been a dinner guest at a collection of notables attending Charles de Gaulle. On that occasion, she delivered a report in fluent French, which evoked the astonished admiration of de Gaulle and the others present.

She was thoroughly a statesman of the highest rank during our century, and also a mother. She loved her sons, and those grandchildren of hers. She read *Fusion,* the magazine of the Fusion Energy Foundation. As a statesman, she was personally committed to those topics in shaping the science and technology policy of her nation. We had the privilege of consulting with her and working with her relevant key people on such projects. As a mother, she directed the youth supplement section of that publication to those grandchildren. She combined this strong sense of family and statesmanship, in the form of a habit of gauging her decisions and policies of today to their consequences for the future of India. She wished to be a friend to President Reagan; it is unfortunate that that sort of collaboration was not permitted to develop.

How our government is run

There is the popularized myth, that I am preoccupied with "conspiracy theories." Much of this originates with members of the Eastern Establishment, who are therefore simply liars when they deny that the most important events in the world are organized through what are fairly described as "conspiracies." Marxist Professor Herbert Marcuse used to begin his series of lectures in Germany, with the assertion that "There are no conspiracies in history." That is standard Soviet "historical materialism," that everything is controlled in the final analysis by the *Zeitgeist,* and, in the lesser degree by those factors of "human nature" recognized by Marxian forms of materialism. One might wonder, therefore, why the Soviets expend so much effort on conspiracies, and why Marcuse devoted his life to operating as part of sundry conspiracies. The circles of wealthy families which exert hegemonic power over nations in the West, and the ruling families of the Soviet oligarchy, the *Nomenklatura,* arrange things through conspiracies most of the time. They believe in the efficacy of conspiracy, obviously: However, they do not wish the general public to understand how these matters work—the enraged public might rouse itself to spoil the conspiratorial games.

You, the ordinary citizen, live most of your private life like a goldfish in a bowl. You have freedom, in greater or lesser degree, to decide which direction you may choose to swim in that bowl. You become accustomed to limiting your attention to those smaller matters over which you can exert personal control; you become accustomed to accepting the proposition that a mysterious agency, which you usually refer to as "they" or "them," determines whether you are moved to a slightly larger or a slightly smaller fish bowl of life, and whether the fish bowl is moved to a sunnier and warmer, or more unpleasant location. Today, if life in the fish bowl becomes unpleasant, or merely unsufferably boring, you can escape of your own free will at almost any time, by turning on the television set, which is entertaining one or more members of the family approximately a dozen hours a day.

Then, between 30 to 40 percent of you adults vote on election days. You vote for candidates, as you believe that you may be placing a candidate in a position of power to control the conditions of your private fish bowl, or simply because you would vote for almost anyone you see with a chance of winning, simply to punish the fellow you helped to elect during the preceding election. The rest of you do not vote; you sense that it makes no difference, that "they" will manage to do as they please, either way. If a majority among you who do vote cast ballots for a certain candidate, that candidate is not necessarily elected. Vote fraud commonly runs to a margin above 5 percent these days, and often much higher. Yet, you wish to believe that, through ballot-democracy, you do exert some significant control over the policy making of our government.

You do exert influence, although most among you do not understand the way in which your vote can count for something. Your influence is negative. Sometimes, the powers-that-be find it prudent to allow the voters to choose between two candidates, each of which is acceptable to those powers. Those powers would usually prefer to have their policies carried out by a candidate who happens to be popular, than one with less ballot charisma. Only when the public is in a very ugly mood, might those powers allow a majority to elect a candidate of which they do not approve—"Let him be elected, and let us deal with the problem afterward," they will instruct one another, when it seems imprudent to enrage popular opinion.

The public is slipping into a very ugly mood today. A majority might succeed in electing me President, in 1988, for example, although the Eastern Establishment and the party machines which they control definitely disapprove of me and will do everything possible to have me dead, preferably dying conveniently in prison, to have me out of circulation before the spring primaries of 1988. The signs of the growing ugliness in the public mood were clear in the November 1986 elections. The public is fed up, enraged, with the President's insistence that a great "economic upsurge" is in progress. The Republicans are becoming about as popular as Herbert Hoover in 1932; one might wonder why any Republican presidential candidates might be thinking of campaigning for their party's 1988 nomination. Given present directions, the next President will be a Democratic candidate, one committed to economic recovery policies as dirigistic as President Franklin Roosevelt's 1940–1943 recovery measures.

A growing portion of the powers-that-be already know this, and even sections of the Eastern Establishment are now preparing themselves for a Democratic President with policies not too far distant from my own today. Twenty years of a "post-industrial" drift, away from manufacturing investments, into low-waged service employment, has proven itself a catastrophe. Even some who were ready to enter into a "New Yalta" agreement with the Soviet monster, have become aware of the real intentions behind Premier Mikhail Gorbachov's public-relations smile. Among the higher echelons of the trans-Atlantic power establishment as a whole, there are developments in progress of a type which have not been seen in those ranks since the 1938–1940 period, during that period when Roosevelt and the British establishment agreed there had to be a war against Nazi Germany, and when the British establishment gradually awakened to the dimensions of that war they had chosen earlier.

Frankly, I don't think it at all probable that World War III will break out under the next U.S. President. We must act as if such a war were in the process of breaking-out; the Soviets are in a prewar mobilization aimed at just such a probability. I think more likely than war, is that we might surrender to Soviet world-domination during the next two years, or, as an alternative, that the West will mobilize to such a degree that the danger of a general war is delayed for a decade or more, and, one might hope, indefinitely. The former of the two alternatives has been greatly shrunken in popularity among the ranks of the power establishment during the course of the past two years, especially so since President Reagan came within an SDI inch of surrendering Western Europe to Moscow at the October Reykjavik "summit." The trend of shifts in factional alignments among the ranks of the trans-Atlantic power establishment, is toward policy orientations consistent with the second of the two options.

By approximately the second half of 1987, I shall either be on my way to being eliminated personally from the scene, or shall be on the way to probable election as President in 1988. If the majority of the power establishment decides upon the second alternative, they shall have to come to agreement on a presidential candidate able to carry through such a policy. Within that faction of the establishment, the dispute will be over two kinds of choices of presidential candidate.

Some might choose a figurehead candidate, such as a Gary Hart for example. Reach down into the ranks of available candidates, and select a suitable dummy. Make this dummy popular, through the usual sort of public-relations buildup, and put him in the White House. Condition him beforehand to the kinds of policy directions he will represent, and surround him with a body of cabinet officers and palace guard, which actually translate policy into the form of decisions this elected dummy will be guided to carry out. The usual sort of selected presidential candidate, such as a Jimmy Carter.

Truman was not a dummy in every respect, of course, but he was totally incompetent in strategic and foreign policy matters, and easily controlled on all important matters. Eisenhower was capable in his own way, but he was picked because he had proven his political adaptability during the war, and was not likely to take his nominal access to great powers of the presidency too seriously. Kennedy was associated with some very positive actions, as well as some cowardly ones; his father, Joseph Kennedy, was no dummy, but Jack was a mental lightweight. Johnson was a wheeler-dealer, with no apparent interest in the serious aspects of strategic policy. Richard Nixon had been broken to harness by the time of his 1968 candidacy.

The President represents great powers, especially under conditions of crisis. These powers a President might be tempted to use, as Franklin Roosevelt did, and in ways in which might not altogether please the establishment. Therefore, a prospective presidential candidate with the knowledge, experience, and temperament for effective sorts of independent leadership, is ordinarily one the establishment will seek to eliminate long before his name might reach the floor of a nominating convention. The establishment seeks to ensure its continued control over the Executive Branch of government, and wishes no President who might have the knowledge and inclination to take the U.S. Constitution too literally. You see, our Constitution makes no allowance for an establishment more powerful than elected government itself.

So, men who are content to enjoy the prestige of being President, even a virtual figurehead President, are much preferred in relevant circles of power. Just to take the sting out of the status of being a figurehead, the President is allowed two things. As far as the public is concerned, he will always appear to be in charge. He will also be permitted to introduce a few of his own pet ideas as policy, provided these do not conflict seriously with those several few policy areas of vital interest to the establishment.

The first impulse of the establishment, is to assemble a short list of politically salable figureheads. That would be the end of the matter this time around, except for one reason. The question arises in these circles: "Can we risk using a figurehead?" This is the worst crisis in the twentieth century; can a presidency built around a figurehead cope with those kinds of challenges? The hardliners of the power establishment are inclined to a real President, not just another choice of figurehead. If that view prevails, I shall probably become the next President. If the opposite view prevails, I might be eliminated from the political scene rather soon, my admirers within the establishment sadly regretting the loss of my useful talents on the scene.

The issue is not merely who is President for the coming four, or even eight years. It is a matter of how our government and much of civilization, is going to be managed over the coming twenty years or more. This brings us back to the subject of the way our government is actually run.

Over nearly all of known history of Europe and the Americas, governments have been managed from behind the scenes by something which might be called a "power elite." It happens, that in the founding of our republic, under George Washington, this power elite and visible government were essentially one and the same. It has not been the same since. The change built up gradually under the Presidents who followed Washington; behind-the-scenes power elites have controlled government since the 1870s.

Our power elite is not a body of uniform interests and opinions. It is a collection of power blocs, each with rather distinct outlooks and policy-making inclinations. Among these power blocs, a kind of pragmatic accommodation has developed. They usually hold in check their endemic inclination to eliminate the other factions entirely from power, and, as the saying goes, "learn to work with one another." It is the usual arrangement in most parts of the world today.

The structure of the power elite is composed of chiefly two elements. The power rests in the control of what might be described as the relevant "interest groups." However, being of great wealth or other sorts of power, does not necessarily enable one to think very well. So, each faction of the power elite, selects a smaller body of persons deemed qualified to perform the function of thinking. These may be members of the powerful to perform the function of thinking. These may be members of the powerful families who are the principal components of the power-elite faction, or they may be selected, hired, groomed, educated, conditioned, and so forth. In feudal times, talented figures from religious orders frequently performed the functions of the special committee to which serious thinking was assigned. Around Venice, for example, the institution of the *fondo* was established, a sort of feudal financial corporation, in which the heirs were more the assets than the owners of the corporation. The *fondo* was actually directed by figures whose functions resemble somewhat a corporate executive, but with much greater personal power than any modern corporate executive.

Below the social level of these two strata of the power elite itself, there are the useful errand-runners, the status of a Henry Kissinger, for example. Henry does not actually do any serious thinking; he is too preoccupied with stealing large sums of wealth and personal prestige, to concentrate in the way required to work through policies. He is too self-interested to think about long-range policy matters. It is the errand-runners who tend to be publicly visible, and who are sometimes mistaken for the thinking portion of the elite by credulous popular opinion. The thinkers are usually found only in the background, rarely in the gossip columns. If they surface in the public, they usually appear in the guise of top figures of major law firms or in a comparable role; they represent real political power in the guise of appearing to be above it.

The interplay among the factions of the power elite, is the real policy-making structure of government, an agency which remains in control, as Presidents come and go.

From the standpoint of the trans-Atlantic power elite as a whole, the recent escalation of strategic and related economic crises signifies that the policy-making structure has failed. By its success in imposing a certain direction in policy over the course of the postwar period, especially the past twenty years, we have successfully a state of affairs which is most unpleasant to a majority of the power elite as a whole. This elite is not so blind to reality, as to fail to recognize that no way out of this mess exists, unless the policy-making structure is drastically altered. To accomplish this, the structure of the power elites must be reorganized. Possibly, no such reorganization can be effected except from the outside.

At various exceptional points in the past 2,500 years, power elites have gone through structural reorganizations effected through outsiders. The idea is by no means a new one. It is an idea being debated among relevant circles on both sides of the Atlantic today.

Our constitutional system of government made a special provision for this sort of reorganization of the elites, in the course of debating such things as the choice between an elected monarch and a presidential head of state. The four-year presidential term is potentially the ideal instrument through which the structure of the power elite can be reorganized. One of the advantages is, that the President leaves after the end of his elected terms. So, his long-range decisions must be made for the advantage of the nation, rather than as to the advantage of himself or the particular faction he happens chiefly to represent.

That is our present system of government at its best. Don't start a war-dance, screaming against elitism and demanding some radical sort of democracy. Our system of government has always been, at its most democratic, a form of representative government. The electorate has the right to choose how it is to be represented. I favor a more democratic form of government than this one; I fight for the kind of reforms in our educational system which qualify secondary-school graduates to understand policy, and thus to exert a more powerful and direct influence on our nation's policy making. If you desire that, as I do, we shall have to build things up appropriately, with special emphasis on creating the qualified teachers, who presently do not exist generally, and in the textbooks and curricula of our public schools. In the meantime, our nation and you, require a government whose actions truly represent your interests and those of coming generations, too.

You have been ruled by an elitist system all your life. Some among you may have objected to this in words, but you have always acted in a way which demands that government be elected and function in just this way. The place to begin, if you wish to make it more democratic, is to make government more representative, by grooming and electing prospective candidates for public office who are the top elite of people with your interest, who can really think through policy, and who must come back to you and give a direct accounting of what they have done in office. If they don't measure up, replace them.

Among all of the power elite, the idea of my being President scares them almost to death. What frightens them has nothing to do with that lying propaganda about me you have seen or heard in most of the news media. They wonder what their power and influence will be under the new organization of our policy-making structures. Put to the wall, a majority of the power elite are not afraid of what I might do as the acts of a President are ordinarily identified. Their concern is how I might reorganize the policy-making structure as it functions ten or twenty years or so ahead. They are not afraid that I might make myself king, or some sort of dictator. Most of the elite have no fear, as a group, of the policies I would implement. Some of it would be tough medicine for some parts of the power blocs, but they know that there is no way to avoid tough medicine of one sort or another, if we are to get out of the presently worsening mess. They are not afraid of me; they are afraid of what they know must be done, even were I not there to do it. The idea of putting the power structure itself through a reorganization, is frightening for the same reason that it is a change.

They fear also that perhaps I am the only person in sight who possesses the tested capabilities for doing what must be done. Such a chore requires a President who understands the long-range implications of a reorganization of the policy-making structure itself. The thinking required is analogous in form to the way the "hereditary principle" of axiomatics expresses itself in the elaboration of successive constructions, in a constructive geometry. For such work, a pragmatist is worse than useless; this is the work suited only to a President who is also a philosopher. I am the only representative of such a breed of political leader today. Either they accept living with my philosophy, or perhaps the lack of any other qualified philosopher means that they have no alternate choice. It is that lack of alternate choice which infuriates and frightens many among them.

My Marriage to Helga 8

My wife was born Helga Zepp, in Trier, the oldest city of Germany, on August 25, 1948. She was the only child of two sweethearts who married immediately after the war, and was born in the darkest moment of postwar German history, during the period of savage hunger called the "Potato Winter" by Americans, and usually referred to among Germans as the "Rubenwinter." When her father died, Helga was supported by her mother, with daytime care provided by help of her mother's aunt and uncle, the latter a skilled restorer of the artwork of cathedrals. Helga became an orphan shortly after completing her gymnasium studies, and has only one known surviving relative today.

Her gymnasium education was a blend of German classical education and pre-scientific training. Her later position as a scholar in the work of Friedrich Schiller and the Prussian reformers, was grounded in a rigorous gymnasium training in Schiller's work. She also qualified for the German equivalent of academic honors in sports.

She went from gymnasium into training as a journalist. When she had completed the training, she went directly into a freelance undertaking, and became the first European journalist to visit China after the peak of the Cultural Revolution. She sold her story after her return, and refused a position with the newsweekly *Der Spiegel,* to undertake higher studies in political science and philosophy at Berlin. It was there, in 1972, that she first intersected my orbit, attending a class on the subject of my work in economics given by Uwe von Parpart.

One incident from the time immediately prior to her coming into my orbit, is both typical of her and characterizes the state of mind which brought her into contact with von Parpart's lectures. She attended a Berlin event organized by admirers of Mao-tse Tung. An address eulogizing the state of affairs in China was delivered by a spokesman for the Maoist students. Helga went to the microphone during the discussion period.

"I have just returned from three months in China."

Hysterical approbation from the assembled multitude.

Addressing the speaker, Helga quickly presented the second of her two sentences: "Nothing of what you have said about China is true."

Hysterical disapprobation.

The curiosity about this strange American provoked the Germans associated with such classes on my economics work, to resolve on sending a delegation to the United States, to inspect this curious fellow at closer range, and to report back. So, the first delegation of such "visiting firemen" from Germany arrived in New York from the Rhineland in 1972. Later, a second group, this time from Berlin, resolved to visit the United States to check up on the accuracy of the report delivered by the first group. This group stayed for a course I was giving at the time, with various jaunts between those classes. They arrived to pick up on the spring 1973 semester, and left shortly after its completion. Helga was among this group.

I had only perfunctory contact with them at first, apart from their attendance at the course on Columbia campus. Toward the close of their visit, two sessions of the group's members with me were arranged. The two sessions were spaced at about two weeks apart; the first was a working seminar on research projects, the second a final meeting before departure.

In the course of their stay, the delegation had resolved to do something in Germany along the lines of the Labor Committees' work in the United States. It was suggested to them, that they begin with studies of certain of the determining parameters of the current situation in their country. Various projects were defined. Helga's was the social structure of employment. The first of the two sessions was arranged to review these research projects.

The discussion of her topic was the first indication to me that she had extraordinary potential as a real leader. At a later time, when she asked me for a personal perspective on her work back in Europe, I responded: "You must take personal responsibility for the fate of Europe and Germany." Only that attitude of mind can build a viable sort of political association, but very few people can accept the psychological implications of such a personal commitment, to commit themselves to this sort of sense of personal identity. I was convinced either that Helga could adopt this sense of identity, or there was the risk that the failure to do so would break her to the extent of precluding the variety of activity which the Labor Committees' style of functioning implies.

I have said that to a few persons, but very few. My own habits of thought incline me to pay more attention to the way in which a person thinks, than the particular opinions they express. I seek the "policy-making structure" in the person's mind, so to speak. By long experience, I am extraordinarily good at that sort of perception. Sometimes, a very clear image is seen. Rarely, I meet individuals in which this quality of the mind is developed to a special intensity of coherence. This I find in accomplished scientific leaders, and analogous cases; usually, these are persons of established creative accomplishment and related achievements. Sometimes, I meet this in a younger person. Ordinarily, I will ask a serious person to face the question of what they wish to make of their lives. Once in a while, the distinctive mind-set of exceptional potential for political leadership is to be seen. In Helga's case, I was certain.

On several occasions, she has related the effect of that advice. At first, her impulse was to run as far from me and that frightening thought as possible. Then, shortly after returning to Berlin, while she was walking her dog in her favorite site there, the area of the Charlottenburger Schloss, she fought the idea through, and came from the walk resolved to adopt that sense of personal identity.

The effects of the decision showed during the meetings at Münchrath, in early summer 1973. In the situation around the case I described earlier, she and Michael Liebig performed an important part in the debriefing, while Uwe Friesecke took a key role in organizing the practical arrangements. The different roles that these three, and others there, assumed in that emergency situation, provided to be indications of some of the specialized roles each of the three assumed in the leadership of the European Labor Committees afterward. I met her briefly again, with several others of the group which at been at Münchrath, during my trip to Reggio Emilia and Milan.

She visited the United States again, for the Labor Committees' conference at the end of 1973. Under the circumstances, we had little occasion to exchange many words. What I recall most vividly was her report of a conversation with Greg Rose, out of which she concluded that his pathological streak worried her. Her observation contributed to my closer scrutiny of the matter, and to the two passing developments which caught my attention, and proved to me that this fellow was to be placed under much closer scrutiny.

During 1974, she assumed a leading role among the group in Europe. But that involves events beyond the scope of my autobiography. During that year, Uwe von Parpart was much more involved in German events from the U.S. side, although I was briefed on developments almost daily. The one incident which is most typically Helga from that year, occurred in Bucharest, Romania, that summer.

The Soviet bloc and Club of Rome staged an international conference, set within the orbit of United Nations activities, at Bucharest, with the late John D. Rockefeller III the principal figure of the conference. Helga, still working then as a professional freelance journalist, was among the journalists attending. At the presentation arranged for journalists, John D.'s penchant for attractive young women prompted him to call upon Helga for the first question.

She challenged him: Was not the effect of the Malthusian policy he outlined simply genocide like something seen recently in Europe? Dame Margaret Mead reacted to Helga's question very strongly. Shortly after that, Mead, brandishing that horned, witch's Isis-staff she affected in later years, went after Helga as if to slaughter her. A highly amused, much more athletic Helga evaded the assault of that evil old witch.

Helga had worked with the embassies in arranging the aborted week-long seminar of November 1975. In the fall of 1977, I suggested that we marry. It was a thought born of a chain of circumstances set into motion by circumstances associated with the events of August 1977. I was a little surprised, but pleasantly, when she agreed. For people who live an ordinary sort of life, December-June marriages must be a prelude to misery. There was nothing ordinary about the lives of either of us, nor was it ever likely to be otherwise. We married in Wiesbaden on December 29, 1977. The service was in German; the official of the *Standesamt* asked me in German, if I knew what was happening. There was laughter about that question among my friends for weeks afterward.

Beginning about 1974, Helga took up studies of the work of Nicholas of Cusa. Her earlier religious studies in Trier had demonstrated that she had a greater talent for theology than liturgy and catechism. Further studies along that line had been terminated then for that reason. Criton Zoakos had insisted that we must organize a more systematic study of Cusa's work. Helga decided that she knew perhaps a bit more of this matter than others among us, and assumed that element of the division of labor as one of her continuing activities. It fitted into the work in philosophy which dominated a good portion of our activity then. She prepared a paper on aspects of Cusa's work, and came into contact with the work of the Cusanus Gesellschaft. She decided to complete her graduate work in this field, on the indirect, but efficient role of Cusa's scientific work on Leibniz and Schiller's method. Today, she is a qualified specialist in this field, as well as the subjects of Friedrich Schiller's work and the Prussian reformers.

Her work, but not always her good disposition, was fostered by the more unpleasant side effect of our marriage. The marriage made her a prime target, too. She has often described this as being "locked up." She is a very active person physically, and one of a very strong inclination for personal independence, in keeping with such events as her trip to China, her two-sentence interview in the Berlin Maoist's meeting, and the matter of Margaret Mead's obscene behavior at Bucharest. Willy Brandt is intellectually terrified of her. Helmut Schmidt recalls her directness vividly, too. She is not a feminist, but she has very strong, and, I find, correct views, on women's abilities to master habits and work of rigorously rational thought and action as well as any man. She has adapted less to what she calls "being locked up" than I have; otherwise, her work-habits are much like my own.

Her most important personal initiatives of recent years

are centered around her founding of the international Schiller Institute, an institution of major and growing importance, in which my own direct role is marginal overall, and limited to a few undertakings she assigns to me.

It started in discussions with the National Security Council back in 1982. She presented an oral briefing on key features of the direction of developments within West Germany, especially ominous tendencies bearing on continuation of the alliance between the United States and Germany. She indicated the need for a new kind of U.S. initiative. Her briefing was well received, and a genuine effort was made by some Reagan administration officials to set the proposed sort of initiative into motion. It was suggested she submit a written presentation. Further action was blocked at the State Department and within specialist circles within the NSC bureaucracy, although, despite this, her analysis of the situation was taken into account to useful, practical effect.

The bureaucratic obstacles put up by the Kissingerian mice and rats inside the administration, persuaded her that the action she had proposed should be launched on a private basis. This decision led to the formation of the Schiller Institute, and also to a byproduct of that effort inside Germany, called Patriots for Germany, and to other developments, which, in total, make the Schiller Institute a significantly influential institution internationally, today.

Helga's line of argument ran as follows. Contrast General Douglas MacArthur's policy in occupied Japan, with the occupation policies typified by John J. McCloy's role in postwar Germany. The U.S. policy toward postwar Germany should have been based on those points in the history of the United States and Germany, at which each culture was at its best. For the United States, this was the period of the American Revolution. For Germany, this was the period of Schiller and his friends among the leaders of the German Liberation Wars against Napoleon Bonaparte. The ideals of the American Revolution and the German Classical Period, had been essentially identical. The latter ideals were those to which German patriots had returned, instinctively, in the educational policies which Helga had experienced in the gymnasium at Trier. This heritage was the great moral potential of the German people, which had been manifest during the immediate postwar period, but to which natural partner of the United States McCloy's occupation policies had been opposed, preferring instead fellows of Willy Brandt's type.

It was not too late, Helga emphasized. It was five minutes to midnight, but still not too late. If the Reagan administration would introduce a new dimension in American-German relations, emphasizing the common themes of the American Revolution and the German Liberation Wars, the majority of German citizens and institutions would respond with joy. A true alliance of the United States and Germany could be developed on this new basis, and the efforts to lure Germans into a gradual strategic decoupling from the United States would be defeated.

Helga was right on all counts. Until Theodore Roosevelt's presidency, the culture of the United States was proud of the contributions of German culture, especially in music and in the physical sciences. Teddy Roosevelt was what is called in Germany a *Deutschenfresser,* a fanatical hater of Germans. This was key to the United States' commitment to Britain and France, well in advance of World War I, that the United States would support a war against Germany. Teddy Roosevelt could not be reelected President, so he launched his Bull Moose, "spoiler" presidential campaign, to ensure that another German-hater, and backer of the Federal Reserve project, was elected. The election of Wilson ensured that World War I occurred. Wilson's policy at Versailles ensured that World War II would occur, and that something like Hitler would rise toward power in postwar Germany. John J. McCloy was owned by the extended family of Teddy Roosevelt, part of the Morgan-centered complex of power in New York City which did back Schacht's proposal to put Hitler into power, the same Morgan-centered crowd which blamed German culture for the Hitler which Morgan et al. had imposed upon Germany.

I have studied conclusive evidence, that the tilt of many factions in Germany toward deals with Moscow today, is a direct result of the cultural policies which the Anglo-American occupation forces imposed upon occupied Germany.

For example, the Anglo-American occupation forces told the Catholic Church in Germany that it had moral responsibility for bringing Hitler to power. Actually Hitler's early backing among German religious groups came from the spinoff of Crowley's theosophists, Rudolf Steiner's anthroposophs, a project backed by the Astor family. The anthroposophs distanced themselves from Hitler before 1933, but the Nazis gained strong support from within the evangelical (Protestant church), the same currents which are today a hard-core of the Moscow-appeasers. The occupation mafia told the Catholic clergy, that it was their Platonic theology which was to blame; it was alleged that emphasis on reason was "authoritarian." The principle of "freedom" in the philosophy of Swiss Nazi sympathizer Martin Heidigger, was suggested as an antidote to be adopted as part of the "liberal reeducation" program. So, Karl Rahner's influence was produced, fostering the "Christian-Marxist dialogue" current largely responsible for the present regime in Nicaragua.

Margaret Mead was part of this kind of action by U.S. occupation authorities. Closely allied to Bertrand Russell since 1938, Mead was a member of the U.S. intelligence organization directing the occupation of Germany. She was interfaced with U.S. agent Hans Haber, the editor of the U.S. occupation-controlled *Neue Deutsche Zeitung,* and was a key figure in Haber's operation against the world's leading conducter, Wilhelm Furtwängler. The

Furtwängler case is typical of the sheer fraud and hypocrisy of McCloy's policies.

Hermann Goering became infatuated with an oompah band leader, Herbert von Karajan. Propaganda Minister Josef Goebbels was part of the operation launched, to replace the conductor of the Berlin Philharmonic Orchestra with Goering's favorite, von Karajan. The German musical community revolted against this disgusting suggestion. Hitler was politically vulnerable enough, especially with his military overthrow lurking in the offing prior to the war, that the Nazis backed off from pushing through von Karajan's replacement of Furtwängler.

After the war, the U.S. occupation authorities insisted that Furtwängler's success in defeating his replacement by von Karajan, "proved" that Furtwängler had been a force within the Nazi apparatus. Hans Haber spearheaded this campaign of twisted libel, and Margaret Mead played a prominent part. The fact that Jewish musicians stepped forward, to testify how Furtwängler had fought to protect them, was brushed aside. After a decent interval, von Karajan gained the post at Berlin which Goering had sought to award him. The heritage of the oompah band Goering so much admired, was brought to the Berlin Philharmonic.

I first recognized Furtwängler in 1946, during my stay at the replacement depot outside Calcutta. The Red Cross recreation center at the camp had a collection of British HMV records. Furtwängler made the slovenly romantic, Tchaikowsky, sound like music. My astonishment and admiration were instant, not for Tchaikowsky, but for this singularly brilliant conductor. On musical grounds, during the late 1940s, I had had no difficulty taking sides for Furtwängler, against the mechanically brilliant but wicked Arturo Toscanini. If there was a true Italian fascist of note among musicians, it was Toscanini; he was the Mussolini of the podium, who made the trains run on time, and whose conception of Beethoven symphonies was high-grade

Mantovani. When the possibility of Furtwängler's appointment to head the Boston Symphony was mooted, I was ecstatic, and lobbied among every influential or possibly influential friend and acquaintance in sight, pushing for the appointment.

Leibniz, Lessing, Schiller, Mozart, Beethoven, the Humboldts, vom Stein, Scharnhorst, Heine, Schubert, Schumann, Gauss, Riemann, Felix Klein: these were German classical and scientific culture. What literate person in the world does not know this? Apparently, not John J. McCloy.

Among the Germans supporting the formation of the Schiller Institute were leaders and veterans of the anti-Hitler resistance organization, the Reichsbanner, Schwarz-Rot-Gold, who led the procession of delegates from fifty nations into the hall in Virginia, during the opening of the first international conference of the Schiller Institute. These were true Germans, who had resisted, and who represented morally all those committed to rebuilding Germany after Hitler on the moral foundations of the German classical tradition.

Helga generalized. In every nation's history, there is a precious period which expresses the cultural heritage of that nation at its best. In the United States, it is the American Revolution. In Germany, it is the seventeenth-century Great Elector, who gave Jews a refuge from oppression, it is Leibniz, Bach, Lessing, and the German classics. It Italy, it is the Golden Renaissance. Relations among nations must be built on the basis of affirmation of the best traditions of each.

On this basis, the Schiller Institute broadened rapidly, from the initial basis of fostering fundamental improvements in U.S.–German relations, to the same kind of relationship among Germany and the United States with other nations.

President Reagan planned a trip to Germany, for the general purposes which Helga had identified as urgent. The

President delivered an address to the youth assembled at historic Marbach castle which justly pleased Helga immensely. The Anti-Defamation League spoiled the effect.

The President's itinerary included a brief visit to the cemetery at Bitburg. Apart from making what I am assured is the best beer in Germany, Bitburg is an exemplary center of postwar friendship between the Germans and the Americans stationed there. There may be a few German localities as friendly to the United States as Bitburg, but not very many. What a hue and cry the friends of the Soviet intelligence around the ADL stirred up.

The ADL does, of course, have German friends, including a branch of the East German intelligence services known as the VVN. The ADL has closer connections directly to the Soviet KGB, connections in common with Mark Richards of the Department of Justice, former Congresswoman Elizabeth "Holtzperson," Henry A. Kissinger, the Office of Special Investigations, and the neo-Nazi and Ku Klux Klan grouplets which ADL coordinates through paid agents such as Jimmy Rosenberg.

The Soviets did not wish President Reagan's visit to interfere with Soviet decoupling efforts inside West Germany. The ADL obliged, just as they gave political support to the narcoterrorist assassins of Prime Minister Indira Gandhi.

Helga asked me to take a leading role in one Schiller Institute project, the creation of a Schiller Institute Trade Union Commission, now a very influential organization in South America, and an important backing for the continental efforts of Peru's President Alan García. One of our beloved friends was rocket scientist Krafft Ehricke, who died at the end of 1984, after completing, more or less, his project for elaborating the industrialization of the Moon. Krafft was a key figure in the Schiller Institute, and among the most lovable personalities I have known. Helga organized a July 1985 conference in Krafft's honor, and asked me to prepare a suitable paper for presentation there. The result was my Moon–Mars Colonization Proposal, of which I shall write later here.

The Schiller Institute is today a growing, worldwide organization. The leadership is Helga's. I sometimes appear as a kind of fifth wheel.

The Patriots for Germany

From the beginning, Bolshevik strategy for Soviet world-domination, has been based on capturing Germany. With Germany in the Soviet orbit, even as a neutral friendly to Moscow, Soviet domination of Western Europe, and the Mediterranean, is a matter of course. With Western Europe under Soviet domination, the economic potential of the Soviet empire becomes immediately the largest concentration of economic power in the world.

Shortly after the war, in 1952, Soviet dictator Josef Stalin made an effort to lure West Germany into neutrality, transmitting a note setting forth conditions for reunification of divided Germany. Konrad Adenauer and Social Democratic leader Kurt Schumacher had joined forces to reject the offer in the note. Now, since Willy Brandt became Chancellor of Germany, things have gradually changed. Gorbachov is scheduled to resubmit the Stalin note of 1952 after the January 1987 West Germany national elections. The Social Democratic Party, the antitechnology Green Party, and Foreign Minister Hans-Dietrich Genscher's liberal party are lined up in support of accepting such an offer. Also, a sizable fraction of the regional party bosses of Chancellor Helmut Kohl's Christian Democratic Union (CDU) has floated a proposal which proposes acceptance of such an offer.

Meanwhile, U.S. influentials such as Henry A. Kissinger and Georgia Democratic Senator Sam Nunn are pushing for U.S. strategic decoupling from Germany about as vigorously as Moscow is. Inside Germany, the leftist

U.S. Ambassador Richard Burt, is working vigorously, even in public, to bring such a decoupling about.

Helga had wind of such trends within the CDU, during the course of a speaking tour in north Germany. During the discussions around the July 1985 Krafft Ehricke conference of the Schiller Institute, a Schiller Institute-sponsored project was launched, in an effort to rally patriotic forces inside the Social Democratic Party and the Christian Democratic Union against this decoupling trend. A German committee of the Schiller Institute was founded, as a nonpartisan political association, to warn against these dangerous trends. A series of newspaper advertisements was published in Germany by this committee, Patriots for Germany, signed by prominent public figures of the nation, including a number of prominent, retired military leaders.

Ambassador Richard Burt and persons of similar ilk deployed against the Patriots. The leadership of the CDU also deployed heavily. As a result, the Patriots moved from a nonpartisan role, to organize a political party in the state of Lower Saxony, and later a national political party.

The leading problem threatening the U.S. position in Germany is Ambassador Richard Burt. Kissinger has deployed repeatedly to Germany in particular, and Europe in general, campaigning for decoupling and against the SDI. The most serious problem is not the Soviet influence as such, but U.S. figures such as Sam Nunn, Henry Kissinger, and Ambassador Burt. The fact that Burt is a Reagan appointee, and that Kissinger is able to represent himself as a power within the Reagan administration, convinces many Germans that the Reagan administration is in the process of abandoning a strategic commitment to Germany. Simply out of fear caused by a combination of U.S. weakness and threats of U.S. decoupling, influential figures of Germany have swung over to seeking friendly terms with Moscow.

Helga and my other friends in Europe are doing everything slightly beyond their means, to attempt to prevent the decoupling from occurring, either as capitulation to a replay of the 1952 Stalin note, sometime later during 1987, or by the process of U.S. troop-withdrawal initiated under Gramm-Rudman rule from the United States.

Helga and I concur in theology. She is a nonpracticing Catholic, although Catholic in theology. I am nominally Protestant, but my theology is what I have already described it to be. In practice, we are both ecumenical, in the sense defined by Nicholas of Cusa's *De Pace Fidei*. That is the way we intend to remain.

Within those constraints, we are very close to Pope John Paul II ecumenically, and to the relevant views of Joseph Cardinal Ratzinger, among other simple priests and higher clergy within the Catholic Church. The center of this convergence in practice, is twofold. Theologically, we defend what is recognized by St. Augustine's principle as expressed by the *Filioque* of the Latin Christian Creed, and as this is the central feature of both Catholic and Protestant Christianity in Europe and the Americas. Otherwise, our views on a new international monetary system coincide with Pope Paul VI's 1967 encyclical, *Populorum Progressio,* an encyclical vigorously affirmed by John Paul II.

Since we are not practicing Catholics, we avoid even the appearance of meddling into the internal affairs of the American Catholic Church. Nonetheless, we recognize the existence of the issue around what has been called "the American heresy" within that Church, since Pope Leo XIII, and are obliged to recognize the way in which this "American heresy" guides certain political actions by some priests, to which we must take strong objection when these extend beyond the Church itself, into the domain of important practical expressions in political affairs. To the extent that the "American heresy" is a problem internal to the Church, that is not our business, no matter how strong our private views on the issues. When the representatives of that "American heresy" promote the rock-drug-sex counter-culture inside the nations of North American or Europe, make common cause with the pro-Soviet activities of the evil ADL, or promote genocidal policies in Central and South America, as Notre Dame's Father Theodore Hesburgh does, these are political issues, not issues internal to the Church.

Some have accused me of being "anti-Catholic," because of my opposition to the counterculture and progenocide policies of some U.S. priests. This allegation is absurd, of course. I have sufficient knowledge of relevant matters, to have replied to such charges by discussing homosexuality among priests and nuns, or elaborating the heretical character of the "American heresy." It would have been truthful, but inappropriate to appear to meddle in internal church affairs, even in face of such extreme provocations.

The defense of the *Filioque,* is not a liturgical issue; it is an issue fundamental to the foundations of western civilization. Eastern religion, including the pseudo-Christian Soviet state church, worships a different God than Christians of the West. Their God is a Babylonian tyrant, like the gods of mythological Olympus, who may play capricious tricks on the pure mortals subject to him. Our God is that of the Gospels and Epistles of St. Paul. For us, each individual person may participate in the work of God, through being guided by knowledge of the Logos, an imperfect knowledge, but a knowledge whose imperfection we may render less imperfect through development and exercise of the divine spark of reason given to us.

This emphasis on the powers and responsibilities associated with the development of our divine spark of reason, is the secret of western civilization, the source of our potential for producing and assimilating scientific and technologial progress, for example. We see other persons, not as like beasts, as creatures merely of hedonistic impulses; we see other persons in terms of the potentials of the divine spark of reason within each. We value ourselves for developing and being governed by that individual capacity for reason, and value others for the same quality. If we ever lose that mooring, western civilization is doomed. That mooring is expressed by the *Filioque* of the Latin Creed. Formally Catholic, the principle expressed is the essence of all that is good within western civilization.

Populorum Progressio, Pope John Paul II, Cardinal Ratzinger, and so on, campaign for the same thing which I have sought since those last weeks of my 1946 stay in Calcutta. They proceed from the fundamental and universal moral law intrinsic to Christianity. My emphasis is on economic science, combined with a sense of simple human justice. Our methods of work differ in detail, but our goal is the same.

As of Protestant upbringing myself, I am deeply ashamed of the Protestant churches generally on this particular issue. On this point, many of the Protestant denominations have exchanged Christianity for Adam Smith's "Invisible Hand." It is impossible to accept the dogma of the "Invisible Hand" and be a Christian. We are each personally morally accountable to God, for the foreseeable consequences of both our actions and our deeds of omission. When some fellow runs around proclaiming that he is a "born-again Christian," and yet condones a policy of following hedonistic impulses which lead foreseeably to mass-deaths through famines and epidemics, and monstrous miseries, I must shake my head sadly, and say, "If you love Christ, why do you not love his sheep?" A pittance of charitable donations, to the casue of feeding famine-stricken Africans, if donated by one who tolerates the U.S. policies which have imposed that famine and epidemic, is not a Christian's act; it is a damnable piece of hypocrisy. I think of a Jimmy Carter, who used to attend satanic-rock sessions, and then teach Baptist Sunday School, and whose administration did more to promote the spread of the drug traffic than anything but Yuri Andropov, at least during this century to date.

Perhaps I recognize this hypocrisy among professed Christians more easily, because I fought through the theological implications in the course of my break with Quaker theology.

After nine years of marriage, it is now difficult to make a distinction between the fruits of Helga's and my own collaboration, and the enrichment of my ideas in the course of that collaboration. Without her contribution, I should be much less than I am today; those who find themselves in that state of mind, know thus that theirs is a good marriage.

My debt to Helga is but a special degree of the general indebtedness of a similar kind which I owe to many among my collaborators. I have an excellent marriage, and, in the same sense, a most fortunate association.

The Founding of a Colony on Mars 9

Beware! If you should discover the Anti-Defamation League torturing your cat, and you should file a complaint against the individuals you have caught in that act, you may find yourself labeled "an anti-Semite" for the rest of your life. If so, curiously nasty things may happen at your bank, your place of employment, and so forth. The ADL is like that.

On the other hand, if you are an unscrupulous and nasty person, and wish nasty things done to some person or group, try to secure the ADL's services to do the dirty job for you. If your victim objects, he will be victimized by false charges of "anti-Semitism," while you sit back and relish the fun.

For the same reason that some hire paid assassins, certain entities which did not desire to be caught on the scene during attacks on me and my friends, retained the services of the ADL in 1978. As soon as word of my 1984 Democratic presidential candidacy was out, in autumn 1983, the ADL was deployed to work with renewed vigor. The impetus for these new attacks came chiefly, and loudly, out of mouths of the ADL's connections in Moscow.

Soviet public attacks on me escalated, from April 1983 into March 1984. The consistent theme of these published and other Soviet operations targeting me, was the Soviet view, that I had been the original author of the policy on which the Strategic Defense Initiative is based. Moscow was resolved that all my influence in and around the U.S. government and among U.S. allies, be destroyed.

The continuing barrage of personal attacks on me in the Soviet press, were in the nature of what are called "signal pieces." Such published attacks are not written for the Soviet domestic audience. They are Soviet official confirmation of what Soviet diplomats are saying, off the record, to diplomats in various parts of the world. Putting such personal attacks officially on the published record, in key publications such as *Pravda, Izvestia, Krasnaya Zvezda, Literaturnaya Gazeta, New Times,* or, more since Raisa Gorbachov's husband came to power, *Sovetskaya Kultura,* automatically alerts sundry Soviet agents and friends scattered about the world. Such public attacks establish the "official Moscow line" concerning the targeted personalities, and thus orient Moscow's sundry channels of influence and action around the world to take appropriate forms of action.

Moscow's highest priority for immediate action, was to drive a wedge between me and the Reagan administration. At the time, NBC-TV was negotiating a potentially lucrative contract for broadcasting from Moscow; NBC-TV accepted the role of conduit for the work of Moscow's ADL assets. The very intimate relationship among Henry Kissinger, the Bronfmans, and Armand Hammer, was the connection immediately behind these actions of the ADL and NBC-TV. NBC-TV's contract negotiations with Moscow during that period, had the effect of integrating NBC-TV News into the new special unit of Soviet intelligence, a unit which has surfaced publicly more recently as Raisa Gorbachov's Soviet Cultural Fund.

Why I ran in 1984

I had not committed myself to run in 1984, until Democratic National Chairman Charles Manatt convened a Washington, D.C. press conference committing all then-listed Democratic candidates to support the "nuclear freeze" policy set into motion in Moscow in March 1982. The leading Democratic contender, Walter F. Mondale, had had such a policy delivered to his Minnesota organization by a visiting Soviet delegation earlier that spring. The leader of the delegation received by Mondale's Minneapolis organization, had been a self-avowed Soviet enemy of mine, KGB official Fyodor Burlatski, then functioning as an editor of the KGB's weekly voice, *Literaturnaya Gazeta*. The two-dozen members of the Soviet delegation were also chiefly known to us as KGB officials. Mondale had adopted Moscow's line on U.S. defense policy as the theme of his campaign. The adoption of the same policy publicly by Manatt, and the full, public endorsement of the policy by all but one timidly reserved Democratic presidential aspirant, forced my decision.

There were important collateral factors affecting my decision. The Reagan economic policy was a catastrophe, and his policy toward Central and South America abominable. He had brought Kissinger into his administration. Yet, it was almost certain that the President would win reelection, and it seemed more useful to work to improve the Reagan administration, and to back the SDI effort, than to run against him in what would almost certainly be a futile effort to bring my nomination to the Democratic convention floor. Besides, my year to run was 1988, not 1984. Only overriding considerations prompted me to become a candidate in 1984.

Apart from winning the election, the only sensible reason for running for major office is to affect the environment of policy making in a significant way. Sometimes, the latter motive is the only reason for campaigning.

If I could presume that Reagan's defense policies would hold up through 1988, I could not presume that Reagan would change his economic policies. Up into spring of 1983, I had thought a change in his economic policies possible. By late summer of 1983, I concluded the possibility of a positive change was slight, even under conditions of a severe general financial crisis. Therefore, I must assume that a worsening economic depression over the coming four years would ensure that no Republican could be elected President in 1988. The nation would require a President who would continue the positive features of Reagan's defense policies, and effect the overdue changes in monetary and economic policies. So, I saw 1988 as my year to run.

However, even if the Democratic candidate lost in 1984, should the full resources of the Democratic Party be mobilized for the Soviet-appeaser doctrines of Mondale and Manatt, the losing Democratic campaign could set into motion strong currents of policy thinking, which could become disastrous during the period of the second Reagan administration. There were two targets to be the focus of the attack: Mondale and Kissinger. Kissingerism embedded in the institutions of government, and Mondale's Soviet-appeaser role, were the two major points of infection which must be exposed, and neutralized to the maximum degree possible. After Manatt's press conference, such a campaign must be run.

The positive features of my campaign were obvious: present the strategic military and economic situation, and the policy to be adopted on these issues.

Moscow used the ADL and NBC-TV to spearhead a pressure campaign against the Reagan administration. The tactic was to convince the administration that my very name was such a public-relations liability, especially during an election year, that the administration must cut off all liaison with me in the most dramatic way. Moscow, which ordered exactly such action from the Reagan administration in the Soviet press, had guessed shrewdly. The administration responded to the pressure tactic exactly as Moscow demanded.

The charges aired by NBC-TV included allegations of major criminal behavior. I was obliged to sue NBC-TV and the ADL for reckless disregard for the truth. I might have guessed that both the judge and jury would be fixed. So, I sat in court the day Indira Gandhi was murdered, and looked across to the defendant's bench, where sat an official of and attorneys for an ADL which had given political backing to the narcoterrorist gang which murdered that dear woman. You see, the U.S. government was protecting an ADL linked, among other things, to the Israeli gun-running lately at the center of "Irangate." To protect the Reagan administration's standing agreements with the ADL during an election year, the court was fixed.

Experience tends to suggest, that there really is very little law in our federal courts these days. The attorneys for the Department of Justice are chiefly hired gun-slingers, of the sort who would frame up and imprison a friend they knew to be innocent, for the sake of improving the score on their career-management program. The record of performance among many of our federal courts today, so that they are the only railroad which runs on schedule nearly every time. The increasing pattern, is "clubhouse justice," the crassest form of rule by men, in place of our constitutional system of rule by law.

There are exceptions to this. Some federal judges still believe in law, although the system as a whole tends to discourage such sentiment, especially in politically sensitive cases. Unfortunately, the question whether a record and testimony of a nominee for the federal bench, is just another "clubhouse judge," or shows a genuine commitment to constitutional law, is the one large area of inquiry in which the Congress seems totally uninterested. The rule in federal court, is that a typical drug runner is out peddling his wares by the end of the same day his bail hearing is conducted, but woe to some innocent, accused of some nebulous offense, who happens to be the target of a politically motivated Justice Department targeting.

Kissinger predicted, during the closing period of the 1984 primary campaign, that I would be "taken care of" by his friends after the election. Kissinger knew what he was talking about; the friends in the Justice Department, from whom he had demanded such action during the summer of 1983, had a neat little frame-up ready to be unleashed right after the November election. Right in the center of directing the Justice Department's frame-up were the ADL and NBC-TV. The prosecuting attorney, William Weld, was an old left-wing enemy of ours from the 1970s, and is also a member, according to his own business records, of a Soviet-controlled network with a nest inside the Harvard Law School where Weld was trained; this Harvard nest is tied very intimately with Kissinger. The U.S. Justice Department official behind the frame-up was Steven Trott, an old-time lefty with former Communist Party ties, with more recent ties to the circles of Soviet agent Armand Hammer.

Both Trott and Weld, incidentally, are up to their necks in the cover-up in "Irangate."

In an FBI document dated from January of 1986, the FBI reported Weld as admitting that he had no case in fact against my campaign or any of the organizations or officials among my friends. According to the FBI report, Weld emphasized that it was essentially to get me before the 1988 election campaign, and appealed to state attorneys general to assist in organizing new frame-ups. Attorney General Ed Meese knew this sort of illegal game was being run out of his department, but refused to interfere with the cover-up of such illegalities. It is, unfortunately, not inconsistent with my past experiences with the Reagan administration.

Nonetheless, facts or not, Trott and Weld moved on October 6 and 7 of 1986, in a 400-man armed raid on my friends' enterprises in Leesburg, Virginia, an operation which had buried within it an optional plan for killing me. This operation was mobilized during August 1986, under heavy pressure from Moscow to have me eliminated.

Weld's stated legal pretext for the raid was perjured allegations by one Forrest Lee Fick, who had served for a time as a hired security guard in aid of my physical security. Fick had been retained in this capacity on the highest recommendation of elements of the U.S. intelligence community. He had been discharged for reason of certain highly irregular behavior, and this disgruntled, discharged former employee had sold himself to the ADL and NBC-TV News. His intelligence background had included working under the cover of membership in neo-Nazi and kindred varieties of grouplets, where he had established a close connection to the ADL, through ADL official Irwin Suall's neo-Nazi employee, Jimmy Rosenberg. The ADL and NBC-TV had passed a Fick desperate for money over to the FBI agent assigned to Weld's attempted frame-up. Fick was prepared to swear to anything his prospective sponsors wished to hear him allege.

The Soviet demand for Trott and Weld's October 6 action, was issued publicly by a Moscow publication controlled by Raisa Gorbachov, the wife of Premier Gorbachov, and a person of higher social rank in the Soviet *Nomenklatura* than her husband. The call for the action was publicized in the August 7, 1986 issue of *Sovetskaya Kultura,* shortly prior to Trott and Weld's initial preparations for the October 6 raid. The demand for the raid was stated more forcefully and explicitly in the *Sovetskaya Kultura* of September 30, 1986, just six days before the raid. In the meantime, the Soviet KGB published an attack on me in the largest-circulation Soviet publication, *New Times,* with a vitriol and length unprecedented for Soviet attacks on any figure in the West. The formulations used to characterize me in the KGB's *New Times* piece, were the theme of a major public address by Premier Gorbachov, on October 3, just three days prior to the raid.

Raisa Gorbachov is the head of a major Soviet strategic operation, called the Soviet Cultural Fund, whose chief funder is longstanding Soviet agent and businessman, Armand Hammer. Hammer has channels of influence into the U.S. Justice Department through the circles of the ADL and Mark Richards, and gained access to influence in the Reagan White House through Charles Wick, the head of the U.S. Information Agency. The Soviet Cultural Fund's operations against me were run chiefly through a subordinate of Soviet chief ideologue Yegor Ligachev, Alexander Yakovlev. Yakovlev ran special operations in both the Geneva and Reykjavik Gorbachov-Reagan summits, and met with Charles Wick at the latter summit. The broad picture of the points of origin, and channels of influence used to conduit the demand for Weld's October 6 action, is sufficiently clear.

The key to the Soviets' sense of urgency in demanding this operation against me and my friends, was the Reykjavik summit itself, held one week after the Leesburg raid. The Soviets entered the summit convinced that President Reagan would agree to trade away the SDI at that meeting. On nearly every Soviet demand but the SDI, the President did capitulate, much to Secretary of State George Shultz's shamelessly expressed delight in his closing press conference there. The President virtually offered to trade away Western Europe, and leading Europeans saw the President's actions in those terms.

Moscow's concern to have me eliminated as soon as possible, cannot be classed as Soviet paranoia. The Soviet concern is twofold. They forecast a devastating economic crisis hitting the United States during the period immediately ahead, and estimate my support among Democratic voters to be already about 30 percent and rising. They have stated to European government officials, that they foresee me as becoming President in either 1988 or 1992, unless I am eliminated earlier. They had indicated their desire for my elimination in the strongest possible terms. They see the SDI becoming institutionalized to such a degree, that unless it is chopped away very soon, its development and deployment is irreversible. They see me as so much a key factor in the authorship and pushing of the SDI, that my elimination is viewed as almost indispensable. For, if the SDI is deployed, as I have indicated, then the Soviets will have to abandon any hopes for gaining world-domination during the years immediately ahead.

My program to colonize space

I have been occupied with the colonization of space for about thirty years. A few elementary calculations then, as today, showed that the colonization of any object more distant than our Moon depends absolutely on powered flight trajectories. Thirty years back, nuclear fission power offered a potential for manned flight to a nearby planetary body. In more recent years, the more I thought about defining a way for driving technological progress on Earth over an extended period, the clearer it seemed to me, that the task of establishing a permanent colony on Mars might seem a roundabout way of effecting the desired improvements on Earth, but perhaps it was really the most direct way. I published a few remarks on that about five years ago. What forced me to get down to working through such a policy, was Helga's request that I prepare an address for the July 1985 Schiller Institute's Krafft Ehricke Memorial Conference.

Others, better qualified for that purpose, would present Krafft's past life and achievements. I wished to produce something that might become a living memorial for Krafft. Krafft had concentrated on the colonization of the Moon. The real function of colonizing the Moon in the way Krafft had worked this through in such detail, is to make possible the colonization of Mars. I have accumulated a fair amount of knowledge of validated space-projects over the years, enough to estimate a feasible series of sequential steps, to arrive at a reasonable date for beginning the permanent colonization of Mars. Putting as much weight as I could, into rallying relevant people to a commitment to such a combined Moon and Mars colonization project, seemed a proper sort of living memorial for Krafft.

The work of putting men on Mars requires a far more elaborate preparation than is needed merely to send an unmanned package there. The logistics of sending and supplying a colony on Mars add up to something massive. We require powered trajectories, which, for various reasons, should be based on inerial confinement fusion power. To found a colony would require about a hundred carriers, each larger than an ocean liner, ferrying back and forth, to and from Mars orbit, for some years. Constructing such ships of materials produced on Earth is prohibitive for the next generation or so, at least. Constructing all but a small fraction of that weight on the Moon, is clearly indicated. An Earth–orbit space station, at a considerable distance from Earth must be constructed, and that, starting from today, is a chore which can be accomplished economically, only through a well-defined series of stages of preparation.

The catch is, that about forty years of stage-by-stage work, is needed to bring us to the point we are ready to begin constructing the permanent colonization of Mars. In one very important sense, I saw that forty-year span as an advantage.

The project as a whole is quite feasible economically. The technology spinoffs of a Moon–Mars colonization project, enable the project to pay for itself in the same way a properly managed SDI project pays for itself. As long as we can pay out the initial cost of each stage of the project, we need not worry about how much the total cost will be: The spinoff benefits will more than repay the costs.

My estimated date of founding of the first element of

permanent colonization of Mars was between A.D. 2025–2027. During 1986, the U.S. Space Commission proposed the same approximate target date. There are differences between my design of the steps of the program and theirs. There are no significant differences in our respective views of the step-by-step progress to a full-fledged, Earth-orbiting spaceport. My spacecraft to Mars are fusion-powered, whereas they base their specifications on fission power. My overall design is superior to theirs, but the general scheme is otherwise similar in all features bearing upon feasibility of the target date. Thus, there is no reasonable doubt of the feasibility of the target date.

The essential difference between their schedule and mine, is that, for the successive steps of implementation between the years A.D. 2005–2025, my design demands a more rapid rate of successive advances in technologies than does theirs. Thus, their settlement on Mars begins at a lower level of technology than does mine. This most essential difference between the two designs results in some significant secondary differences in the detailed specifications. The differences in specifications for the 2005–2025 phases, reflects their neglect of the role of technological spinoffs in generating a payback for the investment in the project as a whole. We agree on the feasibility of the schedule, but we see the significance of the project within differing terms of reference.

My design of the project works simultaneously, from 2027 back to the present, and from the present to 2027. I work backward to define the technological requirements for each step of the program. At the same time that I work backward, I am also working forward: starting with a transatmospheric craft whose highest ascent is the height of a low-orbiting "bus-stop" kind of station above the Earth. The reason for my approach may not seem clear at first. I will try to make it clear as briefly as possible, and in the simplest possible language the subject allows.

My design starts with a commitment to the devel-

314   *Power of Reason: 1988*

opment of four categories of new technologies. 1) Controlled thermonclear fusion and related plasma technologies; 2) The development of coherent electromagnetic radiation of high energy-density cross-section of focus on target, and the development of new qualities of materials and production processes based on this; 3) Optical biophysics, as the basis for management of synthetic "biospheres" in interplanetary travel on spacecraft, and controlled environments in colonies; 4) The increasing role of advanced generations of computer systems. I set target dates for completing specific degrees of advancement of these four classes of technologies. I base the specifications and time schedule for each stage of the project, on the changes in designs made possible by the highest levels of new technologies coming into use at the relevant point in time.

My initial permanent colonization on Mars requires certain levels of advancement of these new technologies. Working backward, stage by stage, I assign a level of sets of technologies assigned to each stage. The time I assign to the beginning of that stage, is a time not earlier than the earliest availability of each and all of the technologies specified. So, up until about 2005, we both rely on technologies already in the process of development, and our designs are most similar to one another's for this initial period of the schedule. After that point, the two designs diverge increasingly, because of my demand for a more rapid rate of development of new technologies beginning approximately 2005.

My design incorporates a characteristic mathematical function in the LaRouche-Riemann method. To introduce this function to students, I make the general point in the following way. This description will be sufficient discussion of that function, for our purposes here.

The term, "technological progress" is commony used in such a loose way of speaking, that it is difficult to see, whether the speaker means just a single step upward in technology, an undefined sort of technological advancement in a general sense, or a series of well-defined upward steps. I use the term to mean the latter; I mean a series of upward steps, to the effect that each step seems to cause the next upward step. The way in which one technology follows another, is determined both by scientific principles, and by the way in which the new production and engineering capabilities required for each stage are developed during the course of the preceding stages. It is a bit more complicated than that, but that gives the general picture.

Generally, unless each upward step in the level of technology introduced causes a significant increase in the average level of physical output per person, the automatic appearance of the next upward step is doubtful. To ensure what might appear a series of rather regular and automatic successive steps upward, we must ensure that each new level of technology does in fact result in a significant rise in physical output per person for that society.

The kind of mathematical function which takes all essential factors into account, assumes that the evolution of the economy satisfies six general conditions:

1) The physical standard of living per capita must rise, on the average, with each increase of physical output per person. Not as much as the increase of physical output per person, but significantly.

2) The amount of energy usefully consumed per person, must increase.

3) The direction of applied technology must be associated with an increase of the energy-density cross-section of energy applied to work.

4) The percentile of the total labor force employed in rural production must decrease, on condition that

the society's production of food and fiber per person increases.

5) The percentile of the urban labor force employed in producing producers' goods must increase, on the condition that the production of consumer goods per person increases.

6) The level of technology used must increase on the average for the society as a whole.

These six requirements, expressed as inequalities ("greater than," "less than"), are named "constraints." Constraints numbered 1, 4 and 5 need not be considered at this moment. We are concerned primarily with the correlation between the sixth constraint and constraints 2 and 3. For convenience, we can rename constraint 2 "energy-density," and constraint 3 "energy-flux density."

Assume that increases in energy-density and energy-flux density, advance in proportion to advances in level of technology. How shall we compare increases in both energy-density and energy-flux density with increases in productivity? Let us use a scale of powers of 10 for measuring increases in both energy-density and energy-flux density. An increase in the power of 10 by 1, is called "order of magnitude." So, 10 is one order of magnitude greater than 1, and 100 is one order of magnitude greater than 10, and so on. Or, the same thing, we can measure these increases on a simple logarithmic scale, or we may shift to a natural-logarithmic scale. Strictly speaking, the natural-logarithmic scale is the correct choice.

In the case of thermonuclear fusion, we must think in terms of orders of magnitude of increase of both energy-density and energy-flux density. In the case of coherent beams, such as laser beams, we must think in terms of orders of magnitude of increase of energy-flux density of the beam's action on its working target. My design is based on driving technological progress in such a way as to increase energy-flux density by as many orders of magnitude as possible, as quickly as it is possible to generate such densities and to control them for productive purposes.

I then base the kinds of materials used on the kinds of materials which can be produced and worked at the available level of energy-flux density. I define other possible choices of requirements in the same general way.

The effect of this on my approach to the Mars-colonization project is as follows. Instead of basing the project's specifications on the kinds of technologies it might be estimated society will have available at each point in time, I say that the technologies which society will have available are those we force to be developed for the purposes of our Mars project. I propose to create the same kind of effect seen in "crash programs" such as the Apollo project, or in "crash programs" to create technological breakthroughs in weapons.

In principle, most of the technologies required for the SDI are expressions of the same scientific principles employed in a Mars colonization project. Similarly, the basic engineering capabilities which must be developed at each stage of the Mars project, and the qualities of production capabilities, cover every technology required for the SDI. However, the Mars project has much broader applications, and far greater benefits for Earth's economy as a whole, than does the more limited SDI.

I said that it was most convenient that we shall require not less than about forty years of work on this project, step by step, to begin the construction of a permanent colony on Mars. I do not mean, of course, that it would not be desirable to reach Mars even much earlier. The point is this: This Mars project gives the United States and its collaborators a consistent, long-range science and technology policy, for not only the first forty years, but for many decades beyond that. Since the Mars project includes the development of every category of advanced technology we can expect to discover during the next fifty years or more, it gives us a long-range technology and economic policy for the next fifty years or more.

This is very important, for many reasons.

For one thing, as I have already pointed out, in order to commit public and private investment in production capacities, we need to know in advance whether those investments are a good choice for a period ahead covering at least half the useful economic life of those capital investments. If we can establish a consensus among government and industries, saying that "this is the general outline of the future economic history of the United States and other nations," then private investment will proceed more or less automatically to take advantage of this commitment.

This does not imply that we can know in advance each kind of product which ought to be produced over even a few years ahead. What we can know, and must know, is what qualities of capacity we require to be able to produce whatever sort of useful product some inventor or production manager might wish to produce within the limits of existing technological possibilities. On the condition that existing production capacities are adequately developed technologically, the tooling of production for any new product within technological possibilities requires at most a few years of preparation before production begins. The point is, to have an investment policy which ensures that we shall have developed the quality of production capacity which can be readily adapted to whatever sorts of products are likely to be designed and required over the half-life of long-term capital investments in plant, equipment, and analogous objects.

The principal tasks of government as a whole—federal, state, and local, in total—include the following:

1) Government, working with the national banking system, must have policies governing the general, long-range policies for generating and lending new

volumes of credit, which will foster economic growth in general, and encourage investments in the direction indicated by the consensus between government and investors.

2) Government must assume responsibility for the Mars project itself, and for the military development programs which generate the desired rates of technological spillover.

3) Government must assume responsibility for the required direction and scale of development of basic economic infrastructure, either as government programs, or through promoting such work by public utilities.

4) Government must attune educational programs to the requirements of the kinds of technology emerging during the next two generations.

5) Government must design its policies of taxation, both to fit the priorities identified by our six constraints, and to the priorities placed on the general direction of industrial and other investments by the consensus on the Mars project.

6) Other policies of law making by government must be attuned to these realities.

If we adopt such policies in conjunction with a Mars project, we need not worry about details of other aspects of the shaping of policies of government. The adjustments in policy-making structures, which result from the adoption of a popular consensus centered around such a design of the Mars project, are the key. It is our policy-making structure, which determines the philosophy of policy making in every aspect of life. Instead of attempting to define in advance every particular policy issue we might imagine, as Stalin planners attempted to work out the fine details of every Five Year Plan, assume that if the philosophy of government is right, that each particular decision made down the line, will be at least a good one, if not exactly perfect.

The philosophical standpoint of policy making, and law making, implicit in our outline of the Mars Project, is that our national philosophy of government is centered on developing the mental potentialities of every individual, and promoting useful employment opportunities enabling every individual to have equal opportunity for using his or her developed potentialities. At the same time, the idea of personal social achievement is focused increasingly on pride in the indispensable contributions we are either making today, or preparing to make through education, because of the benefits these will mean for our children and grandchildren. We need not fear the kinds of decisions which would be made in the future, by a government whose policy-making structure is consistent with that philosophy of government.

The founders of our nation thought along similar lines, in drafting the Preamble to our federal Constitution, and in the reflections of Christian natural law in the composition of the Declaration of Independence. Our nation has drifted far away from that Preamble and Declaration of Independence. We must resume that commitment, not in the terms of 1776–1789, but in the terms of the coming fifty years. The way in which to accomplish such a result, is to rebuild our policy-making structures around a grand design such as the Mars project.

The function of the next President of the United States is to create a new national consensus consistent with such changes in our policy-making structure, and to use his personal influence to reorganize the existing elements of the power elites in a new way, a way consistent with this practical philosophy of national purpose.

Are you not tired of economic decay, of growing seas of worsening impoverishment, as I am? Are you not tired of the stink of pessimism, a pessimism which causes so many of our youth to believe that they have no future, as I am? Are you not disgusted with the lack of any governing sense of moral purpose in Washington, as I am? Are you not tired of fear, as I am? Are you not enraged by the fact, that your personal life seems to be going nowhere, as I am? Then, are you ready to join me in getting you out of the fish bowl in which you live? We could not hope to make such changes, except under conditions of a monstrous crisis. The crisis is here. Now is the time to move to make the change.

In conclusion, I repeat what I have said in other published locations, on the purpose for the Mars project, and also on what we must do about this disease which now threatens to wipe out the human species, AIDS.

I am in the advantageous position to know, how the next great revolution in fundamental scientific knowledge will be reached. The principles which determine how sweeping scientific revolutions are accomplished are proven by history, especially by the internal history of science over the recent six hundred years. Those are principles at the center of my own discoveries in economic science. I am also privileged to know concrete lines of current investigation leading in the direction of the next great sweeping revolution in science. The Mars project is essential to making that next revolution possible.

I have already reported, that modern science has proven conclusively, that the fundamental laws of the universe are negentropic, not entropic, as a modern view of Kepler's discoveries implies this to be the case. These negentropic laws are presented to us experimentally in the most immediate and direct way, by fundamental research into three areas of physics: the extremes of astrophysical scales of phenomena, the extremes of the microphysical scales of phenomena, and a focus upon those aspects of biological phenomena which express living processes as a negentropic function. To prove that a hypothetical principle of science is either valid or false, experimentally, we must be able to test that hypothesis in all three of these areas, more or less simultaneously.

As we enter now into the region which will be opened up to us by development of gamma-ray lasers, we shall open up to experimental view the seeming mysteries of the inner structure of the atom's nucleus. A limited, but insistent resurgence in optical biophysics, aided by our ability to measure a single quantum of coherent radiation generated within, for example, the DNA, of a small living organism, means a revolution in experimental biology over the years ahead. To establish the basis for a new scientific revolution, beyond that presently in progress of emergence, we must make a leap in astrophysics.

The refinement of astrophysics requires measuring the full range of electromagnetic radiation from very distant objects, with a magnification factor way beyond anything possible, either from observatories on Earth, or even in Earth orbit. We know already everything essential to the design of such observatories. However, we cannot build and operate such observatories and the laboratory stations associated with them, until we are able to sustain populations of scientists and technicians at a significantly greater distance from our Sun than Earth's orbit.

The kind of "telescope" we require, is a coordinated collection of parts, spread over areas comparable in width to the diameter of the Moon, for example. To maintain the system of observatories and space laboratories our scientific objectives demand, includes the requirement of sustaining perhaps thousands of scientists and technicians at great distances from the Earth.

To sustain such a "colony" of scientists and technicians at such distances, we must establish a supporting logistic structure. The manning of such a logistic structure, defines a colony on the scale of a sizable city on Earth. For obvious reasons, this requires basing the colony on some planet which can be made artificially habitable. The only feasible choice of base for the foreseeable future, is Mars.

So, the almost self-sufficient Mars-base colony, is linked by regular travel to and from a manned space station orbiting Mars. The "telescopes" and so forth, are placed within "commuting distance" from the space station. There are reasons I would place a network of "telescopes" and laboratories within the Mars orbit of the Sun, but that need not be discussed here.

So, the development of a permanent colony on Mars, is a critical bottleneck on the road to the next major breakthrough in science, beyond that emerging at the present time. Once we have the observatories in the vicinity of Mars operating for a few years, we may expect the threshold of that next scientific revolution to be reached. Before we establish those Mars-based facilities, astrophysical work based in Earth-orbit and on or near the Moon, will have enabled us to formulate a range of very crucial experimental questions. Immediately on establishing the Mars-based observatories, we shall focus most of the work of those observatories on better answers to these questions. We know enough about the nature of those questions presently, to state with reasonable assurance, that a major breakthrough in science will erupt about fifty years ahead.

I repeat here what I have stated in several published accounts earlier. Do not expect that space exploration will pay for itself by means of minerals and so forth brought back to the surface of our planet. The exports from space colonization to Earth, will be knowledge-exports. Space will pay for itself in terms of great advances in productivity which space science makes possible on Earth.

There is another, very deep motive for exploration and colonization of space. We must uplift mankind's image of itself. As mankind plays an increasingly active role in space, the popular conception of mankind will change for the better, to a large degree. Man will understand more easily, the principle of man's duty to participate in God's work in the universe at large. Those petty, hedonistic concerns which dominate the motives and attention of most of us, most of the time, will slip back to that lesser degree of importance they deserve. Already, during the course of the coming fifty years of a Mars project, individuals whose imagination is caught up by the idea of being a necessary actor in the forty- to fifty-years' work of initial colonization of Mars, will begin to make such a shift in sense of personal identity and personal self-interest. The school children two generations ahead will be as familiar with the principal features of the known universe, as literate pupils have been familiar with the principal landmarks of our planet. Not only will they think of such matters; their sense of what is important work, will be emotionally engaged with man's exploration of space.

Our government, and many other institutions of the world, have been chiefly lying wildly about the nature and danger of AIDS. First, as I have said, unchecked spread of AIDS, without a cure or vaccine, means the extinction of the entirety of the human species within thirty-five to forty years, more or less. Second, there is no known basis for assuming that a vaccine or cure is in sight earlier than five, or, more probably, ten years, and even that is more an optimistic guess than based upon any proofs. Third, a great deal of effort has been expended, arguing that AIDS is essentially a sexual disease; AIDS is not a sexual disease, but essentially a blood-transmitted disease. The same type of disease exists among sheep, cows, and horses, among other species, as well as among monkeys and apes. We know in the forms found among cattle, that the arguments issued by governments and leading bodies of medical institutions, are essentially absurd. We also know that government and medicine have not a single experimental fact to support their claim that AIDS is primarily a sexual disease.

Given the known facts, humanity has no foreseeable

defense against approximately a doubling of total number of infected persons every six to eight months, for not less than five to ten years, except public health measures based on identifying the persons already infected, and preventing infected persons from spreading their infection to others.

We also know, that the basic research which needs to be done, if we are to understand the infection adequately, and to discover vaccines and cures, is not medical or pharmaceutical research in the ordinary sense, but is rather emphasis on biological research. Presently, the vastly insufficient total sums available for AIDS research, are being gobbled up by medical and pharmaceutical research programs, while the more essential biological research projects are dying for lack of funding.

We have the situation today, in which governments and so-called medical authorities rush about, shouting hysterically wild claims about AIDS, while those so-called authorities have not a single experimental fact in support of those hysterical assertions. Worse, those same authorities refuse almost to spend a single penny on those experiments, never yet conducted, which would test the truth or falsehood of what those so-called authorities are insisting, without a shred of proof, to be proven facts.

What we require is a "crash program" on AIDS and related problems, modeled on the Apollo project. Every useful area of investigation must be run in parallel, with central coordination of, results pooling and sharing of every fact developed in one research program, which might be useful information for other programs. I would insist, that a very substantial portion of that "crash program" effort, should be relevant fundamental research in optical biophysics. To put the point very simply, we need a new theory of the cell. We must see the existence of cells as merely a subsumed aspect of the process of mitosis, and must correlate cell chemistry, over the entire process leading from one cell to its daughters, with a very fine-grained study of the spectroscopic characteristics of each stage of that process. It is probable, that if everything else were to fail, the electrodynamics of the mitosis-defined cell-reproduction process, would probably show us a way to conquer AIDS. If there are alternative solutions, the optical biophysics research would be of enormous help in discovering those alternatives.

This brings us back to the Mars project. The ability to engineer the development and maintenance of required kinds of artificial biospheres, in extended space flight and in colonies on planets and moons, depends greatly upon fundamental advances in biophysics. The optical biophysics work, already so promising in work on cancer, and indicated as of first-rate value for AIDS research, is the same work needed as part of the exploration and colonization of space.

The Mars project typifies the positive roadway leading up out of our presently worsening condition; the failure to face the apocalyptic reality of AIDS, typifies the abolute breakdown of presently existing policy-making structures. The link between the scientific work needed for the Mars project, and the scientific work needed as part of the conquest of AIDS, expresses the efficiency of the approach I have outlined, both to build the future, and, simultaneously, to ensure that a future exists to be built.

For Further Reading

By Lyndon H. LaRouche, Jr.

"Beyond Psychoanalysis," *Campaigner,* Vol. 6, Nos. 3–4, September–October 1973.

"The Case of Ludwig Feuerbach," Part I: *Campaigner,* Vol. 7, No. 2, December, 1973; Part II: *Campaigner,* Vol. 7, No. 3, January, 1974.

The Case of Walter Lippmann: A Presidential Strategy, University Editions, New York, 1977.

(Published as Lyn Marcus), *Dialectical Economics,* D. C. Heath and Company, Lexington, Massachusetts, 1975.

A Fifty-Year Development Plan for the Indian-Pacific Oceans Basin, Executive Intelligence Review, Washington, D.C., 1983.

Imperialism: The Final Stage of Bolshevism, New Benjamin Franklin House, New York, 1984.

Operation Juárez, Executive Intelligence Review, Washington, D.C. 1982.

The Power of Reason: A Kind of an Autobiography, New Benjamin Franklin House, New York, 1979.

"The Sexual Impotence of the Puerto Rican Socialist Party," *Campaigner,* Vol. 7, No. 1, November, 1973.

So, You Wish to Learn All About Economics? A Text on Elementary Economics, New Benjamin Franklin House, New York, 1984.

What Every Conservative Should Know About Communism, New Benjamin Franklin House, New York, 1980.

Will the Soviets Rule During the 1980s? New Benjamin Franklin House, New York, 1979.

By LaRouche associates

Carter and the Party of International Terrorism, U.S. Labor Party, New York, 1976.

Chaitkin, Anton, *Treason in America: From Aaron Burr to Averell Harriman,* New Benjamin Franklin House, New York, 1986.

Colonize Space! Open the Age of Reason: Proceedings of the Krafft A. Ehricke Memorial Conference, New Benjamin Franklin House, New York, 1985.

Editors of Executive Intelligence Review, *Dope, Inc.: Boston Bankers and Soviet Commissars,* New Benjamin Franklin House, New York, 1986.

Editors of Executive Intelligence Review, *LaRouche: Will This Man Become President?* New Benjamin Franklin House, New York, 1979.

Executive Intelligence Review Economics Staff, *EIR Quarterly Report, October, 1985: The Political Economy of AIDS and How to Fight It,* Executive Intelligence Review, Washington, D.C., 1985.

LaRouche, Helga Zepp, editor, *The Hitler Book,* New Benjamin Franklin House, New York, 1984.

The Independent Democrats' Platform: Five Crises Facing the

Next President, Independent Democrats for LaRouche, New York, 1984.

Parpart, Uwe, "The Concept of the Transfinite," *Campaigner,* Vol. 9, Nos. 1–2, January–February 1976.

A Program for America, LaRouche Democratic Campaign, New York, 1985.

St. Augustine: Father of European and African Civilization: Proceedings of the Sixth International Conference of the Schiller Institute, Rome, 1985. New Benjamin Franklin House, New York, 1985.

Schiller Institute, *Friedrich Schiller: Poet of Freedom,* New Benjamin Franklin House, New York, 1975.

Scientific staff of the Fusion Energy Foundation, *Beam Weapons: An Alternative to Nuclear Destruction,* Aero Publishers, Fall Brook, California, 1983.

Spannaus, Nancy, and White, Christopher, editors, *The Political Economy of the American Revolution,* University Editions, New York, 1975.

Other source material

Cantor, Georg, "Foundations of a General Theory of Manifolds," translated by Uwe Parpart, *Campaigner,* Vol. 9, Nos. 1–2, January-February 1976.

Carey, Henry, *The Harmony of Interests,* Augustus M. Kelley, New York City.

Carey, Mathew, *Essays on Banking,* Ayer Company Publishers, Salem, New Hampshire.

Dante Alighieri, *The Divine Commedy,* translated from the Italian by Allen Mandelbaum, University of California Press, Berkeley, 1980.

Feuerbach, Ludwig, *The Essence of Christianity,* Peter Smith Publishers, Magnolia, Massachusetts, 1958.

Fromm, Erich, *The Art of Loving,* Harper & Row, New York, 1974.

Furtwängler, Wilhelm, *Concerning Music* (translated by

L. J. Lawrence), Greenwood House, Brooklyn, New York.

Gauss, Karl Friedrich, *Werke (12 Bände), König liche Gesellschaft der Wissenschaften zu Göttingen* (text in German), Olms, 1973.

Hamilton, Alexander, *The Federalist Papers,* Random House, New York.

Hilbert, David, *Methods of Mathematical Physics,* (2 Vols.), John Wiley & Sons, Inc., New York.

Homer, *Odyssey,* Ohio University Press, Columbus, 1978.

James, William, *Varieties of Religious Experience,* Macmillan, New York, 1961.

Kant, Immanuel, *Critique of Practical Judgment,* Oxford University Press, New York, 1952.

Kepler, Johannes, *The Secret of the Universe (Mysterium Cosmographicum),* Abaris Publishing, New York.

Keynes, John Maynard, *General Theory of Employment, Interest, and Money,* Harcourt, Brace, Jovanovitch, New York, 1965.

Kubie, Lawrence S., *Neurotic Distortions of the Creative Process,* Farrar, Straus, and Giroux, Inc., New York City.

Leibniz, Gottfried Wilhelm, *The Clarke-Leibniz Correspondence,* Everyman Classics, London, 1973.

Leibniz, Gottfried Wilhelm, *Monadology,* Everyman Classics, London, 1973.

Leibniz, Gottfried Wilhelm, *Theodicy,* Open Court Publishers, Peru, Illinois, 1985.

List, Friedrich, *National System of Political Economy,* Augustus M. Kelley, New York.

Marcuse, Herbert, *One Dimensional Man,* Beacon Press, Boston, 1966.

Marx, Karl, *Capital,* Random House, New York, 1977.

Nicholas of Cusa, *De Docta Ignorantia,* Banning Press, Minneapolis, 1985.

Pascal, Blaise, *Physical Treatises,* Hippocrene Books, New York.

Philo of Alexandria, *Philosophical Works,* Howard University Press, Cambridge, Massachusetts.

Plato, *The Collected Dialogues,* Princeton University Press, Princeton, New Jersey.

Plato, "Timaeus," *Campaigner,* Vol. 13, No. 1, May 1980.

Riemann, Bernhard, "Fragments of a Philosophical Contents," translated by Uwe Parpart, *Campaigner,* Vol. 9, Nos. 1–2, January–February 1975.

Smith, Adam, *Wealth of Nations,* Modern Library, New York, 1977.

Turgot, Robert A., *Reflections on the Formation and Distribution of Wealth,* Augustus M. Kelley, New York City, 1898.

Wiener, Norbert, *Human Use of Human Beings: Cybernetics and Society,* Avon Publishing, New York, 1980.